TRANSLATION STUDIES

THEORIES AND APPLICATIONS

Edited by
Sunil Sawant

ATLANTIC
PUBLISHERS & DISTRIBUTORS (P) LTD

ATLANTIC
PUBLISHERS & DISTRIBUTORS (P) LTD

7/22, Ansari Road, Darya Ganj, New Delhi
Tel.: +91-11-4077 5252, 2327 3880
E-mail: orders@atlanticbooks.com
Web: www.atlanticbooks.com

Reprint 2025

Published by Atlantic Publishers & Distributors (P) Ltd.

Printed & bound in India by Atlantic Print Services

Dedicated to

Dr. Laxmi Shanker,
Former Editor of
Synthesis and *Punya Bhoomi*

Preface

It is a pleasure to place in the hands of the readers, *Translation Studies: Theories and Applications*.

Over the years, Translation Studies has developed into an interdisciplinary area of research, taking in its stride Comparative Literature, Applied Linguistics and Culture Studies. The present anthology offers a variety of theoretical approaches and a number of their applications.

In my own article, I propose a new research model for conducting Translation Studies consisting of such parameters as (1) the condition of the receiving system; (2) the intentions of the receiving system; (3) the needs and attitudes of the receiving system; (4) the politics of cultural transfer in importation; (5) power equations; and (6) agency.

David Bellos from Princeton University (USA) enumerates different strategies used to represent the foreignness of the foreign in the receiving language such as the use of selective foreignism by retaining original titles and ranks, by leaving common words and phrases in the original language. He also highlights the difficulties in representing the foreignness of foreign languages or the meaning of a foreign text.

Sachin Ketkar provides a critique of the linguistic sciences oriented approaches to translation and argues that, despite some attempts to bridge the gap between the linguistic sciences oriented approaches and the approaches that emphasize the target culture system or the political dimension of translation as a product, a comprehensive General Theory of Translation where all the approaches agree on one infallible approach, is a distant dream.

Amar Singh explores the challenges involved in translating texts that are inscribed with many languages and cultures, i.e. with hybridity. Deepak Borgave discusses some of the problems that could emerge while translating Source Language (SL) texts and also the problems about how the Target Language (TL) texts are received, the problems of cultural contextualization, decontextualization and reconextualization in translation.

Rajiv Ranjan Dwivedi shows how translation involves two texts and their multiple intricacies, idiosyncrasies and subtleties associated with language, culture, context, style, theme, etc. and core issues like loss and gain, untranslatabilty, equivalence, etc. which constantly question the identity of translation as a creative exercise. His is an attempt to examine the veracity of the question of equivalence in translation and the issues associated therewith.

Meena Edith Keller examines details of translation, its kinds, problems, solutions and the latest trends. Laxmi Shanker and Anubha analyze the most frequent translation difficulties which are obviously of a semantic and cultural nature: "Linguistic untranslatability" (cognates, i.e. true and false friends, calques, and other forms of interference; institutional and standardized terms, neologisms, aphorisms, etc.) and "cultural untranslatability" (idioms, sayings, proverbs, jokes, puns, etc.).

Satyendra Singh studies the challenges and strategies in translating texts from one language to another. B.O. Satyanarayana Reddy proposes a comprehensive approach to translation which highlights the nature and standard of the culture of the translator which influences the understanding of the source language text and the target language text. B.N. Gaikwad explains different definitions of translation and takes a review of the changes in translation practices across the 18th, 19th and 20th centuries. Mallikarjun Patil also takes a review of different definitions of translation proposed by Paz,

Collingwood, Wilmovitz, Wittgenstein, Heidegger, Sujit Mukherjee and others.

Vandana Pathak examines two Marathi Dalit autobiographies translated into English, viz. Laxman Mane's *Upara* (An Outsider) and Laxman Gaikwad's *Uchalya* (The Branded). She shows how the figurative language used in both these Dalit autobiographies imparts polysemy to these texts and how both self-narratives contain idiomatic expressions and heteroglossia. She concludes that in spite of the use of the devices of code mixing, code switching or borrowing, English translations of these Marathi autobiographies have failed to provide exact equivalents to vernacular words and idioms.

According to Neeta Modi, translation involves a lot of "spilling over" not only of languages but also of cultures. It is almost impossible to translate words, phrases and elements that are heavily and exclusively grounded in a culture. A translator has to face many problems and challenges while rendering a Hindi or any Indian language text into English. The problem of untranslatability increases all the more if the differences between the SL and the TL and their cultures are vast. She explores the issue of untranslatability and the cultural snags faced by a translator while translating Munshi Premchand's famous Hindi novel *Godaan* into English.

Sarita Mane examines parallel corpora, the extracts drawn from both Tennessee Williams' *A Streetcar Named Desire*, the source text and Vijay Tendulkar's *Vasanachakra*, the target text, and studies it in relation to the sociocultural context.

A.K. Farakate examines the nature of equivalences established by Vilas Salunke in his translation "The Marching Song of Columbus" of the well-known Marathi poem "Kolambasache Garvageet" written by the Jnanpeeth Awardee poet, Kusumagraj. His paper is an attempt to comment on how strategically the translation has been attempted, the nature of compromises made by the translator and finally to appreciate the worth of the translated text as a parallel creativity or a transcreation.

J. Samuel Kirubahar and Ms. M. Muktha Manoj discuss transcreation/interpretation as the two grounds in Indian context and argue that in Tamil poetics, translation as a discipline has been felt right from the time of the earliest known grammatical 'urtext' *Tolkappiyam*. Sangeetha Jayakumar makes an attempt to evaluate the success of the translated version by Karthik Narayan of Kalki's *Ponniyin Selvan* which carries the diversity, the richness and the depth of Tamil culture, tradition, art and religion to the world around.

Informed by the theories of Linguistics, Discourse Analysis and Pragmatics, A.M. Sarwade's article probes into the ways English language is used in *Difficult Daughters* by Manju Kapur in order to depict the socio-cultural background of Indian characters and their ethos.

Manoj Gujar presents an experiment of applying certain procedures of translation suggested by Vladimir Ivir in his essay "Procedures and Strategies for the Translation of Culture" published in 1975 in *Indian Journal of Applied Linguistics* while translating Renu Gavaskar's *Amcha Kai Gunha?* as *What's Our Crime?*

Shirish Chindhade and Apara Tiwari relate a few experiences of authors while engaged in the activity of translation.

I thank all the contributors for their valuable papers. I hope that readers and researchers will find this book intellectually stimulating and practically useful.

Sunil Sawant

Contents

1

Comparative Studies vis-à-vis Translation Studies

Sunil Sawant

For a long time, Comparative Literature was largely confined to histories of literatures, showing patterns of connection and influence, laying emphasis on sources, on documenting how texts came to be read across cultural and linguistic boundaries, on tracing origins and establishing the cultural basis of national consciousness (Bassnett 1993: 34). It was Henry Remak, the founder of the idealistic transnational approach of the Great Books, who proposed that comparative literature "is the comparison of one literature with another or others, and the comparison of literature with other spheres of human expression" (Remak 1961: 3). This formalist model too avoided socio-economic or political issues.

In the West, comparative literature has now been called into question by the alternative schools of thought such as structuralism, post-structuralism, feminism, deconstruction, semiology, psychoanalysis, etc. Much of the critical space previously occupied by comparative literature has been now largely swept by Literary Theory, Women's Studies, Semiotics, Film and Media Studies and Cultural Studies. Susan Bassnett writes: "...the term 'comparative literature'...has little meaning today (not that it ever had much meaning from the outset)...comparative literature as a formalist exercise is in decline" (Bassnett 1993: 158).

Derived from author studies, thematic studies, genre studies, etc., conventional methodologies of comparative literature set up canons of primary and secondary authors, greater and lesser texts, stronger and weaker cultures, majority and minority languages without consideration of ideological implications of such hierarchization. Contemporary methodologies, on the contrary, have been derived from gender studies, cultural studies and postmodernist theory and they thereby expose subtexts beneath the apparently innocent details.

Comparative literature next started:

(a) the radical reassessment of Western cultural models;

(b) the transcendence of disciplinary boundaries through new methodological insights supplied by gender studies or cultural studies; and

(c) the examination of the processes of intercultural transfer that are taking place within translation studies. (*ibid.*: 47)

More exciting and dynamic areas of comparative cultural research became:

(a) the definition of culture;

(b) the construction of otherness;

(c) the horizon of reader expectation;

(d) the processes of textual transfer through translation;

(e) the relationship of language and place; and

(f) the relationship of language and identity. (*ibid.*: 68)

Today, comparative literature has almost given way to Translation Studies.

Werner Koller defines Translation Studies as "a collective and inclusive designation for all research activities taking the phenomena of translating and translation as their basis or focus" (quoted by Holmes in Venuti 1972/2000: 184). James Holmes further makes the distinction between Descriptive Translation Studies (DTS) or Translation Description (TD) and Theoretical Translation Studies (ThTS) or Translation Theory

(TTh) (Homes 1972/2000: 184). Accordingly, the two main objectives of these two branches of pure translation studies are:

(1) to describe the phenomena of translating and translation(s) as they manifest themselves in the world of our experience, and

(2) to establish general principles by means of which these phenomena can be explained and predicted. (*ibid.*: 184)

Of the two, Description Translation Studies, which constantly maintains the closest contact with the empirical phenomena under study, consists of three major kinds of research: product-oriented (which describes existing translations), function-oriented (which describes the function of translations in the recipient socio-cultural situation) and process-oriented (which is concerned with the process or act of translation itself) (*ibid.*: 184).

The Polysystem Model

Sharing Holmes's vision, Itamar Even-Zohar, a Scholar from Tel Aviv, established a new paradigm for the study of literary translations during the 1970s. Adopting the notion of system from the Russaian Formalists, he viewed translated literature as a system in its own right. Even-Zohar argues that translated works do correlate in at least two ways: (a) in the way their source texts are selected by the target literature, the principles of selection never being uncorrelatable with the home co-systems of the target literature...; and (b) in the way they adopt specific norms, behaviours, and policies—in short, in their use of the literary repertoire—which results from their relations with the other home co-systems (Even-Zohar in Venuti 2000: 199-200). Thus, translated literature does not function in isolation. It fully participates in the history of the literary polysystem, as an integral and as a most active system within it, related with all the other co-systems.

Even-Zohar's theory of the polysystem further sees translated literature as one system among many other co-systems in the constant struggle for the central position. When translated literature succeeds in maintaining the central position in the literary polysystem, it

(a) participates actively in shaping the centre of the polysystem;
(b) is by and large an integral part of innovatory forces;
(c) is identified with major events in literary history;
(d) is produced by the leading writers;
(e) is likely to become one of the means of elaborating the new repertoire;
(f) introduces new features (both principles and elements) into the home literature;
(g) introduces new models of reality, a new (poetic) language, or compositional patterns and techniques; and
(h) is compatible with the new approaches within the target literature. (*ibid.*: 200)

Whether translated literature will form part of the polysystem's prestigious centre or remain a peripheral phenomenon depends upon the specific circumstances operating in the polysystem. While a peripheral position is of course normal, Even-Zohar identifies three sets of circumstances in which it can occupy a more central position: (a) when a polysystem has not yet been crystallized, that is to say, when a literature is "young," in the process of being established; (b) when a literature is either "pheripheral"...or "weak," or both; and (c) when there are turning points, crises, or literary vacuums in a literature (*ibid.*: 200-01).

Translated literature which maintains a peripheral position within the literary polysystem

(a) employs secondary models;
(b) has no influence on major processes;
(c) is modelled according to norms already conventionally established by an already dominant type in the target literature;

(d) adheres to norms which have been rejected either recently or long before by the (newly) established centre;

(e) no longer maintains positive correlations with original writing;

(f) becomes a means to preserve a traditional taste;

(g) becomes a factor of preservation of unchanged repertoire; and

(h) exists as an ossified systeme d'antan, often fanatically guarded by the agents of secondary models against even minor changes. (*ibid.*: 202)

Translated literature may not be either a central or peripheral system, but, like any other literary co-system, it comprises its own stratified polysystem. Hence it is possible that within the sub-system of translated literature one section of translated literature may assume a central position, another may remain quite peripheral (*ibid.*: 202). For instance, in the stratified system of translated literature within Marathi Literary Polysystem, translated American popular literature of Pearl S. Buck, Maria Susanna Cummins, Louisa May Alcott and Marjorie Kinnan Rawlings assumed an unmistakably central position, while translated literature of moral ambiguity or male adventure written in the tradition of the mainstream American novel assumed an obviously peripheral one (Sawant 2007: 162).

After the 'cultural turn' in Translation Studies, translation is no longer seen as a mere transformation of a text from one language to another, but rather the production of a target text that can function within a different context for recipients from a different culture.

Taking a point of departure from the polysystem model, Jose Lambert and Rik Van Gorp suggest the following valuable areas of research:

(a) the study of the vocabulary, style, poetical and rhetorical conventions of both source and target systems;

(b) the analysis of how a translated text is termed in the target system, and its role and status in that system;
(c) the study of the history of translation theory and criticism in particular literatures at particular times;
(d) the study of the emergence of groups or schools of translators and the significance of such; and
(e) the study of the role of translations in the development of a literary system with a view to establishing whether translation plays a conservative or an innovative role, etc. (in Hermans 1985: 44-45)

Translation Studies has developed a methodology of its own that draws on both comparatistics and cultural history:

> Translation Studies...effectively offers a new way of looking at cultural history, taking into account both the implications of socio-cultural changes that affect literary production in different cultures and the linguistic structuring of a text as it is transposed across language boundaries. (Bassnett 1993: 11)

Bassnett (1997: 1) further asserts,

> Translation is about wanting to cross boundaries and enter into new territory, whilst the study of translation involves mapping the journeys texts undertake.

Lefevere (1997) makes a distinction between translation 'praxis' and translation 'practice' in which the former involves the process of taking into account what actually happens (or happened in various moments of history) in the translation process and the reasons why. Hermans (1999: 5) further states that the questions that DTS scholars ask themselves are

> geared not so much to gauging the quality of individual translations, upholding particular principles as to what constitutes a good translation, or guaranteeing the quality of new translations to be made. Rather, the aim is to delve into translation as a cultural and historical phenomenon, to explore its context and conditioning factors, to search for grounds that can explain why there is what there is.

The aim of DTS is thus 'to arrive at a better understanding of languages, cultures and translation phenomena and behaviour' (Ulrych in Riccardi, 2002: 200). DTS thus adopts a methodology which offers a diachronic rather than purely synchronic perspective to undertake radical revisions of cultural and literary history.

The Comparative Model

Andrew Chesterman (2000) describes three models of translation used in Translation Studies research: The Comparative Model, the Process Model and the Causal Model. Of these, the comparative model examines translation in terms of correlation with source or other texts. It studies translation, generally involving analysis of certain features of the source language or text and comparison with their translation into a target language or text. This model has been extensively used in the contrastive analyses, the detailed micro-shift and macro-shift analysis, discourse analytical approach, translation quality assessment and other contemporary approaches.

Mona Baker's corpus-based studies in translation (1993, 1995) highlights an interest in the translation as a text in its own right, not as derivative of a source text. Baker advocated a new perspective on the study of translations, namely "...a shift away from comparing either ST with TT or language A with language B to comparing text production per se with translation" (Baker 1995: 233). This kind of study required "two separate collections of texts in the same language: one corpus consists of original texts in the language in question and the other consists of translations in that language from a given source language or languages" (*ibid.*: 234). Baker thus proposed the study of non-translated language and non-translated texts along with translated language or the language of translation to capture "patterns which are either restricted to translated text or which occur with a significantly higher or lower frequency in translated text" (*ibid.*: 235). Baker posits a number of features of translation that could be investigated using comparable corpora (Baker, 1996); for example, that translations tend to be more explicit on a number of levels than non-translated texts (explicitation), that their content or form is simplified compared with non-translated texts (simplification) or that translations use language in a more conventional or normalized way than non-translated texts (normalization). Most of the research in Translation Studies is concerned with identifying and finding evidence for these features.

The Process Model

The process model looks at the translation process over time. Translation process research identifies, describes and analyses what happens during translation, i.e. the cognitive processes at work during translation. The empirical study of the translation process uses introspection (in particular the think-aloud method of data elicitation. The introspective studies, which are largely data-based and descriptive, often focus on specific aspects of the translation process, for example, the use of reference material, decision-making criteria. The most important drawback of the think-aloud methodology, pinpointed by the critics of this methodology, is that this data elicitation method cannot provide access to thought processes that are subconscious or automated. However, Olohan and Baker (2000) have referred to 'subconscious' processes of explicitation, hypothesizing that translators may unintentionally use language in certain ways that increase the explicitness of the text, without setting out to do so.

Bell (1991) has suggested an alternative approach to studying the translation process. His model of the process combines induction (i.e. inferring processes from the product) and deduction (i.e. using introspective data such as diaries). He suggests drawing inferences from the observation of translator performance. He proposes to study the translation process by analyzing the translation product: 'by finding features in the data of the product which suggest the existence of particular elements and systematic relations in the process' (*ibid.*: 39). A number of researchers use translation product analysis to know about the translation process. Gideon Toury (1995), for example, suggests studying translation without studying the source text. However, there are some researchers who insist that the relationship between source and target text needs to be analysed to discuss the translation process.

The Causal Model

The causal model focuses on the causes and effects of translation in domains ranging from textual to social to cognitive. Chesterman (2000) proposes four types of hypotheses that can be tested (interpretive, descriptive, explanatory and predictive). The comparative model can accommodate interpretive and descriptive hypotheses, but falters with explanatory and predictive hypotheses. Chesterman finds the causal model the most fruitful because it, he claims, allows us "to make statements and hypotheses about causes and effects" (*ibid.*: 21), to formulate and test explanatory and predictive hypotheses. It can accommodate all four types of hypotheses and can contain the other two models (comparative and process). The causal model can easily be used to explain and predict causes and effects. It can tell us why a translation or translated language is the way it is, or it can tell us what effect a translation or translated language will have. Jeremy Munday (2000) has tried to develop this kind of comprehensive causal model by bringing together corpus linguistic techniques, systemic functional linguistics and the consideration of wider sociocultural contexts.

The foregoing review of various models in Translation Studies helps us to arrive at certain useful generalisations. The functional approach proposed by Itamar Even-Zohar and Gideon Toury is more accommodative as it views all translation activity (whether it involves producing, using or commenting on translations) in terms of the norms, value scales and models prevalent in a polysystem. Nevertheless, a comprehensive model of translation evaluation can hardly be derived only from the polysystem model. The contributors to the anthology *The Manipulation of Literature* (1985) demonstrated that different social institutions use translations to 'manipulate' a given society in order to 'construct' the kind of 'culture' desired. In the introduction to *Translation, History and Culture* (1990), Susan Bassnett and Andre Lefevere expressed the need to explore the role of 'the vagaries and vicissitudes of the exercise of power' in the production of culture in general and the production of translations in particular. Gayatri Spivak (1992, 1995) and Homi Bhabha (1994) apply postcolonial theory and practices to translation and focus on questions of power and colonialism. Taking a point of departure from this 'power turn' in Translation Studies, I would like to argue, the intercultural and interlingual relationship between the two parallel literary polysystems can be properly comprehended only in terms of a set of parameters such as:

(1) the condition of the receiving system;

(2) the intentions of the receiving system;

(3) the needs and attitudes of the receiving system;

(4) the politics of cultural transfer in importation;

(5) power equations; and

(6) agency.

It goes without saying that these parameters do not fall into watertight compartments, nor do they fall into a lumpish totality. Depending on the relationship between the source and target literary polysystems and depending on the changing dynamics of the target literary polysystem and its relationship with the subsystem of translated literature, the degree of their functional relevance would vary from one historical moment to another.

References

Baker, M. 1993. "Corpus Linguistics and Translation Studies: Implications and Applications", in M. Baker, G. Francis and E. Tognini-Bonelli (eds.), *Text and Technology: In Honour of John Sinclair*. Amsterdam: John Benjamins, pp. 17-45.

———. 1995. "Corpora in translation studies: An overview and some suggestions for future research". *Target* 7: pp. 223-43.

———. 1996. "Corpus-based Translation Studies: The challenges that lie ahead", in H. Somers (ed.) *Terminology, LSP and Translation: Studies in Language Engineering in honour of Juan C. Sager*. Amsterdam: John Benjamins, pp. 175-86.

Bassnett-McGuire, Susan and Lefevere, Andre, (eds). 1990. *Translation, History and Culture*. London: Pinter Publishers.

Bassnett, Susan. 1993. *Comparative Literature: A Critical Introduction*. Oxford and Cambridge: Blackwell.

Bassnett-McGurie, Susan. 1997. 'Introduction.' "Intricate pathways: observations on translation and literature." *Translating Literature*. Ed. By Harold Somers. Cambridge: P.S. Brewer.

Bell, R.T. 1991. Translation and Translating: *Theory and Practice*. London: Longman.

Chesterman, A. 2000. "A causal model of translation studies", in M. Olohan (ed.) *Intercultural Faultlines. Research models in translation studies I: Textual and cognitive aspects*. Machester: St. Jerome, pp. 15-27.

Hermans, Theo (ed.). 1985. *The Manipulation of Literature*. London: Croom Helm.

Hermans, Theo. 1999. Translation as Systems: Descriptive and System-oriented *Approaches Explained*. Machester: St. Jerome.

Lefevere, Andre. 1997. "Concezione della tradizione in cina e in Occidente", in Tradurre, Unapproccio multidisciplinare. Ed. By Margherita Ulrych. Turin: UTET.

Munday, J. 2002. "Systems in translation: A systemic model for descriptive translation studies", in T. Hermans (ed.) *Crosscultural Transgressions. Research models in translation studies II: Historical and ideological issues*. Manchester: St. Jerome, pp. 76-92.

Olohan, M. and M. Baker. 2000. "Reporting *that* in translated English: Evidence for subconscious processes of explicitation?" *Across Languages and Cultures* 1: 141-72.

Remak, Henry. 1961. "Comparative Literature, Its Definition and Function", in Newton Stallknecht and Horst Frenz (eds) *Comparative Literature: Method and Perspective*. Carbondale: Southern Illinois Press.

Sawant, Sunil. 2007. "The Tradition of the American Popular Novel in Marathi", in Rambhau Badode, Afzal Khan and Arvind Mardikar (eds) *New Directions in Comparative Literature*. New Delhi: Macmillan India Ltd., pp. 153-164.

Toury, Gideon. 1995. *Descriptive Translation Studies and Beyond*. Amsterdam/Philadelphia: John Benjamin's publishing Company.

Ulrych, Margherita. 2002. "An evidence-based approach to applied translation studies," *Translation Studies: Perspectives on an Emerging Discipline*. Cambridge: The University Press.

Venuti, Lawrence. 2000. *The Translation Studies Reader*. London and New York: Routledge.

2

Fictions of the Foreign

David Bellos

For most of the last century reviewers and laymen have customarily declared in order to praise a translation to the skies that it sounds as if it had been written in English. This is hollow praise indeed, since the self-same community of reviewers and laymen has often shown itself unable to tell when an alleged translation *was* written in English. All the same, the high value placed on target language fluency—"domesticating translation", in translation studies jargon—is a strong feature of the language culture of the English-speaking world throughout the 20C and 21C. But there have also been dissident voices. If a detective novel set in Paris makes its characters speak and think in entirely fluent English, even while plodding along the Boulevard Saint-Germain, drinking Pernod or scoffing a *jarret de porc aux lentilles*—then something must be wrong. Where's the bonus in having a French detective novel for bed-time reading unless there is something *French* about it? Don't we want our French detectives to *sound French*? Domesticating translation styles that eradicate the Frenchness of Gallic thugs have been attacked by some critics for committing "ethnocentric violence".[1] An ethics of translation, such critics say, should restrain translators from deceiving readers with inauthentic simulacra of the foreign.

How then should the foreignness of the foreign best be represented in the receiving language? The easiest way to make a text sound foreign is to leave parts of it in the original. Such was the convention in England in the Romantic era. In the earliest translation of *Dangerous Liaisons*, for instance, characters refer to and address each other by their full titles in French (*monsieur le vicomte*, *madame la présidente...*) and use everyday expressions such as *Allez! parbleu!* and *ma foi!* within sentences that are in other respects entirely in English.[2] Similarly, in recent translations of the novels of Fred Vargas, the lead character Jean-Baptiste Adamsberg retains his French rank of *commissaire* in charge of a clutch of *brigadiers*, but he talks to them in English.[3] Following to the same logic of selective foreignism, German officers in most WWII movies made in Hollywood speak perfect English interrupted at regular intervals by *jawohl, Gott in Himmel* and *Heil Hitler*.

This "mishmash" manner of representing the foreignness of foreign texts relies on a number of unspoken conventions in the language culture of the receiving language. These conventions are not easily laid bare, but they call for some kind of explanation. Otherwise, asserting that a translation *sounds just like English* or alternatively *sounds as if it had been written in French* will remain what it has in fact been all along—words in the air with no demonstrable meaning at all.

It is a challenge, but not an insurmountable one, to write something that *sounds like English* to the ears of speakers of foreign languages without writing English at all. English is heard around the world in pop songs, commercials, TV news broadcasts and so on by millions of people who do not understand the words of the song lyrics, jingles and news reports. As a result there are large numbers of people who recognize the phonology of English—the kinds of sounds English makes—without knowing any English vocabulary or grammar. Hundreds of millions of teenager have been listening to global pop in exactly that way for many decades. Some forty years ago, an Italian rock star performed a musical routine in which he pretended to be a teacher of English showing his class that you do not need to understand a single word in order to know what English sounds like. And this is what he sang, to a catchy tune and rhythm:

Ai ai smai sesler eni els so co uil piso ai
in de col men seivuan prisencolinensinainciusol ol rait
ai ai smai senflecs eni go for doing peso ai
in de col men seivuan prisencolinensinainciusol ol rait

That's what *English sounds like* if you don't speak English—but only if you vocalise this transcription (aloud or in your head) according the standard rules for vocalising Italian script. In other words, Adriano Celentano's *Prisencolinen sinainciusol, ol rait* is an Italian "fiction of the foreign".

It is equally possible to produce gibberish that *sounds foreign* to English-language ears. A famous and splendid example is the song sung by Charlie Chaplin in *Modern Times* (1936). Having got a job as a singing waiter, the hapless wee fellow finds himself on the restaurant dance floor with the band thumping out a French music-hall tune, *Je cherche Titine*—but he does not know the words! Chaplin dances, mimes, looks perplexed. His girl-friend in the wings mouths the word "Sing!" The inter-title reads:

Sing! Never Mind the Words!

Chaplin then launches into a ditty in Generic Immigrant Romance, which as readers and speakers of English we might represent thus:

Se bella giu satore
Je notre so cafore
Je notre si cavore
Je la tu la ti la toi

La spinash o la bouchon
Cigaretto Portabello
Si rakish spaghaletto
Ti la tu la ti la toi

Senora pilasina
Voulez-vous le taximeter?
Le zionta su la sita
Tu la tu la tu la oi

Sa montia si n'amura
La sontia so gravora
La zontcha con sora
Je la possa ti la toit

Je notre so lamina
Je notre so consina
Je le se tro savita
Je la tossa vi la toit

Se motra so la sonta
Chi vossa l'otra volta
Li zoscha si catonta
Tra la la la la la la

That sounds like French—or Italian, or perhaps Spanish— to an English speaker with no active knowledge of the language, only a familiarity with what French (Italian, Spanish) *sounds like*. The words have no meaning, of course, and only a few of them are actually words of French (Italian, Spanish). The point is this: you do not have to make any sense at all to sound foreign. For the ancient Greeks, of course, the sound of the foreign was the unarticulated, open-mouthed blabber of *va-va-va-*, which is why they called all non-Greek speakers *varvaros*, that is to say, barbarians. To "sound foreign" is to mouth gibberish, to be dim, to be dumb: the Russian word for "German" is indeed немец, from немой, "dumb, speechless", and in an older form of the language it was used for any non-Russian speaker.

However, since the 1980s a number of modern European classics have been retranslated into English and French by translators whose expressed ambition was to make much-loved works like *Crime and Punishment* or *The Metamorphosis* "sound more foreign"—although they certainly did not wish to make them sound dumb.

One traditional way of achieving this effect is to leave common words and phrases in the original language, as 19C translators of French novels into English frequently did. However, contemporary "foreignising" retranslators do not do this. When Gregor Samsa wakes one morning and finds that he has turned into an insect overnight, he does not exclaim *Ach Gott!* in Stanley Corngold's retranslation, as he does in the original; nor does Ivan Fyodorovich say *Это вот как* in Richard Pevear and Larissa Volokhonskaya's foreignising version of *The Brothers Karamazov*. Had these novels been written *in French* and translated *into English* by the conventions of the 1820s, we can be fairly sure that Gregor Samsa would have said *Oh mon Dieu*! and Ivan Fedorovich would have said *Alors, voilà* in the English translation.

Things have changed, not in French, German or Russian, but in English. In the language culture of today, English-language readers are not expected to know how to recognise conversational interjections like "Good God!" or "Well, now" when spoken in German or Russian; whereas within the language culture of 19C Britain, educated readers were held to be familiar with everyday French expressions of that kind.

There was and still could be a distinct educational and social purpose in maintaining items of the source text in the translation. It allows readers to acquire what they had not learned at school, or to recover or refresh their memory of long-forgotten lessons. Retention of the original expression in narrowly delimited and effectively self-glossing speech situations—such as greetings, apostrophes and interjections—provides readers with something they might well want to glean from reading a translated work: the vague impression of having read a novel in French. In a social world where the ability to read in French is a mark of cultural distinction, this can be a very satisfying feeling indeed.

The "mishmash approach" of selective and decorative foreignism is available only in translating between languages that have a well-established relationship. For many centuries, knowledge of French was part of the panoply of advanced education in the English-speaking world, and to some extent it remains so today. Little bits of French are therefore part of the educated English-speaker's general linguistic resource. What those fragments of the other language signify most of all is simply, *This is French!* together with the pleasing corollary, *I know some French*! The effect on the reader's self-esteem is not seriously affected if the exact meaning of phrases like *parbleu* and *ma foi* has been lost. When a mastery of French was the hallmark of the educated classes, part of the point of reading a French novel in translation for those whose education had not been quite so complete was to acquire the cultural goods that the elite already possessed. Thus the more the translator of a French work left in French, the more he or she served the reader in the quest for higher status.

You can't do that with Russian or German any more, which is why contemporary foreignising styles of translation have to use other tactics. These languages are taught to only tiny groups of students nowadays. Knowledge of either or even both has no relation to cultural hierarchies within the English-speaking world—it just means you are some kind of a linguist, or maybe an astronaut or an automobile engineer.

Nonetheless, the retranslators of Kafka and Dostoevsky do believe that they know what German or Russian *sounds like* in English. Such a belief can only be grounded on the view that within our imagination of the foreign there is a latent memory of the sound patterns and rhythms of those two specific languages—gleaned perhaps from WWII movies or else from Cold War dramas like *Dr Strangelove*. Or it might be the other way round: to the extent that Corngold's *Metamorphosis* and Pevear's *Karamazov* do not sound as if they had been written in English, they may serve to inform us what German or Russian *would sound like* if German or Russian were written in English.... But that's ridiculous! Kafka and Dostoevsky wouldn't sound like *that* at all if they had been to Eton. At all events, in both these cases of retranslation, foreign-soundingness is achieved principally by altering the natural word order of sentences in English.

But why should we want Kafka to sound German? It would be rather naive to think that "sounding German" gives us a more authentic version of the original. In German, after all, Kafka doesn't sound "German" at all—he sounds like Kafka! But to the ear of an English speaker who has learned German but does not inhabit that language entirely naturally, everything Kafka wrote "sounds German" to some degree, precisely because German is not quite that reader's home tongue. Making Kafka "sound German" in English is perhaps the best way that a translator can communicate to the reader his or her own experience of reading Kafka in the original. Nothing suggests that this is identical or even close to the experience of reading Kafka for a natural speaker of German.

Foreign-soundingness can be achieved when translating from a language with which the receiving language and its culture have a real or imaginary relationship. The longest and most extensive relationship of that kind in the English-speaking world in general is with French; but nowadays, especially in the USA, Spanish has breached the Rio Grande to a spectacular degree and is by far the most familiar foreign tongue for the vast majority of younger readers. Through a thousand years of physical proximity, commercial interchange, cultural rivalry, intellectual admiration, political hostility, and tourism, English has acquired many ways to represent Frenchness, and American English now also has a panoply of devices for representing Spanishness. To a lesser degree, we can represent Germanness, and, to a rather limited and usually comical degree, Italianness as well. But what of Yoruba? Marathi? Chuvash? or any one of the nearly seven thousand other languages of the world? There is no special reason why anything within the devices available to a writer of English should "sound just like Yoruba" or give a more authentic representation of what it feels like to write in Chuvash. We just have no idea. The project of writing translations that preserve *in the way they sound* some trace of the work's "authentic foreignness" is only really applicable when the source language is not *altogether* foreign.

Some knowledge of the source language is surely necessary for the "foreign effect" to exist. In order to even notice that this sentence from German a foreignizing translation is you have to know that in German subordinate clauses their verbs to the end leave. Otherwise it is gibberish.

The BBC Television comedy series *Fawlty Towers,* set in a second-rate boarding house in a second-rate English seaside resort, features an immigrant waiter from Spain, called Manuel. Manuel does not speak English very well and has a limited range of expressions, pronounced with non-native accent and diction. His most famous recurrent line is *I know nothing!* Although the actor who played this role was a Londoner, his pronunciation of *I know nothing* was intended to be and was universally heard to be Spanish-sounding. The series was exported all over the world and dubbed into many languages, in most of which the voice of Manuel was profoundly *altered* to correspond to the conventions for Spanish-soundingness appropriate to the receiving culture. But what of the Spanish-language version of *Fawlty Towers*? How could Manuel be made to sound Spanish *in Spanish*? Well, obviously, he couldn't be. The Spanish *Fawlty Towers* has a dim-witted immigrant waiter from... Italy.

Fawlty Towers, *Modern Times* and Adriano Celentano play entertaining games with foreign-soundingness quite literally, in sung and spoken speech-sounds. Corngold's *Metamorphosis* could of course be read aloud or sounded out in the reader's head in a non-native phonology. Gregor Samsa's first words in direct speech—

> "Oh God," he thought, "what a grueling job I've picked! Day in, day out—on the road",

would then be taken as a written representation of sounds more recognisably transcribed as

> "Och Gott," e saut, "vot a kruling tschop aif picked! Tay in, tay out—on ze rote."

This is surely very silly: neither Corngold nor any other serious translator ever intended his work to be sounded out with a conventional source-language accent. But it's a silly idea that nonetheless forces us to ask a real question: if that is *not* what is meant by foreign-soundingness in the translation of a foreign literary or other text, then what exactly *is* foreign-soundingness? By what criterion—by what means—can foreign-soundingness be perceived or judged? After all, written texts have no *sound* at all. To talk of some written sentence as "sounding like English" or "not sounding like English" must be a figure of speech—and most likely, speech with forked tongue.

Let us examine a passage of translated prose to see if we can define what it might mean to say that it does or does not "sound" like its original or its receiving language independently of any implied oral realization:

> The positive and the classical sciences of writing are obliged to repress this sort of question. Up to a certain point, such repression is even necessary to the progress of positive investigation. Beside the fact that it would still be held within a philosophising logic, the ontophenomenological question of essence, that is to say of the origin of writing, could, by itself, only paralyse or sterilise the typological or historical research of *facts*.

> My intention, therefore, is not to weigh that prejudicial question, that dry, necessary, and somewhat facile question of right, against the power and efficacy of the positive researches which we may witness today. The genesis and system of scripts had never led to such profound, extended, and assured explorations. It is not really a matter of weighing the question against the importance of the discovery; since the questions are imponderable, they cannot be weighed. If the issue is not quite that, it is perhaps because its repression has real consequences in the very content of the researches that, in the present case and in a privileged way, are always arranged around problems of definition and beginning.[4]

It is not because this passage is hard to follow that it "sounds like" English or not-English—Celentano's old song shows how easy it is to make completely meaningless concatenations sound like perfect English if phonetic English-soundingness is all you want to achieve. What marks it as a translation *from French*, however, is the anomalous use of the word *research* in the plural, matching a regular usage of a similar-looking word in French, *recherche*. Obviously, that can be seen only by a reader who knows French as well as English: the foreignness of "researches" is not self-evident to an English-only speaker, who may well construct quite other hypotheses to account for it, or else accept it as a special or technical term belonging to this particular author. But if the bilingual reader also has some additional knowledge of French philosophical terminologies, then the word *positive* preceding *researches* becomes quite transparent. It stands to reason to a bilingual reader that *postive researches* in the English represents *recherches positives* in the source. What that French phrase means, however, is something else. It is how you say *empirical investigation* in plain French.

Two views of this are available to us. We can say that *positive researches* is a poor English representation of a straightforward French phrase that the translator seems not to recognize; or else we can see it as the trace inside English of the authentic sound of the original. Indeed, unless an English phrase *is* perceptibly anomalous, we would not be able to see it as containing any trace of not-English. But it is equally clear that we would not be able to see the "Frenchness" of the phrase if we had no knowledge of French.

Foreignizing translation styles bend English into shapes that mirror some aspect (but by no means all aspects) of the regular forms of the source. But they rely entirely for their foreignizing effect on the reader's prior knowledge of the approximate shape and sound of the foreign language—or if we are to take Spivak's translation of Derrida as a case in point, on detailed items in the grammar and lexis of the foreign tongue.

For a counterfactual demonstration of this, imagine a novel translated from Hindi. Hindi has not one, not two but three ways of saying "you": *tu, tum* and *ap*, corresponding to the intimate, the friendly and the formal (all three may be used for single or plural addressees). Let us say a translator tries to import into a foreignising English translation from Hindi some linguistic anomaly in English that corresponds to this triple division of "you". (After all, alternation between the three forms of address might be really important for understanding the dynamics of interaction between the novel's characters in dialogue passages, and a legitimate object of the translator's effort.) But would we notice? Yes, if the chosen anomaly was really way out. Would we know that it was a mark of Hindi? Not at all! That is because we do not know any Hindi....

On the other hand, there are many historical and cultural circumstances where knowledge of items or elements of a foreign language is quite widely shared. In fact, most translations take place between languages spoken by communities that have quite a lot to do with each other, culturally, economically, or politically. In the 16C a great deal was translated from Italian into French, just as many Italian craftsmen were brought in to beautify palaces and castles across the land. The translators of that era wrote French with a whole raft of Italian words and turns of phrase, because they felt that their readers either did or really should know the words and phrases they imported. More than that: they thought French would be positively improved by being made a little more like Italian. And in fact the process of making French more like Italian has continued down to the present day. Limiting ourselves to words beginning with the letters *ca-*, a not very large dictionary lists the following Italianisms—many of them introduced by translators—that have enriched the French language over the past five hundred years:

caban, "pea-jacket" (from Sicily, originally Arabic)

cabinet, "office" (It. *cabine*)

cabriole, "summersault" (It. *capriola*, from *capra,* "goat")

cadastre, "survey" (from Italian via Provençal)

cadre, "frame" (It. *cuadro*, from Lat. *quadrus,* "square")

caleçon, "underpants" (It. *calza,* "footwear")

calepin, "notebook" (from the name of Calepino, a famous Italian lexicographer)

calfater, "to caulk" (via Italian from Arabic)

calmar, "squid" (via Italian from Lat. *calamus,* ink or pen)

calque, "copy" (via Italian from Lat. *calcare*)

camérier, "steward" (from It. *camera.* "bedroom")

campagnol, "vole" (from It. *campagna,* "countryside")

campanile, "bell-tower" (It. *campana,* "bell")

canaille, "rabble" (It. *cane,* from Lat. *canis,* "dog")

canette, "duck" (*canna*, Genovese dialect)

cantabile, "singable" (It. *cantabile*)

cantaloup, a type of melon (from an Italian place-name, Cantalupo)

cantate, "cantata" (from It. *cantare,* "to sing")

cantatrice, "female singer"

cantine (It. *canto,* "corner")

capital, "capital" (It. *capitale,* "principal")

capiteux, "heady" (via Italian from Lat. *caput* "head")

caporal, "corporal" (It. *caporal*)

cappuccino, a type of coffee drink (It. *cappuccino*, diminutive of *capucin*, monk) caprice, "caprice" (It. *capriccio*)

carat, "carat" (via Italian from Arabic *qirat*)

cardan, "universal joint" (from the name of an Italian scholar, Girolamo Cardamo)

carène, "hull" (ultimately from Lat. *carena*, the half-shell of a walnut)

caresse, "cuddle" (It. *carezza,* from *caro,* « dear »)

caricature (from It. *caricare*, "to mock")

carmagnole, name of a revolutionary song (probably from an Italian place-name)

carnation, "ruddy tint" (from It. *carne* « flesh »)

carnaval, "carnival" (from It. *carne,* "flesh" and It. *levare*, "to stop": an end to the meat fast)

carpaccio, "thinly siced beef" (after the name of an Italian painter)

carrière, "career" (It *carrier*a "chariot path")

carrosse, "coach" (It. *carrozza*)

carrousel, "roundabout" (a game played in Naples, from It. *caruso,* shaven head)

carton, "cardboard" (It. *carta*)

cartouche, "cartridge" (It. *carta)*

casanier, "home-bound" (from It. *casa* « home »)

cascade, "waterfall" (from It. *cascare* "to fall")

casino, "casino" (diminutive of It. *casa,* "house")

casquer, "to catch, imprison" (from It. *cascare* "to fall" (into a trap)

cassate, "cassata"

castrat, "castrato"

catafalque, "ceremonial funerary urn"

cavale, "ride" (It. *cavalla*, from Lat. *caballus, "horse"*)

caviar (via It. from Turkish.)[5]

At a similar moment in the linguistic history of another European language, German translators consciously imported a quantity of words from Greek, French and English not only to make European classics accessible to speakers of German, but also to improve the German language by extending its range of vocabulary. The issue as they saw it was like this. French and English were international languages already, propped up by powerful states. That was why non-native speakers learned French (and to a lesser extent, English). How could German ever be the vehicle of a powerful state unless non-natives learned to read it? And why should they learn to read it—unless it can easily convey the meanings that arise in the transnational cultures held to represent the riches of European civilization?

A similar argument has been put forward by the contemporary French writer who goes by the name of Antoine Volodine. He has the striking aim of writing in French (his native language) as if it were a foreign language. Why so? For Volodine, French is not only the language of Racine and Voltaire. Because translation exists, and has existed for a very long time, French is also the language of Pushkin, Shalamov, Li Bai and Marquez. Far from being the privileged vector of national identity, history and culture, French is a language that transmits cultures, philosophies and concerns that have nothing to do with the habits of French society or the Francophone world.[6] It is not that French is by its nature or destiny an international language: on the contrary, only the practice of translation into French makes the language a tool of internationalism in the modern world. Thanks to its long history of translation from exotic languages, French is now a possible vehicle for an imaginary, infinitely haunting literature that Volodine would like to consider absolutely foreign to it.

It would therefore be quite wrong to see the progressive interpenetration of English, French, German, and Italian together with terms and phrases from the ancient source tongues, Latin and Greek, and (in Volodine's rather special case) Russian and Chinese too, as the sole product of what is now called globalisation. In any case, globalisation does not spread only English into other languages and cultures: it could just as well be exemplified by the spread of pizza-language and the vocabulary of pasta (along with pizze and pasta as well) into every corner store and fast food joint in the developed world as by the penetration of English-sounding pop lyrics in all the European languages. It is more significantly the result of long efforts by translators to raise their national languages to international status. They did not necessarily seek to make their translations "sound foreign". Indeed, if that is what they were really trying to do, their success has made mincemeat of their ambition, because the words they imported or mimicked have now become part of the receiving language to such an extent that they are no longer foreign at all, as the list of Italianisms in French given above amply demonstrates.

Translators' campaigns to make German more like English or French more like Italian are however quite different from contemporary efforts to produce translations into English that keep something "authentically foreign" about them. The foreignizers of today are not campaigning to make English an international language—English *is* the international language of the present. Nor are they consciously seeking to enrich English with the linguistic resources afforded by languages that are distant from it. What they are doing, it seems to me, is seeking to share with their readers some of the feeling that they themselves have when reading a foreign text. Do these feelings—of strangeness, perhaps of mild frustration—come from not being completely at home in the source language? Richard Pevear has stated publicly many times that he is not a very fluent speaker of Russian: as David Remnick wrote of him in a now-famous *New Yorker* profile, "he has certainly picked up a great deal of Russian, but not its outlandishly rich vocabulary, the complicated grammar, with its maddening various verb conjugations, shades of tense, reflexivities, cases, endings, gerundial gymnastics";[7] he relies on his partner Larissa Volokhonskaya to provide a "bare bones" translation for him to work into a literary version. Something similar may be true of other proponents of less-than-fluent, awkward and foreign-sounding translation styles. If that were so, then the very project of writing translations that do the least "ethnocentric violence" to the original would dissolve into something altogether different—an imitation not of what the source text says, but of the funny ways foreigners speak. In this roundabout way, contemporary translation studies seems to license and promote an inadvertent return to the kind of language games played to brilliant and comic effect by Chaplin and Celentano.

It is not easy to represent the foreignness of foreign languages in complete seriousness. All that a translation really can do is represent the meaning of a foreign text. And that's quite hard enough.

Notes

1. The term probably originates with Antoine Berman, *L'Épreuve de l'étranger. Culture et Traduction dans; Allemagne romantique* (Paris: Gallimard, 1984), but has been given wider circulation by Lawrence Venuti, especially in *The Scandals of Translation. Towards an Ethics of Difference* (New York: Routledge, 1998).
2. Dangerous connections: or, letters collected in a society, and published for the instruction of other societies. By M. C**** de L***. [Choderlos de Laclos, a translation from the French]. London, 1784.
3. Fred Vargas, *Have Mercy on Us All.* Translated by David Bellos. London: Harvill, 2003.
4. From Chapter Two of Jacques Derrida's *Of Grammatology* (1967), translated by Gayatri Chakravorti Spivak. Johns Hopkins UP, 1974.
5. Adapted from Mariagrazia Margarito, "Une valise pour bien voyager...avec les italianismes du français", *Synergies* 4 (2008): pp. 63-73.
6. Antoine Volodine, "Écrire en français une littérature étrangère", *chaoïd* 6 (2002).
7. David Remnick, "The Translation Wars", *New Yorker*, November 7, 2005.

3

Translation Studies and Language Sciences

Sachin Ketkar

Before Translation Studies was recognized as an autonomous area of inquiry, translation received a good deal of theoretical attention as a branch of applied linguistics and as an area of 'influence studies' within the discipline of Comparative Literary Studies. The approaches based on linguistics considered translation primarily as a verbal activity and a linguistic process. It does not mean that the early linguists overlooked the cultural dimensions of translation. Theorists like Quine (1959/2000) or Jakobson (1959/2000) went beyond formal linguistics in approaching translation and were aware of the problems involved in considering translation merely as a verbal act. All this was before what is called 'cultural turn' in translation theory.

Roman Jakobson's famous 'On Linguistic Aspects of Translation' (2000: 113-118) is a seminal statement not only in the linguistic theorizations of translation but also in Translation Studies as a whole. As he approaches his subject from a semiotic perspective, he is able to locate translation in the broader framework of culture, and at the same time expand the conventional understanding of the activity. His renowned tripartite classification of the activity into (i) Interpretation of verbal sign by means of other signs of the same language or Intralingual translation (rewording), (ii) interpretation of verbal signs by means of some other language or Interlingual translation (translation proper), and

(iii) interpretation of verbal signs by means of signs of nonverbal sign systems or Intersemiotic translation (transmutation) has had a tremendous impact on the later development of Translation Studies. Due to the first and the last categories of translation, the meaning of the term 'translation' itself is greatly altered and broadened. This extension of the sense of the term 'translation' makes it extremely elastic and inclusive. After Jakobson's theorization, it becomes possible to consider the things like commentary, explication and rephrasing as forms of translation. It also becomes possible to see adaptations of texts to different mediums like films or plays as a form translation. In many ways, Jakobson anticipates and probably influences the later theories of translation like Lefevere's theory of translation as 'rewriting'.

Jakobson's position is also very useful for its discussion of the major problems of translations like 'the dogma of untranslatability', especially the kind posed because of the Sapir-Whorf thesis. The thesis states that different languages shape different cognitive 'realities' and that communication between two people who do not share the same native language, is impossible because the cognitive function of language is dependent on the specific grammatical patterns of that language. The implication of this is particularly negative for translation. The Sapir-Whorf kind of 'incommensurability thesis' is also at the basis of Quine's statement on translation (2000:94-112) which states that it is not possible to decide what is a correct translation as, "What is really involved is difficulty or indeterminacy of correlation. It is just that there is less basis of comparison—less sense in saying what is good translation and what is bad—the farther we get away from sentences with visibly direct conditioning to nonverbal stimuli and the farther we get off home ground." (Quine, 2000:112). Quine seems to be pointing out that because two statements in two different languages cannot be really compared, as there is no firm ground for comparison, the question of equivalence becomes a meaningless question.

On the other hand, Jakobson argues that "languages differ essentially in what they must convey and not what they *may* convey.... In its cognitive function, language is minimally dependent on the grammatical patterns because the definition of our experience stands in complementary relation to metalinguistic operation-the cognitive level of language not only admits but directly requires recoding interpretation i.e., translation. Any assumption of ineffable or untranslatable cognitive data would be a contradiction in terms." That comprehension itself is impossible without interpretation is a well-known fact and hence the act of translation that is 'interpretation of verbal signs' by means of other verbal signs is inevitable and integral to the use of language. Jakobson's extension of the meaning of the term 'translation' enables him to bypass the Sapir-Whorf 'incommensurability thesis' which actually denies the possibility of translation. When you think of rewording or even intersemiotic adaption as translation, there is more scope for equivalence, a greater possibility for translation.

The question of possibility of translation ceased to remain the most pressing issue for later development in linguistic theorization of translation. The focus of the later theorization was on translation as a process and the means of defining, describing and modeling this process in linguistic terms. The emphasis of theorization moved away from the cultural dimension and closer to formal linguistics. However, Jakobson is skeptical about the utility of linguistics theory for studying literary translation.

J.C. Catford's remarkably lucid *A Linguistic Theory of Translation* (1965) can be seen as a typical case of movement towards more formal approach to translation. He sees translation primarily as 'an operation performed on languages' and hence feels that 'any theory of translation must draw upon a theory of language, a general linguistic theory'. He defines translation as "the replacement of textual material in one language (SL) by equivalent textual material in another language (TL)." The use of the term 'textual material' instead of the word 'term' is particularly significant because in 'normal conditions', Catford explains, it is not the entirety of a SL text which is translated, that is, replaced by TL equivalents. The key term in Catford's theorization is 'equivalence'. He states that "the central task of translation theory is that of defining the nature and conditions of translation equivalence." Catford goes on to provide an interesting way of looking at the notion of equivalence. He says, "A textual translation equivalent is thus: that portion of TL text which is changed when and only when a given portion of the SL text is changed," a textual translation equivalent being any TL form (text or portion of text) which is observed to be equivalent of given SL form (text or portion of text).

The notion of equivalence has remained central to linguistic approaches to translation theory and most of the technical jargon used to address the problems of equivalence seems to be saying more or less the same thing in spite of terminological differences. Most of the theories tend to become prescriptive and advice ancient compromise formula suggested by Horace of avoiding literalism and remaining faithful to the 'spirit' of the original without damaging the structure of the target language. For instance, Eugene Nida's (1974: 200-01) distinction between two types of equivalences, formal and dynamic equivalence based on the principle of equivalence effect, does not seem to be very original. Formal equivalence or correspondence is one in which "the features of the form of the source text have been mechanically reproduced in the receptor language". Nida points out that this formal correspondence distorts the grammatical and stylistic patterns of the receptor language, and hence distorts the message, so as to cause the receptor to misunderstand or to labour unduly hard. He contrasts this formal correspondence with the dynamic equivalence which is "a quality of a translation in which the message of the original text has been so transported into the receptor language that the RESPONSE of the RECEPTOR is essentially like that of original receptors. Frequently, the form of the original text is changed; but as long as the change follows the rules of back transformation in the source language, or of contextual consistency in the transfer, and of transformation in the receptor language, the message is preserved and the translation is faithful." In some respects, Nida's classification resembles Dryden's famous classification of translation into metaphrase, paraphrase and imitation. Paraphrase, in Dryden's scheme, is a compromise between word for word metaphrase and 'free' imitation. Dynamic equivalence aims at complete 'naturalizing' of a message from source language in the receptor language. Nida says, "a translation of dynamic equivalence aims at complete naturalness of expression, and tries to relate the receptor to modes of behavior relevant within the context of his own culture; it does not insist that he should understand the cultural patterns of the source-language context in order to comprehend the message."

Nida's distinction also is similar to Newmark's (1982:39) distinction between Semantic and Communicative translation. Newmark notes that, "communicative translation attempts to produce on its readers an effect as close as possible to that obtained on the readers of the original. Semantic translation attempts to render, as closely as the semantic and syntactic structures of the second language allow, the exact contextual meaning of the original.... Semantic translation remains within the original culture and assists the reader only in its connotations if they constitute the essential human (non-ethnic) message of the text. One basic difference between the two methods is that where there is a conflict, the communicative must emphasize the 'force' rather than the content". One also recalls Vinay and Darbelnet's (1958/2000, 84) distinction between 'literal' and 'oblique' translation. The two modes of translation resemble Schleiermacher's (1993) distinction. Schleiermacher observed that there are two ways of translating: "either the translator leaves the writer alone as much as possible and moves the reader towards the writer or he leaves the reader alone as much as possible and moves the writer towards the reader."

This compromise formula seems to be proverbial old wine and the new bottle kind of thing. One of the severe limitations of this type of approach was that in spite of the rhetoric of rigour and discipline it did not go much beyond the pre-linguistic theories and only managed to provide a long list of specific strategies and manuals for the translators and the approach which began as descriptive ended up being covertly prescriptive and normative. The norm is usually what Venuti (1995) calls the norm of fluency or naturalizing of the alien text, which aims to conceal the fact that the text is a translation by ironing out stylistic oddity or 'foreignness' and create an illusion that the text is 'natural' and not translated. Venuti points out that such a norm is product of commercial and market forces and aught to be challenged.

Martindale (1984: 47-72) actually makes a case for literalism and 'metaphrase'. He notes that it is merely Nida's prejudice against literal correspondence, because there can be equally good reasons in the support of the very literal correspondence. Schleiermacher, too, favours the method that emphasizes the idea of drawing out the readers from the linguistic world they inhabit. Venuti and Martindale's argument seem to hold good for literary translations, and linguistic approaches to translation have not exclusively dealt with literary translation. However, intervention like Venuti's is important because it exposes the fact that though linguistic approaches claim to be descriptive and neutral, they are covertly normative.

Henry Schogt (1992: 193-203) examines the relationship and the scope of using the semantic theory for translation theory and comes to the conclusion "for texts where cognitive meaning prevails and formal expression of that meaning has no other function than expressing that meaning, the semantic theories are helpful, and are adequate for describing the double process of encoding and decoding. For literary texts, it is precisely the literariness that falls outside the domain of semantics."

Some of the other preoccupation of theorists of such orientation like Nida or Roger Bell (1991) is the attempts to formulate a sort of descriptive model of the whole process of translation and integrate various language sciences like linguistics, pragmatics, semantics and even psycholinguistics and neurolinguistics. However, the models in spite of intricacies and complex terminology fail to describe what actually goes on in the 'mind' of the translator when he or she switches over from one language to the other in search of possible equivalents. This becomes a sort of 'black box'. The actual 'event' of 'going across' and beyond the boundaries of languages remains veiled and unarticulated. Many, like Theo Hermans (1985: 9-10)consider the approach to be too sterile and endlessly caught in the inexorable discussions that come with new vocabulary while the concepts, of course are not very new. Lawrence Venuti (1998: 1) points out that such approach, "offer truncated view of the empirical data they collect...and remain reluctant to take into account the social values that enter into translating as well as the study of it."

G.N. Devy (1993: 140-141)objects to these linguistically oriented theories by pointing out that the Western linguistics is too much obsessed with monolingual situations and is monolingual in its orientation. It refuses to look at the fact that languages are 'open' to each other in socio-linguistic sense; that is, they interact very frequently with one another and have a historical relationship. He believes that if we think of a 'translating consciousness', which exploits the potential openness of language systems, and conceptualize a whole community of "translating consciousnesses, taking lead from Phenomenology, it should be possible to develop a theory of inter-lingual synonymy."

Hewson and Martin (1991) have attempted to bridge the gap between these two types of theoretical perspectives. They formulate a two-tier model for analyzing and explaining the translation phenomenon. While the first tier focuses on the range of linguistic possibilities available to the translator and the choices, he or she makes while the second tier deals with the institutional, cultural contextual factors that influence the range of choices as well as the actual decisions made by the translator. Basil Hatim and Ian Mason (1990: 3) also endeavor to bridge the gap between the linguistic sciences oriented approaches and the approaches that emphasize the target culture system or the political dimension of translation as a product. They view translation as a process involving the negotiation of meaning between producers and receivers of texts and consider translating as a communicative process that takes place within a social context. Corpus translation studies or CTS seeks to combine the cultural studies model and the concepts from corpus linguistics and computational linguistics. This approach aspires to be rigorously scientific by using the statistical tools, computers and database to uncover the same general laws of translation. However, a comprehensive General Theory of Translation is a distant dream where all the approaches agree on one infallible approach.

References

Baker, Mona. Ed. *Routledge Encyclopedia of Translation Studies.* London and New York: Routledge, 1998.

Bassnett, Susan. *Translation Studies.* London and NY: Methuen, 1980.

Bell, Roger. *Translation and Translating: Theory and Practice.* London and New York: Longman, 1991.

Catford, J.C. A Linguistic Theory of Translation: An Essay in Applied Linguistics. London: Oxford University Press, 1965.

Devy, G.N. *In Another Tongue: Essays on Indian English Literature.* Madras: Macmillan India, 1993. pp. 117-52.

Hatim, Basil and Ian Mason. *Discourse and the Translation.* London and New York. Longman: 1990, p. 3.

Hewson, Lance and Jacky Martin. *Redefining Translation The Variational Approach.* London and New York: Routledge, 1991.

Hermans, Theo. ed. The Manipulation of Literature: Studies in Literary Translation. New York: St. Martin's Press, 1985.

Jakobson, Roman. 'On linguistic aspect of translation' in Venuti ed. 2000.

Martindale, C. 'Unlocking the word-hoard: in praise of metaphase' in E.S. Shaffer. 1984, pp. 47-72.

Newmark, Peter. *Approaches to Translation.* Oxford: Pergamon, 1982.

Nida, E.A. Towards a Science of Translating: with Special Reference to Principles and Procedures Involved in Bible Translating. Leyden. Brill. 1964.

Nida E.A. and C. Taber. *The Theory and Practice of Translation.* Leyden, Brill. 1974.

Quine, Willard V. 'Meaning and Translation' in. Venuti ed. 2000.

Schleiermacher, F. 'From "On the Different Methods of Translating" Translated by Waltraund Bartscht.' in R. Schulte and J. Biguenet eds. 1993. pp. 36-54.

Schogt, H.G. "Semantic Theory and Translation Theory" in R.S. Chulte and J. Biguenet eds. 1992 pp. 193-203.

Schulte, R. and Biguenet. J. eds. *Theories of Translation: An anthology of Essays from Dryden to Derrida.* Chicago, University of Chicago, 1992.

Shaffer, E.S. ed. *Comparative Criticism.* Vol. VI, Cambridge: Cambridge University Press, 1984.

Venuti, Lawrence ed. *Translation Studies Reader*. London and New York: Routledge and Kegan Paul, 2000.

Vinay, Jean-Paul, and Jean Darbelnet. "A Methodology for Translation". In Venuti ed. 2000, p. 84.

4

Translation, Hybridity and Transcreation

Amar Singh

In general, translation is considered an act of rendering a text written in one language belonging to a certain culture into a different language belonging to another culture. But what happens if the source text is replete with several languages and cultures? How does one translate a text whose untranslatability is aggressively inscribed within it in the form of French/Italian/American English words? In other words, what are the challenges involved in translating texts that are inscribed with many languages and cultures?

In the context of post colonial studies, Homi Bhabha refers to hybridity as a state—"a third space" from where the dynamics of colonial authority can be contested. It is in this zone, characterised as the zone of negotiation, contest and exchange that a translational culture emerges. In his text entitled "Cultural Diversity and Cultural Differences" Bhabha underlines the interdependence of the colonizer and the colonized and argues that any claims to the inherent purity and originality of cultures are invalid. It is hoped that by exploring the 'Third Space', we may elude the politics of polarity. Embracing the hybridized nature of cultures will steer us away from the problematic binaries that have until now framed our notions of culture[1] (Bhabha 1995: 206-09).

Today, hybridity is closely linked with the phenomenon of globalization. The mass movement of population and products across the globe has resulted in the hybridization of cultures. There is no single culture which has not been adulterated by contact or intermingling, or not influenced by the foreigner (s). The idea of a culture as an envelope which securely binds all the members of a national community within the same coherence of meaning today belongs to the realm of myth, which has been aptly pointed out by Sherry Simon in her eloquent essay on "Translating and Inter-lingual Creation in the Contact Zone"[2] (Simon 1999b: 58-74). The great migrations of the post-colonial age have shaped a new socio-demographic situation and most nations now have increasingly mixed populations. The ease and rapidity of global communication has created an international mass culture which competes and interacts with local forms and thus the idea of culture as a set of fixed and consistent values, behaviours or attitudes, has given way to the idea of culture as, *"evolutive"*, and in constant *"negotiation"*.

Hybridity is different from multiculturalism which conceives cultures as autonomous bodies; i.e. each group representing one culture that is different from others in terms of its habits, beliefs, and customs. Multiculturalism is each for 'himself' in an empire of differences, whereas hybridity is interpenetration and contamination. It is against two extreme world views: the leveling of differences (i.e. homogenization) and the inverted movement of hyper differentiation[3] (Simon 1999a: 19-36).

If hybridity is defined as "a third space"—"a space in between"—how would one define a hybrid text? In the context of postcolonial writings, the hybrid text is often defined as one written by the ex-colonised in the language of the ex-coloniser, thus creating a 'new language' and occupying a 'space in between'. In the words of Mehrez:

> These post colonial texts frequently referred to as 'hybrid' or 'metisses' because of the culturo-linguistic layering which exists between them, have succeeded in forging a new language.[4] (Meherz 1992: 121)

These texts written by postcolonial subjects create a language *"in between"* their own and that of the colonizer and therefore come to occupy a space *"in between"*. In most cases, the challenge of such a space has been double: these texts seek to decolonise themselves from two dominating forces, namely the ex-coloniser and the *"traditional, national"* cultures. Therefore, a hybrid literary production can be viewed as resistance to the hegemony of the colonizer and the colonised, the dominant and the dominated. The ultimate goal of such literature is to subvert hierarchies by bringing together the *'governing'* and the 'governed' by exploding and inter signification[5] (*ibid.*: 120-138). Hybrid texts are thus not drawn from one culture, one language, but manifest the presence of more than one culture, one linguistic code within the same text. Hybridity in these texts may be termed as the creation of new trans-cultural forms.

It is important to note that hybridity is closely linked with cosmopolitan spaces which are contact zones of negotiation, dialogue and intermingling of individuals of all kinds irrespective of their colour, religion, race and gender. Being transient, evolutive and *'anational'* in nature, hybridity contests conventional linguistic and cultural identities based on simplistic binary categories. It thrives in *'contact zones'* which are spaces of multiplicity, exchange, renegotiation and discontinuities.

The concept of transcreation is closely related to the issue of the practical "Indianisation" of English by creative writers in their work. Raja Rao famously argued in 1938, in the preface to his novel *Kanthapura,* for using English, but an English adapted to Indian conditions:

> English is not really an alien language to us. It is the language of our intellectual make-up-like Sanskrit or Persian was before—but not of our emotional make-up. We are all instinctively bilingual, many of us in our own language and in English. We cannot write like the English. We should not. We can only write as Indians.... Our method of expression...will some day prove to be as distinctive and colourful as the Irish or the American.[6] (Rao, Preface. 5)

Kanthapura has often been seen as being written in an English modified to South Indian condition that reflects Kannada speech rhythms. Indeed, in a later essay, "In Search of—My Bride" (1978), in which he recalled the history of his writer's vocation, Rao went so far so far as to advocate a "*Sanskritic*" English:

> I will have to write my English after all—and how soon we forget it-is an Indo-Aryan tongue. Thus to stretch the English idiom to suit my needs seemed heroic enough for my urgent most demands. The Irish, remember, had done it (...) So why not Sanskritic (or if you will, Indian) English?[7] (Rao 1996: 147)

English is also placed in relation to Sanskrit in a different context by A.K. Ramanujan, in an essay entitled "*Is There an Indian Way of Thinking?*" published in 1989. Ramanujan argues, somewhat provocatively, for a contextual or socio-linguistic analogy between English and Sanskrit:

> When English is borrowed into (or imposed on) Indian contexts, it fits into the Sanskrit slot; it acquires many of the characteristics of Sanskrit, the older native father tongue, its pan- Indian elite character as a medium of laws, science and administration, and its formulaic patterns; it becomes part of Indian multiple diglossia.[8] (Ramanujan 437)

This position highlights the relative formality of Indian English—an aspect on which other analysts concur and thus adumbrates what we may call a *socio-linguistic* approach to the phenomenon.

Sarangi, paying particular attention to bilingualism or multilingualism as a key given in multiple language situations in India, including the creation of literary works, marshals a number of basic socio-linguistic concepts, including *code-switching* (moving from one language to another) code mixing (including elements of more than one language in the same utterance, *role-relationships* (the structuring of dialogue according to the speakers' different roles in society) and *turn taking* (the social conventions governing who speaks when). He applies these concepts to a series of IWE works. With specific regard to Indian English and its literary manifestation in IWE, Sarangi offers a number of important observations from the inside, which we may place alongside those made, rather more from the outside, by the non-Indian scholars David Mc Cutchion and Dora Sales:

> In the linguistically and culturally pluralistic Indian subcontinent English is used as the Second Language (L2), which is acquired after one has learnt the First Language (L1). This co-existence...results in interference from one's First Language in the Second Language. Through a large-scale socio-cultural interaction with regional contexts English becomes Indianised. A Variety of English albeit non-native, lexically, morphologically, syntactically, stylistically and socio-linguistically different from the Standard British form has come to be known as the Indian Variety of English....[9] (Sarangi 17)

Bandyopadhyay, applying her theoretical postulates to a corpus different from but comparable to Sarangi's (there is some overlapping of authors and texts between the two), takes an approach in many ways similar but rendered distinct by its emphasis on Indian English as a *specific variant of International Standard English*. Her analysis of specific texts stresses such features of Indian English, many of them socio-linguistic, as Indianisation of vocabulary, loan translation, use of repetition, formality of register and linguistic creativity. She writes:

> The term "Indian English" refers to the variety of English which is learnt and used by a large number of educated (in the conventional sense, someone who has undergone and intellectual and moral training). Indians as a second language.... Indian English has the status of an Indian language, serves the international role of communication with the global community of nations and intra-regional roles of link language among people of diverse linguistic backgrounds.[10] (Bandyopadhyay)

Considering standard Indian English as a variant of standard International English, we may provisionally suggest, in a non-exclusive list, nine lexical strands as being specific to

Indian English, which we shall now describe in turn: (a) pan-Indian terms, or words from Indian languages absorbed into Indian English as lexical items and understood throughout India—e.g. *lakh; crore; dhoti; dhobi; mali;* (b) *Indian "localisms"*, pertaining to a specific language or cultural area, e.g. to take two south Indian culinary items; *idli; dosa;* (c) native Indian words that have been absorbed beyond India into general International English e.g. through Indian restaurants or musical styles- e.g. (first type) *wallah; pukka; dekko;* (Second type) *chapatti; biryani; bhangra.* (e) transplanted Britishisms (words, idioms, acronyms) still used in the UK and recognizable as such to a reader from that country- e.g. *GP* (general practitioner); *snazzy; culture-vulture;* (f) "old" Britishisms, that is, terms that now seem dated or anachronistic to a British reader but are still current coin in India- e.g. GPO (General Post Office); thrice (for three times); doing bird (=being in jail); chip off the old block (=like father, like son); (g) American or other neologisms pertaining to International English and often associated with globalisation or with the journalistic register- e.g. MBA; start up; (h) coinages or acronyms formed from within the usual rules of English but unique to India- e.g. scheduled castes; shirtings; in-charge; NRI (Non-Resident Indian); (i) cases of such coinages that have passed into International English, e.g. Bollywood; Goa trance. In its very richness and creativity, Indian English emerges from this descriptive analysis as a specific form of English that may legitimately be considered as important a variant of the international language as American or British English. It will, therefore, inevitably generate a number of translation problems of a specific nature, whatever the language translated into.

If there are two challenges that permanently face the translator of IWE works into any non-Indian language, they are, on the one hand, the presence of lexical Indianisms, embedded in the text, and the need to find appropriate translation strategies to communicate their sense and flavour; and, on the other, the strong tendency of IWE texts to deploy to the full the idiomatic resources of International English, with a marked continuing influence of British English, a characteristic which forces the translator to decide how far each such idiom should or should not go into a similar register in the target language. Today, translation of Indian Writing in English, for all its challenges and difficulties, has a major role to play in communication, to as wide an audience as possible, the richness and complexity of Indian culture, in an evermore globalised world to which that culture will have a remarkable contribution to make as the twenty-first century unfolds.

By depicting more than one culture, more than one language, more than one world experience, the hybrid Quebecker texts very often defy the very notion of an 'original work' and its translation. Hence in many, these plurilingual texts demand of their readers to be like themselves: 'in between', at once capable of reading and translating. For a multi-lingual Indian reader this experience may not be unique or new but it is challenging since it involves reading and rendering of new power dynamics between languages and cultures.

Analyzing hybrid texts translated into a secular Hindi has made me realize that a translator's job has become more and more challenging especially in the context of cosmopolitan zones. Earlier when boundaries were clear, nations neatly defined, a translator had to navigate within two shores (source to target). In the heterogeneous global village of today where the concept of nation has been complicated by mass migrations and development of multi-cultural societies and where the boundaries between the languages have become hazy and blurry, the translator has to acquire special skills and expertise in multiple areas and languages to understand the myriad linguistic-cultural layerings inscribed in hybrid texts.

References

1. Homi, Bhabha. 1995. "Cultural diversity & Cultural differences" in Bill Ashcroft et al. eds. *The post-Colonial Studies Reader*. London and New York: Routledge.
2. Sherry, Simon. 1992. "The language of Cultural Difference: Figures of Alterity in Canadian Translation" in *Rethinking Translation*. Eds. Lawrence Venuti. London: Routeledge.
3. *Ibid.*

4. Samia, Mehrez. 1992. "Translation and the Postcolonial Experience: The Francophone North African Text" in *Rethinking Translation*, Ed. Lawrence Venuti. London and New York: Routeledge. pp. 120-38.

5. *Ibid.*

6. Raja, Rao. 1938/2001. *Kanthapura*. New Delhi: Orient Paperbacks.

7. *Ibid.* (1996)

8. A.K. Ramanujan, "Is There An Indian Way of Thinking?: An Informal Essay" 1989/2001. In Chaudhuri, Amit (ed.). *The Picador Book of Modern Indian Literature*. London: Picador, 2001. pp. 420-37.

9. Jaydeep, Sarangi. *Indian Novels in English: A Sociolinguistic Study*. Bareilly: Prakash Book Depot, 2005.

10. Sumana, Bandyopadhyay. 2007. "Indianisation of English: Analysis of Linguistic Features in Selected Post-1980 Indian English Fiction." Ph.D. thesis. Kanpur: Indian Institute of Technology Kanpur.

5

Literary Translation: An Overview

Deepak Borgave

What is translation? on a platter
A poet's pale and glaring head,
A parrot's screech, a monkey's chatter,
And profanation of the dead
Reflected words can only shiver
Like elongated lights that twist
In the black mirror of a river
Between the city and the mist
This is my task; a poet's patience
And scholastic passion bent-
Dove-droppings on your monument (Nabokov, 1975)[1]

Though the art of translation is as old as written literature, it was, until recently, not considered to be an ideal discipline in comparison with linguistics and literary studies, perhaps because the translators and translating culture were always placed at a lower end. Robert Frost's epigram, 'What is left out in translation is poetry' is a well-known example of such 'misgivings'.

But as M. Snell-Hornby (2006:133) holds that the developments since the industrial revolution have influenced the practice of translation, nurturing schools, professional associations and standards. Translation has become a very significant instrument of international communication in all branches of human knowledge and experience in recent years. There has been an increased commitment being found in the area of translation theory and practice and the study of translation has emerged as a discipline with renewed vigor now. These attempts are inadequate; they generally clarify the principles, structures and categories of the process of practical translation. An exploration of problem areas would therefore be the first step towards a systematic and scientific study of translation. Based on the explanation and understanding of the problems identified, a good deal of research is yet to be conducted in respect of language pairs to enumerate, describe and explain the processes and products of translation.

Translation of literary works, (novels, short stories, plays, poems, etc.) is considered a literary pursuit in its own right. It is a tool used to introduce literature of an alien language into one's own and hence a serious activity.

A Historical Perspective

The history of translation practice is quite old both in the West and the East. Cicero and Horace have been regarded as the first theorists. Cicero was sensitive to alter anything in the order of wording if compelled by necessity and Horace too was aware of the dilemma and advised not to be a slave to the original text (Bassnett 1991: 43-44). The Bible translations in the early period were used as a weapon against the dogmatic beliefs prevalent in the Church. John Wycliffe, who was first to translate Bible into English (1580-84), compared the previous versions to establish the original text. George Chapman states in the preface to his translation of *Iliad* that a translator must reach the 'spirit' of the original and avoid 'word for word' translation.

Rationalism, inductive reasoning, rules of aesthetic production and notions of 'imitation' and 'decorum' gained ground around the mid-seventeenth century. John Dryden outlined a rough theory of translation in his preface to *Ovid's 'Epistles* (1680). He distinguished between metaphrase, imitation and paraphrase. It was a prescriptive programme. 'Metaphrase' referred to a word by word and line by line translation of a text whereas 'imitation' referred to free translation. Cowley's Renderings of Pindar (1656) was a sort of imitation in terms of Dryden who viewed it as transgression. Alexander Pope too favoured Dryden's views on translation and wanted the spirit of the original text to be captured with emphasis on stylistic details of the text. Dr. Johnson also held the view in his *Life of Pope* (1779-80) that a translator has the right to read in his own terms. Large-scale translations came out in the eighteenth century and they played a pivotal role in shaping the contemporary taste and language of the period.

The first study of its kind on translation, Alexander Fraser Tytler's *The Principles of Translation* (1791) mentions three basic principles (a) the translation must retain the complete idea of the original (b) the style and manner of writing should be the same type as the original (c) the translation should have the ease of the source language text. Dryden's concept of paraphrase was not favoured by Tytler; he conceived it as loose translation. He, however, favoured 'omissions' and 'additions' in the translation to clarify ambiguities.

New twists on the art of translation during the early nineteenth century were given by the Romantics; rejecting rationalism of the eighteenth century, they dumped these as junk theories and emphasized the crucial role of 'fancy' and 'imagination' (S.T. Coleridge), the latter leading to powers of creativity. The Romantics, thus viewed translation in terms of imagination, i.e. as a higher creative activity. T. Webb (1976) shows from Shelley's writings that Shelley appreciated translations for their ideas and other literary features.

The expression of the remoteness of time and place of the original text in translation was the main concern of the Victorian translators which added a new dimension to literary translation i.e. the clement of archaism. In a series of lectures that Mathew Arnold delivered *On Translating Homer* (1862), he appears to be closer to the neo-classical perspectives; he held the view that a translator must serve the original text, and the target text reader must be brought to the source language text through the translation. Edward Fitzgerald in translating *Rubaiayat of Omar Khayyam* (1858) demonstrates that instead of leading the TL reader to the SL text, it was possible to bring a version of the SL text into the TL culture as a 'Living Entity', for he preferred 'a live sparrow to a stuffed eagle'.

Speech Culture and Linguistics

With the emergence of the discipline of linguistics, there has been the most far reaching impact on the twentieth century translation theory. Most linguistic theories developed during the twentieth century were developed in isolation from the main stream translations of literary theories. The American structuralism, Chomskyan 'Transformational Theory', Hallidayan 'Systematic' theory made attempts to combine both linguistic and literary theories of translation; literary texts are now seen to be rooted in the cultural metrics of a speech community.

Speech-acts, speech-patterns-rhythms are important in language because writing is finally derived from the metrics of speech-culture; different civilizations, different epochs do not produce the same speech-mass. Certain cultures speak less; some modes of sensitivity prize taciturnity and elision, others reward prolixity and semantic orientation.[2]

Ramchandra Sharma (1999: 124-130), while mediating between English and Kannada and translating poetry from both languages, finds rare relevance with reference to the behavioural patterns of speech between English and Kannada. How do Indians converse in a public place or at home? Sharma finds similarities in speech patterns in Indian, African and Latin American languages. Indians, Africans and Latin Americans speak loud in gross gestures, in larger exaggerated movements of both words and hands while communicating with others and obviously the same characteristics appear in our writing. We have no use for whispers.

Linguistic behaviour and climatic conditions are also interrelated with each other. Why are the Europeans found reserved natured and unspeakable and why do they speak lesser in amount as compared to the Indians and Mediterraneans? Is it due to the cooler climate? It is also possible to predict that the behavioral pattern of a language is governed by the fact that how late the printing facilities appeared in the history of a language. The lack of printing devices enforces the oral literary traditions; it would obviously put a great deal of pressure on a speech community to be louder or that whatever is to be said must be said forcefully without any ambiguity and say it in a louder linguistic gesture. The translators thus confronted several problems while translating such texts produced in a pre-printing era or in a specific cultural milieu.

Culture Contexts

Fidelity (or "faithfulness") and fluency are two qualities that, for millennia, have been regarded as ideals to be striven for in translation, particularly literary translation. Sometimes, especially in inexperienced hands, the two ideals are at odds. An example of one such translation is Nicol Macnicol's translation of a seventeenth century Marathi saint poet Tukaram's Abhangas a seventeenth century text oriented in oral literary tradition (There is often a feeling that the seventeenth century Marathi texts were oriented in oral literary tradition)[3]. The translation, through "formal equivalence" sought via literal translation, attempts to render the text literally.

When the renowned poet, Dilip Chitre, writing both in Marathi and English (Chitre, 1999) took to the task of translating the *Abhangas* he was confronted with the problems of contextualization of the SL text. Chitre's translation is faithful as it takes us closest to the SL text; it cannot tolerate loud gestures of the SL text. Subsequently, the SL texts wear overtones of dispiritedness and flatness, probably failing to bring up the vitality and loud gestures of the seventeenth century Marathi text. Similar observations have been made in respect of the English translations of Gopalkrishna Adiga's poems from Kannada by A.K. Ramanujan and M.G. Krishnamurthy (Ramchandra Sharma, 1999: 128). However, in translating poetry (Newmark, 2010: 6) creative deviations have to be considered as normal deviations as there are more poetic constraints such as rhyme, meter, assonance, alliteration, onomatopoeia, etc.

Promod Talegiri (1999: 85–88) considers embeddedness of a literary text in a cultural context. Word, he considers, as an inseparable agent of cultural memory or social history. Hermeneutics underlines the participatory experience of the SL culture; the translator is expected to recontextualize it. The SL text of one's own culture is decontexualized in the TL translation. Paul Ricoeur (1999: 87) identifies a similar process in the case of interpretation of the written text vis-à-vis the oral discourse. He points out that the written documentation of the living world, even of fictional world, creates a distance from the immediacy of the oral expression.

The structure of a literary text is organized in a peculiar way and such a structure does not merely put a meaning into a word, but it creates an associative horizon of understanding, in which this meaning gets contextualized. There is no meaning in a text as such, for it always is conditioned by a context. This is crucial for translation as the recreating process of translation takes place in a bicultural context. The constitution of meaning goes via a reference; without a reference the texts become dumb. The presence of the referral framework has particular significance that the meanings can never become visible or perceptible in their assumed ontological form, but only in their 'colouring'; there is no meaning of a text which is completely independent of the references.

There are two chief implications as far as the distance between the SL and TL text are considered. First, the written fixation is alienated from where the oral discourse has emerged and secondly the writing decontextualizes the earlier oral discourse. A similar process is involved in literary translation. The translational transfer of the context oriented text affects a distanciation from the characteristics of the original contextual situation of the SL culture. This distance becomes greater, when more heterogeneous elements of the SL text (language and content) are in a way adjusted to a TL contextual situation. So, one can assert that the process of the translation, in a sense, decontextualizes it in the SL text in order to recontexualize the TL text. Talegiri (1991: 88) holds the view that the entire field of translation is confronted with the basic consciousness of hermeneutic problems of interrelation of text. The hermeneutic alienation about which Paul Ricoeur speaks is very much a part of the literary translation, since the entire translational techniques are employed within the dialectics of two heterogeneous contextual situations and therefore two heterogeneous cultural sensibilities are juxtaposed in this process. The perception of reality is possible only through a referential framework which is culturally conditioned.

While the dialectics of two heterogeneous cultural sensibilities raises several problems, the problems of interpretation of text equally would be determined by class consciousness. Mangesh Padgaonkar, a prominent Marathi elitist poet while translating Kabir into Marathi largely fails in bringing up the wrath, anger and outbursts of Kabir; his docile and refined Marathi cannot tolerate Kabir's wrath. Gauri Deshpande, another elitist bilingual creative writer (Marathi and English) gets into certain deviations, however justifiable, while translating Jaywant Dalavi's *Chakra*, a well known Marathi novel on the Bombay shanty life of Dharavi.

Considering Theoretical Elements

Udaya Narayan Singh (1999: 18-29) identifies some of the problems that confront the theorists and proceeds to build up a theory of translation. He enlists a ten-point programme[4] and argues that a contemporary theory of translation could be a combination of these ten action nominals. There can indeed be a scientific theory of translation for non-literary texts; however the difficulty would arise when it is concerned with the literary texts.

Translation could at best be an approximation. It is always likely that there could be a considerable degree of change in meaning more often not leading to meaning loss but at times contributing to meaning gain.

There is no single method of translation; the SL text types, its wider range and variables would be different and so there would be equally varied methods to be employed in the context of the corresponding translation criteria. It is also equally true that there are always possibilities of multiple translations of the same SL text and they would contribute to the different interpretations of the text.

It is an understanding among the scholars that the unconscious competence of a translator is the most significant element and the centre of translation activity; however in theorizing translation one could keep adding principles of translation, an idea of framework, rules and hints for translating texts or criticizing the translated texts.

The 'Politics of development' and the 'politics of choice' (Singh 1991: 19) is another important factor in translation; it plays a pivotal role and is fundamentally involved in the process of translation activity. (Chitre employs such adjectives as 'battered and beaten' for Tukaram's 'ranjale ganjale' p. 150.) That's why a translator chooses a particular lexical item, a phrase, an expression or an adjective etc; these are the issues that could be raised in the post-colonial contexts and The Third World Literature.

Translation as De-leeching and Problems of Innovations

Rolland Barthes (1986: 352-53) employs a metaphor of 'leech' in order to explain the nature of understanding texts. He says that ideas cleave and cohere to the body of language like a leech does and 'the enigma is doubled when a language-system of demystification, of criticism which in principle is de-leeching language itself becomes a stickiness by which the militant subject becomes the happy parasite of discourses.'

The processes of de-leeching SL and TL texts therefore become crucial in translation. The problems of innovation, lexical choice or word combination create an entirely novel concept, a new name or expression where a translator is likely to favour a semantic extension of an existent form rather than opting for a neologism; new coinages or promoting an element from sub-language or naturalizing a borrowed expression may bring the TL text and SL-text closer to each other in terms of content and form. Assimilation of innovations and the degree of allowance that the society gives the translators are also factors to be considered in these respects as no two languages or cultures would like to be same or tolerate an extreme convergence. A kind of compromise must be brought about by the translator between the SL and TL and the compromise should be adequately controlled by innovations neither affecting over translation nor under translation of the SL texts.

Translation thus is a multidimensional activity; it involves linguistic and extra-linguistic factors, so no single method would be sufficient. The modern translation theoreticians, therefore, seek and derive more ideas not only from linguistics, psycho-linguistics and socio-linguistics but also from culture studies, anthropology and allied disciplines in order to move towards a more flexible theory of translation.

Notes

1. MD. Q.R. Al-zoub and Rajul Bhargava quote the poem in the article, *Some Constraints, Problems and Misconceptions in Literary Translation* in Literary Translation (ed). R.S. Gupta.
2. Ramchandra Sharma refers to Steiner in his article. Speech-culture and behavioural patterns in a community with reference to language use are in co-ordination with each other. Oral literature (of course not all) which is later transformed into written form and when the same is to be translated, several problems configure in terms of culture, semantic and socio-linguistic codes.
3. Dilip Chitre in Introduction to *Says Tuka* talks about the oral literary traditions and the milieu in which Tukaram produced his works. Tukaram's manuscripts of *Abhangas* were destroyed; they were drowned in Indrayani river. However, the Tukaram texts were recovered and recollected from the existing folks who had known these texts probably by heart; this implies that the canonization of the texts has been based on the oral literary traditions.
4. Uday Narayan Singh gives some of the following nominals on which a translation theory may be built up:
   - (a) A paradigm of evaluation to sift out the hack works in the name of translation from the work of the true interpreter
   - (b) A set of language-particular and culture-dependent rules
   - (c) A means to understand an alien culture, a distant author or an otherwise unavailable document
   - (d) A frame of reference for comparative literature and literary studies
   - (e) A document of contemporary cultural patterns of a speech community
   - (f) An evidence of pluralism
   - (g) A test case for semanticists

(h) A prescription for the professional: a checklist of techniques or a set of rules of thumb

(i) An instrument for retaining/eliminating/using/misusing/creating/suppressing ambiguities in a sensitive text.

References

Barthes, Rolland (1986) *The Rustle of Language*. (Tr. By Richard Howard) Oxford: Basil Blackwell.

Bassnett, S. (1991) *Translation Studies*. London/New York: Routledge.

Chitre, Dilip (1991) Says Tuka: Selected Poetry of Tukaram. New Delhi: Penguin Books.

Dalawi, Jayawant (First pub: 1963, reprint 2008) *Chakra*. (A novel in Marathi) Mumbai: Majestic Publication.

Deshpand, Gauri (First pub Orient 1974, reprint by Disha: 1993) *Chakra* (Tr. of Marathi novel by the same title) Bombay: Orient Longman.

Nabokov, V. (1975) *Eugene Onegin*, Princeton: Princeton Uni. Press.

M. Snell-Hornby, (2006) The Turns of Translation Studies: New Paradigms or Shifting Viewpoints Philadelphia: John Benjamins.

Newmark, Peter (2010) "No Global Communication Without Translation" in Gunilla Auderman and Margaret Rogers (eds) *Translation Today* New Delhi: Viva Books (by arrangements with Multilingual Matters Ltd. London).

Sharma, Ramchandra (1999) "Mediating between English and Kannada" in R.S. Gupta (ed.) *Literary Translation*. New Delhi: Creative Books.

Singh, Uday Narayan (1999) "Thoughts on Literary Translation: Search for a Theory and an Aesthetics" in R.S. Gupta. (ed.) *Literary Translation*. New Delhi: Creative Books.

Tytler, A.F. (1978) The Principles of Translation. Amsterdam: John Benjamin's B.K.

Webb, T. (1976) *The Violet in the Crucible*. London: OUP.

6

Translation and the Question of Equivalence: To be or not to be?

Rajiv Ranjan Dwivedi

Translation has emerged as a new discipline in its own right. It is a complex creative process, rather than a mere act of transference of words and ideas of one language into another. The whole process of translating is so unusually complex that Richards went on to say, it "may very probably be the most complex type of event yet produced in the evolution of the cosmos".[1] And yet, since the very beginning, a debate over the status of translation as a creative activity has consistently taken place. The major source of this debate is the issue of fidelity to the original. It is the hot button which initiates the discussion of loss and gain in translational activity. The question of loss and gain is primarily inspired by the problem of equivalence that a translator has to rigorously wrestle to solve, with a question flung open whether this fidelity to the original by finding equivalence is a justifiable demand in an ever-evolving concept of translation.

Since translation is about at least two languages and literatures, its recognition cannot be made in isolation. It offers a comparative and contrastive space as it involves two texts, two languages and their multiple intricacies, idiosyncrasies and subtleties associated with language, culture, context, style, theme etc for an agreeable evaluation of any endeavour of this kind. J Levy opines in this context:

> A translation is not a monistic composition, but interpenetration and a conglomerate of two structures. On the one hand there are the semantic content and the formal contour of the original, on the other hand the entire system of aesthetic features bound up with the language of the translation.[2]

In such a comparative and contrastive purview, the translational activity is challenged by a number of core issues like loss and gain, untranslatability, equivalence, etc. which constantly question the identity of translation as a creative process.

Previously, the question of loss in translation was inspired by the low status accorded to the practice and a sense of inferiority was implanted in translation as any kind of endeavour. It had been perceived as a marginal activity. The inequality of status thus had often left the Source Language (SL) with the impression of 'superior original' and the Target Language (TL) with the impression of 'inferior copy'. Consequently, the hard-pressed need for the translator was to remain faithful to the original to carve out any identity of the translated text of its own, meaning thereby that fidelity to the original, by finding optimal equivalence in the TL was the secret of success for both the translator and the translated text. But simultaneously the hackneyed idea of translation as the mirror of the original usually tended to confine the calibre of the translator to the mechanical task of decoding and recoding. Any distinction between writer (of the original) and the translator proved detrimental only to the latter. It had been constantly perceived as a subsidiary act and derivative, hence deprived of the dignity of the original. So, the problem of evaluation in translation is ultimately connected with the problem of low status of translation. This enabled critics to make pronouncements about translated texts from the position of assumed superiority. Sometimes the translators were branded as traitors while at other times they were expected to show a dog-like devotion to the original. Amidst this prevailing situation an ontological uncertainty loomed large on translation as a creative process.

However, the notion has changed in the recent past. Translation is no longer considered a secondary, subordinate or subservient activity. It is now universally acknowledged as an independent, self-sufficient discipline in itself and even contributory at times to the original. Rabindranath Tagore's *Geetanjali* is a case in point. The cannibalistic theory of textual consumption advocates and acknowledges the creativity and the independence of the translators. The previous emphasis in this regard was on comparing the original and translation, critically analyzing what is lost and betrayed and finally evaluating with a value judgement. But today's approach rejects the conviction and holds the view of: (a) foregrounding the manipulative power of the translator, (b) translation as a bridge- building across the space between SL and TL and (c) identifying the shifts of emphasis from the supremacy of the original to the genuinity of the translation. In the new, post colonial perception of the relationship between source and target texts, that inequality of relationship has been rethought. Both original and translation are now viewed as equal products of the creativity of writer and translator. However, Octavio Paz in this respect holds a little different opinion as follows:

> It is up to the writer to fix words in an ideal, unchangeable form and it is the task of the translator to liberate those words from the confines of their source language and allow them to live again in the language into which they are translated.[3]

Thus the translator is seen as a liberator, someone who frees the text from the fixed signs of its original shape making it no longer subordinate to the source text but visibly endeavouring to bridge the space between source author and text and the eventual target language readership. This revised perspective emphasizes the creativity of translation, seeing in it a more harmonious relationship than the one in previous models that described the translator in violent images of 'appropriation', 'penetration', 'possession', etc.

Translation, as it is often argued now, ensures the survival of a text. It effectively becomes the after-life of a text, a new 'original' in another language. This positive view of translation serves to reinforce the importance of translating as an act both of inter-cultural and inter-temporal communication. As a matter of fact, the old arguments about the need to be faithful to the original start to dissolve. Lawrence Venuti too *'insists upon the creativity of the translator and upon his or her visible presence in a translation'*.[4] Translation according to Venuti, with its allegiance both to source and target cultures *'is a reminder that no act of interpretation can be definitive'*.[5] It is therefore a dangerous act, potentially subversive and always significant.

Translation has perennial challenges posed by the linguistic and cultural aspects of the two texts. It is pestered by their peculiarities and limitations resulting most often in the untranslatability of the words and sentences of a given text. Expecting equivalence in such a context is not only undesirable but also atrocious. Susan Bassnett has rightly remarked in this regard:

> Equivalence in translation, then, should not be approached as a search for sameness, since sameness cannot even exist between two versions of the same text, let alone between the SL and the TL version.[6]

In fact, a translator is not only supposed to be bi-lingual but also bi-cultural. No language can exist unless it is steeped in the cultural flavour and, of course, no culture can exist which does not have at its centre the structure of a natural language. So a translator has to discharge dual responsibilities, rather manifold responsibilities, i.e. s/he has to know the SL, the Source Language Culture (SLC), the TL and the Target Language Culture (TLC). On the linguistic level, untranslatability occurs when there is no lexical or syntactical substitute in the TL for an SL item. For instance, Hindi has a specific linguistic structure, with its lexis, grammar, syntax, etc. totally different from English or any other language. The usage like *'chaay-waay'*, *'genius-wenius'*, *'kahte kahte'*, etc. are language specific. Similarly, Hindi follows the common syntactic structure of 'subject+object+verb' which readily gets subverted into with 'subject+verb+object' in English. Syntactically speaking, on the other hand, Sanskrit is more flexible than either Hindi or English. Syntactic patterns in Sanskrit are controlled by the precise forms of different words, and not by their very order in a sentence. It could be verified in the examples like *Aham pustakam pathami* or *pustakam pathami aham* or *Pathami aham pustakam* or *Pustakam aham pathami.* All these structures communicate the same meaning, i.e. *I read a book.* The change in word-order does not at all affect the meaning of any of the sentence patterns. Moreover, the gender distinction is identified by the form of the principal verb in Hindi syntax whereas it is done so by the change in pronouns in Sanskrit syntax, and not by any change in the form of the verb. In Hindi, for instance, we say, *Woh jal peeta hai* and *Woh jal peeti hai* translated into Sanskrit as *Sah jalam pibati* and *Saa jalam pibati* respectively, whereas there is no such distinction identified by the change in the form of verb in English syntax, however, we have he and she as pronouns to identify the gender distinction in English. Addressing elders in plural verb forms has a rare reverential echo in Hindi language.

Now the cultural untranslatability occurs due to the absence in the TL culture of a relevant situational feature for the SL text. The cultural words or the language embedded in cultural features create untranslatability. For instance, four types of culturally defined 'uncles' are in use in major Indian languages whereas English 'uncle' has only one generic meaning. A translator is always under fear of failure, if not exposed to cultural contexts of the two languages in conveying the real relational network in the TL. Names like Garima, Kirti, Pawan, Pankaj, Shashi, Pratibha, etc. in Hindi are linguistically cultural elements with their associative values. No formal expressions like 'good morning', 'good evening', 'have a nice day', 'sorry', 'thank you', etc. are much prevalent in Indian culture. The list goes limitless when we garner issues like dress code, ornaments, food-habits, custom and tradition, beliefs and feelings, religious elements, myth and legends, etc.

Apart from the cultural and linguistic worries, geographical and environmental elements which, however, affect both language and culture, are a major consideration in translation. *Shall I compare thee to a summer's day* is a difficult poetic line to translate. However, poetry in general is notorious for its untranslatability. But the given line cannot be translated into a language where summers are quite unpleasant.

The translator's task becomes even more troublesome when he is called upon to render proverbs, idiomatic expressions and figures of speech of one language into those of another language. The English expression *mouse potato* has nothing to do with the *potato,* and its literal translation would only produce ridiculous effects. This is also true of some well-known expressions from Hindi like *'nau do gyarah', 'ghar ki murgi daal barabar', 'naak ka baal hona'* and so on. There are some idiomatic and proverbial expressions in Hindi and English which can be paired together and which, notwithstanding differences in associations and exact nuances, express more or less similar sense. For example, *Oont ke muh me jeera* parallels with *A drop in the ocean. Chor ki dadhi me tinka* can be loosely rendered as *A guilty mind is always suspicious* and *Nach na jane aangan tedha* can be accepted as an equivalent of *A bad workman quarrels with his tools.* But since proverbs and idioms are repositories of the cumulative inherited wisdom of the speech community, they cannot be translated easily. The pragmatic aspects of these expressions have got to be taken care of by the translator. What is *A nine day's wonder* in England is *Char din ki chandani phir andheri raat* in India.

Translating elements like collocations, cohesives, phatic expressions, terms of politeness, and endearment, 'cultural fillers' slangs, speech fillers, kinship terms, colour words, jokes and figurative expressions, especially similes and metaphors pose equally difficult problems for any translator. In this context, M.B. Dagut opines:

> Since a metaphor in the SL is, by definition, a new piece of performance, a semantic novelty, it can clearly have no existing 'equivalent' in the TL...what is unique can have no counterpart. Here the translator's bilingual competence...is of help to him only in the negative sense

> of telling him that any 'equivalence in this case, cannot be found, but will have to be created.'[7]

This also applies to the other items listed above. 'Some elements have to be left untranslated by the translator', (International Journal of Translation, pp. 1-12) his primary aim being to attain a fit between formal and functional equivalence drawing on both socio-semantic and socio-linguistic dimensions. Warrd and Nida are very correct with their view in this respect as stated below:

> The crucial problems of translation are often stated in terms of a conflict between formal correspondence and functional equivalence.[8]

While talking about the 'dynamic equivalence' based on what Nida calls 'the principle of equivalent effect', where the relationship between receptor and message should be substantially the same as that which existed between the original receptors and the message, he opines that the message has to be tailored to the receptor's linguistic needs and cultural expectation and 'aims at complete naturalness of expression'. Naturalness is a key requirement for Nida. Indeed, he defines the goal of dynamic equivalence as seeking the *closest natural equivalent to the source-language message.*[9] This receptor-oriented approach considers adaptations of grammar, of lexicon, and of cultural references to be essential in order to achieve naturalness; the TT language should not show interference from the SL, and the 'foreignness' of the ST setting is minimized in a way that could be criticized by later culturally oriented translation theorists. Nida could also be taken to task by certain religious groups who maintain that the word of god is sacred and unalterable, the changes necessary to achieve dynamic equivalence thus verging on the sacrilegious.

Thus, even dynamic equivalence sought to be achieved through the closest natural equivalent is not quite safe and sufficient for the one who is ambitious regarding any translated work. In fact, any such ambition is untrue and undue in light of the cumbersome exercise of a translator putting in his best effort, yet not meeting the expectations quite undesirable. The translator in his/her serious venture of translation experiences the throe of a woman who undergoes a *twin-delivery* in the process of attaining her maternity. The biggest question here is whether to seek any kind of equivalence is reasonable amidst the constraints of translation practices. On the contrary, the practice should be commendable before the mammoth nature of the translation work. It's not at all necessary to find equivalent in the TL (translation) to maintain fidelity to the SL (original). The great poet Kabir used to say that it was not necessary for him to go on chanting the name of God to please Him, for Indian wives who devote their whole existence to their husbands, never call them by their name.

Translation as a new writing is, what P. Lal coines the term, *transcreation.*[10] And transcreation, as the term suggests, is an evolution, a new birth, hence, translation a new original in another language. It should not undergo any comparative assessment with the SL text. As such, it is no longer a second rate task and, therefore, deserves optimum appreciation due for an original work of art. One can just imagine the possibility of translating Shakespeare's line about an infant *Mewling and puking in the Nurse's arm* (As You Like It, 2.7). Does it have a sense in a country like ours where the child continues to have a life-long deep attachment with the mother and not the nurse? If not, then, isn't it absurd to advocate for equivalence in such cases of translational pursuits? Shouldn't the translator here be free to exercise his creative potential to render an alien cultural context into the native (TL) textual creation for its wide readership? Then, would it be an act of transgression? Certainly not. Rather, given the liberty, a translator can work wonder with his own acumen and thus can do great service to the TL readers.

The inter-textual re-creation, while minimizing the faithfulness to the original text, can be in many ways an enriching experience. Rushdie remarks:

> It is generally believed that something is always lost in translation; I cling to the notion-and use, in evidence, the success of Fitzgerald-Khayyam- that something can also be gained.[11]

The rudimentary principle of translation is thematic and, hence, its success rests on what we say *Bhavanuvaad,* and not *shabdanuvaad* (literal). As such, translation like God covets emotions or feelings of love (*bhav ka bhookha*), and not alone reason and intelligence. A text translated with this perspective not only retains the essence of the so-called original but also falsifies and condemns the statement that the sole task of a translator is to show a dog-like devotion to the original. What is meant by *'original'* after all? Paz in this context has a quite veritable remark as stated below:

> Every text is unique and, at the same time, it is the translation of another text. No text is entirely original because language itself, in its essence, is already a translation: firstly, of the non-verbal world and secondly, since every sign and every phrase is the translation of another sign and another phrase. However, this argument can be turned around without losing any of its validity: all texts are original because every translation is distinctive. Every translation, up to a certain point, is an invention and as such it constitutes a unique text. [12]

Hence, it's not a dog-like devotion. What can be a dog-like devotion is to try to find equivalence off and on and thereby maintain fidelity to the original. On the contrary, it's God-like devotion when one pours out his best in the service of the original ahead of him and yet oblivious of it while translating. And this is how a text could be transcreated and not translated, and the person could be called a transcreator and not a translator. Defending the point, in regard to the translation of poetry, Sri Aurobindo is said to have remarked that *A translator is not necessarily bound to the original he chooses; he can make his own poem out of it, if he likes, and that is what is generally done.*[13]

Notes

1. I.A. Richards. *Toward a Theory of Translating,* in A.E. Wright (ed.), Studies in Chinese Thought, Chicago: University Press, 1953, pp. 247-62.

2. J. Levý. *Umeni prekladu* (*The Art of Translation*) (Prague, 1963), cited in J. Holmes (ed.), *The Nature of Translation*. The Hague: Mouton, 1970.
3. Octavio, Paz. "Translation: Literature and Letters" transl. Irene del Corral, in Rainer Schulte and John Biguenet eds. *Theories of Translation: An Anthology of Essays from Dryden to Derrida*. Chicago: University of Chicago Press, 1992, pp. 36-55.
4. Lawrence, Venuti. *The Translator's Invisibility: A History of Translation*, London and New York: Routledge, 1995, cited in Susan Bassnett, *Translation Studies*, Routledge, London and New York, 2003, p. 9.
5. Lawrence, Venuti. *The Scandals of Translation*, London and New York: Routledge, 1998, p. 46.
6. Susan, Bassnett. *Translation Studies*, London and New York: Routledge, 2003, p. 36.
7. Quoted in Susan Bassnett–Mcguire, *Translation Studies*, London: Methuen, 1980, p. 24.
8. Warrd, J. de and E, Nida, *From One Language to Another*, London: Nelson, 1986, p. 36.
9. Nida, E., *Toward a Science of Translating*, Leiden: E.J. Brill, p. 166.
10. Quoted in Sujit Mukharjee, "Translation as New Writing" in *Translation as Discovery and Other Essays on Indian Literature in English Translation*. New Delhi: Allied Publishers/London Sangam Books, 1981, 2nd ed. New Delhi: Orient Longman,1994, p. 64.
11. Rushdie, Salman. *Midnight's Children*, Delhi: Rupa, 1983, p. 29.
12. Octavio, Paz. *Traducción: literatura y literalidad,* Barcelona: Tusquets Editor, 1971, p. 9.
13. Quoted in Prema Nandkumar, *Translation: A Creative Process*, Cygnus 2/2 (1981), p. 65.

7

Translation—Trends, Problems and Solutions

Meena Edith Keller

Communication is a necessity; so man invented languages. The lower form of living beings make their interest known by various sounds and non-verbal methods.

Only human beings have been able to organise their various modes of expression into a language. All human languages are learnable and unlike an animal, man can learn other tongues also. Languages are productive, creative and symbolic. Learning languages is a complex process. Just as mother tongue has to be acquired, other languages have to be learned. That was the reason why translation began.

The Latin word 'translatio' means "carrying across" or "bringing across." Translation connotes the art of recomposing a work in another language without losing its original flavour. The text that is translated is called the 'source text' and the language that it is translated into is called the target language. The product is called target text. Translators play an important role in the evolution of languages and culture. The art of translation is as old as written literature; parts of the Sumerian epic of Gilgamesh is among the oldest known literary works that have been found in translations into several Southwest Asian languages of the second millennium B.C. There is difference between Greek translation and English translation. Greeks emphasized on metaphrase (literal translation) and paraphrase was adopted by the English poet and translator

John Dryden (1631-1700) who blends when selecting, in the target language "counterparts" or equivalents for the expressions used in source language. A widely recognised icon for the practice and historic role of translation is the Rosetta Stone, which in the United States is incorporated into the coat of arms of the Defence Language Institute.

Every translation activity has one or more specific purposes but the main aim of translation is to serve as a cross-cultural bilingual communication vehicle among people. In the past few decades, this activity has developed because of rising international trade, increased migration, globalization, the recognition of linguistic minorities and the expansion of mass media and technology. For this reason the translator plays an important role as a bilingual or multilingual cross-culture transmitter of culture and truths by attempting to interpret concepts and speech in a variety of texts as faithfully and accurately as possible.

The consequences of wrong translations can be catastrophic if done by laypersons—and mistakes made in the performance of this activity can obviously be irreparable. Just think of what could happen in cases of serious inadequacy in knowledge areas such as science, medicine, legal matters or technology. A poor translation cannot only lead to hilarity or to minor confusion but it can be a matter of life and death. While training a translator, care should be taken not only in the acquisition and command of languages, translation strategies and procedures but also in specific knowledge areas and what is equally important in professional ethics. It should be accepted that in the art or skill of translating translators come across assorted and numerous obstacles. 'Translation is an arduous job that mortifies you, puts you in a state of despair at times, but also an enriching and indispensable work, that demands honesty and modesty.'

The first problem regarding translation is related to reading and comprehension ability in the source langauge. The next most frequent translation difficulties are of a semantic and cultural nature. One should adopt a very cautious attitude towards these words or expressions so as to avoid interference or language misuse. Consulting an expert in the topic or a native speaker of the source language can provide us with a solution to convey an accurate meaning when we run into those painful "not found" terms. The greatest virtue of a good translator is what is called contextualized intuition i.e. the ability to find the nearest common sense interpretation of the "not found" element within its context. Whatever the difficulty may be in the translation process the procedure must aim at the essence of the message and faithfulness to the meaning of the source language text being transferred to the target language text. In the words of Nida and Taber (1974), "Translating consists of reproducing, in the target language, the nearest equivalent to the message in the source language, in the first place in the semantic aspect and in the second place in the stylistic aspect."

The quality of translation will depend on the quality of the translator i.e. on her/his knowledge, skills, training, cultural background, expertise and even mood. Newmark (1995) distinguished some essential characteristics that any good translator should have:

(a) reading comprehension ability in a foreign language;
(b) knowledge of the subject;
(c) sensitivity to language;
(d) an excellent command of the language into which the translation is being carried out;
(e) a profound understanding of the etymological and idiomatic correlates between the two languages;
(f) a finely tuned sense when to metaphrase (translate literally) and when to paraphrase to assure true equivalents;
(g) competence to write the target language dexterously, clearly, economically, and resourcefully.

In addition, intuition or common sense is the most common of all senses, in other words making use of that sixth sense, a combination of intelligence, sensitivity and intuition. This phenomenon works very well if handled cautiously.

The transfer process is a difficult and complex approach mechanism, one in which one must make use of all one's intellectual capacity, intuition and skill.

The special role of the translator in society is aptly described as: "Translation is in fact an art both estimable and very difficult and therefore is not the labour and portion of common minds. It should be practiced by those who are themselves capable of being actors when they see greater use in translating the works of others than in their own works, and hold higher than their own glory the service that they render to their country" (Ignacy Krasicki).

"Fidelity" and fluency are the two qualities that have been regarded as ideals to be striven for in translation. Fidelity pertains to the extent to which a translation accurately renders the meaning of the source text without, adding to or subtracting from it, without emphasizing or do emphasizing any part of the meaning and otherwise without distorting it. Fluency pertains to the extent to which a translation appears to a native speaker of the target language to have originally been written in that language and conforms to the grammatical, syntactic and idiomatic conventions of the language. The translation that meets the first criterion is said to be a faithful translation and a translation that meets the second criterion, an idiomatic translation.

During the 18th Century many translators stepped beyond the bounds of translation proper into the realms of adaptation. The Indian epic, the *Ramayana* appears in many versions in the various Indian languages and the stories are different in each. Another kind of translation is back translation which refers to translation into the language of the original text without reference to the original text. Mark Twain issued his own back translation of a French version of his famous short story 'The Celebrated Jumping Frog of Calaveras County' into 'Private History of the Jumping Frog' into English.

A common misconception is that anyone who can speak a second language will make a good translator. It is generally accepted that the best translations are produced by persons who are translating into their own native languages, as it is rare for someone who has learned a second language to have total fluency in that language. A good translator understands the source language well, has specific experience in the subject matter of the text and is a good writer in the target language. The best translation is obtained through the combined application of good technical-terminology skills and good writing skills.

Translation has served as a writing school for many prominent writers. Translators, including monks who spread Buddhist texts in East Asia and the early modern European translators of the Bible, in the course of their work have shaped the very languages into which they have translated. They have acted as bridges for conveying knowledge and ideas between cultures and civilizations. Along with ideas, they have imported, into their own langauge, loan words and calques of grammatical structures, idioms and vocabulary from the source language.

In today's world of advanced technology machine translation has been brought to a large public by tools available on the Internet, such as Yahoo!'s Babel Fish, Babylon and Star Dict. These tools produce a 'gisting translation'—a rough translation that, with luck, 'gives the gist' of the source text. Google translation has a "read—a loud feature" that assists pronunciation in learning a language. But with regards to texts with limited ranges of vocabulary and simple sentence, structure machine translation can deliver results that do not require much human intervention to be useful. So the use of a controlled language, combined with a machine-translation tool, will typically generate largely comprehensible translations. It is certainly true that even purely human-generated translations are prone to error. Therefore to ensure that a machine generated translation will be useful to human beings and that publishable quality translation is achieved, such translations must be reviewed and edited by a human being. Claude Piron states that machine translation at its best automates the easier part of a translator's job the harder and more time-consuming part usually involves doing extensive research to resolve ambiguities in the source text, which the grammatical and lexical exigencies of the target language require to be resolved.

Computer-assisted translation, also called 'computer-aided translation', 'machine-aided human translation' and 'interactive translation' is a form of translation wherein a human translator creates a target text with the assistance of a computer programme. The machine supports a human translator. Computer-assisted translation can include standard dictionary and grammar software. This includes translation-memory terminology-management, concordance and alignment programmes.

With the internet, translation software can help non native-speaking individuals understand web pages published in other languages. Whole-page translation tools are of limited utility. However since they offer only a limited potential understanding of the original author's intent and context, interactive translation with pop-up windows are becoming more popular. These tools show one or more possible equivalents for each word or phrase. Human operators need to select the likeliest equivalent as we glance over the foreign language text.

There is a historical change in languages. All languages undergo gradual changes in vocabulary, pronunciation, grammar and idioms with the passing of time. Yet strict literal translation is apparently quite impossible. Every translation is an interpretation. Thus as stated earlier the translator must first understand the writer's intent and then compose text in the target language. That is why it is rightly said that 'Translation connotes the art of losing its original flavour.' Thus translators should observe that the essence in terms of meaning and sense, register and style and layout of the original text in terms of format i.e. sources, paragraphs, indentation, columns, tables, etc., is properly adhered to in the translated unit.

To conclude, translators, like all 'professionals', must undergo permanent training. Their productive capacity, however, should not always be measured or weighed in terms of pages, words or hours done, but rather taking into account the quality of the output or finished work. No doubt machine translation has facilitated translation but it has come to solve their translation problems. Those of us who are acquainted with translation software know the enormous output difference between a machine-translated text and a human translated text. In order to solve translation problems, a human translator must make use of his/her cleverness, creativity, curiosity, intuition, ingenuity, reflection, resourcefulness as a machine, however well-fed, is unable to discriminate and discern.

References

Bell, Roger T., *Translation and Translating*. Longman Group U.K. Ltd. 1994.

Kasperck, Christopher, "The Translator's Endless Toil", *The Polish Review*, Vol. XXVIII, No. 2, 1983.

Kussmaul, Paul, *Training the Translator*. John Benjamins Publishing Co. 1987.

Nida, E. and Taber, *The Theory and Practice of Translating*, Brill Leiden. 1998.

Wilson, Andrew, *Translators on Translating: Inside the Invisible Art*, Vancouver. CCSP Press, 2009.

8

Impediments to Literary Translation

Laxmi Shanker and *Anubha Sharma*

Is the translation of a literary text, above all of a poetic text, impossible? And if it is, why? Linguists, translators, philosophers, social scientists and the critics engaged in practical criticism independently and collectively all over the world are engrossed in diagnosing the 'noisy' elements in effective communication between the readers of two languages through translation. Their efforts are directed towards the easing of the translation of literature, a subtle form of torture, an arduous job that mortifies and puts in a state of despair at times. As the two expressions associated with translation "*formal* equivalence" and "*dynamic* equivalence" are applicable to any translation, the translation process, and procedures, as Nida & Tyber (1974: 12) believes, must aim at the essence of the message and faithfulness to the meaning of the source language text should be transferred to the meaning of the target language text:

> Translating consists of reproducing, in the target language, the nearest equivalent to the message in the source language, in the first place in the semantic aspect and, in the second place, in the stylistic aspect.[1]

Kussmaul (1995: 65) also talks about an important area: Translation Pedagogy. His focus on the mental processes used by translators is especially insightful: "One should adopt a very cautious attitude toward these words or expressions so as to avoid interference and/or language misuse."[2]

Moreover, linguist Greenberg (1996: 108-109), who put the languages of different origins under 3 separate groups, has found that often a concept lexicalized in one of a particular group of languages does not have a corresponding lexical unit in a language of another group and thus presents a translation difficulty, because such an expression causes a lexical gap. Greenberg's classification of languages into groups is based on the word order of declarative sentences:

> **Group I:** Arabic, Hebrew, Ancient Egyptian, Celtic, Polynesian languages.
>
> **Group II:** Romance languages, English, Russian, Chinese, Germany, Albanian, Greek, Khmer, Vietnamese, all Thai languages except Khamti, Malay, Dutch, Icelandic, Slavonic, Norwegian, Swedish, Danish, Finnish, Estonian.
>
> **Group III:** Japanese, Korean, Turkish, Burmese, Hindi, Navaho, Tibetan, most Australian languages.[3]

According to Heilbron (1999: 429), book translations constitute a cultural world-system "based on a core periphery structure, [that] accounts for the uneven flows of translations between language groups as well as for the varying role of translations within language groups".[4]

It may be observed that English language is an open language which has had accommodated the words from other languages of the world. Still, as the fact remains, there are hundreds and thousands of words in the Vedic literature, *Mahabharata*, *Ramayana*, texts related to Indian System of medicine, spiritual experience and mysticism, Sanskrit literary criticism, Kanarese poetics and prosody, Telugu prosody, etc. without appropriate equivalents in English. An example will make the point clear. In Bharat's *Natya Sastra* rendered into English the translator mentions the four kinds of musical instruments used during a dramatic performance in the following manner: "Musical instruments are of four kinds: (1) stringed like a lute (2) like a drum covered with a hide

(3) solid like the cymbals; and (4) hollow like a flute." The translator has not been successful in finding appropriate equivalents for the Sanskrit words used in the nomenclature of movements and positions of hand, eye, glances, eyebrows, the dilation and contraction of nostrils, the cheeks, etc. and of the constant and inconstant modes-their sensors, etc.

It may be seen that it is necessary for a literary translator to adopt a very cautious attitude towards calques, idioms (for which there are no equivalents in L_2) slangs and lols, phrases borrowed by English from foreign languages, similies, metaphors, imagery (especially conceptual, emotional and compound images), personifications, hyperboles, exemplifications, parallelisms, transferred epithets, hypallages, irony, ambiguity (contextual and semantic), allusions, bombasts, adjectives, alliterations, archaisms, concrete nouns, datives of interest, dialects and epigrams, neologisms, aphorisms, etc. and other forms of interference; institutional and standardized terms frequently become difficult to translate. Then there are "not found" expression terms. Here is an example:

> The Nigerian writer Chinua Achebe's novel *Things Fall Apart* (1958) is full of Igbo names and customs, which by the author's own acknowledgement is his way of reclaiming and preserving his cultural and traditional roots. In the first two editions (1958 and 1959), Achebe offers only a brief one-page glossary of these names and terms, hoping that his readers, even from dominant cultures, in order to reach a clearer understanding of the novel will have to make further efforts to find out more information about the Igbo society, hence allowing that culture to be preserved in the cultural memory of the world as well. (Simon Gikandi wrote a very detailed Introduction to the novel and Igbo society that appeared much later, in the 4th edition (1996) of the novel.) Another example of a postcolonial writer resisting Western cultural domination is that of the Kenyan writer Ngugi wa Thiong'o who, after writing in English for many years, decided to write in his native language

> Gikuyu so that his work could be read by the people he was writing about. His refusal to write in English becomes a strategy of resisting imperialistic demands of foreign cultures that want him to say what he wants to say in English. Instead, by choosing his national language, Ngugi compels his foreign readers to undertake or rely on translations if they want to read what he has to say. Also, when Ngugi wrote his novels like *A Grain of Wheat* and *Weep Not, Child*, he used many Gikuyu words and phrases without offering any explanation and thus remained faithful to his own culture even while writing in English.

Emotional disturbances and feelings have been expressed in most of the narratives (e.g. *Kanthapura* (Raja Rao), *Tamas* (Bhism Sahni) by breaking up of the English syntax. The novelists have taken many words from local Indian languages. Novelists like Bapsi Sidhwa and Anita Rau Badami have used nativized form of English to make their novels appealing to different classes of society. They have used a wide range of local lexical items of Urdu, Hindi and Punjabi origin to display the profundity of her experience of an Indian tradition that create images of Indianness in words and action in novels like *Ice-Candy-Man* and *Tamarind Mem.* Raja Rao has used the words like Harikatha, Mandap etc. which have no equivalents in English. The novelists have used such words 'as they are'.

Here are a few examples from Bapsi Sidhwa's *Ice Candy Man:*

Indian Eatables:

1. 'Aren't you making the halva for my birthday? (p. 141)
2. 'She goes in and fetches a plate of almond fudge and sweet lentil ladoos. (p. 168)

Indian Religion and Culture:

1. Hindus, Muslims and even the Sikhs are going to jockey of power'. (p. 36)

2. "I feel a great swell of fear for Hari: and a surge of loathing for his bodhi." Why must he persist in growing it? and flaunt his Hinduism? (p. 117)

Indian Dress:

1. "I see the wisdom of these baggy shalwars and long kamizes as I fidget in the grass, tugging at my dress." (p. 54)
2. "Ayah notices it and, drawing me to her, cover my head with her sari palloo." (p. 28)

Syntax: According to Oxford-Advanced Learner's Dictionary, syntax is the rules of grammar for the arrangement of words into phrases and of phrases into sentence. Katie Wales (1989: 72) in her *Dictionary of Stylistics* describes it as:

> "the traditional term in grammar for the core component of sentence structure; the way the words, phrases and clauses are ordered and formally grouped; syntax provides the skeleton frame work of the sentence and plays a key role in the distribution and focusing of information"[5]

Sidhwa takes liberty with the language to the extent it serves her purpose, and her purpose is to evoke an Indian atmosphere throughout the novel to a possible extent. That she is successful in her effort, may be seen in the following examples in which Indian variants are noticeable in the structures and patterns of the language.

1. Compound nouns with vernacular modes of expression:

'For a week, Doctor Shahib, the man says.' (p. 12)

"Gandhijee Visists Lahore." (p. 85)

2. Deletion of 'OF' in Indian English Collocation:

"Wollen-Dhurrie." (p. 11)

"Palm leaf Punkah." (p. 33)

3. Transliteration:

"She not walk much...... She get tired." (p. 2)

"I break your neck, you naughty birds ! You do too much chi chi!" (p. 25)

Semantics: Apart from the syntactic and lexical levels, the English language has been exploited by Sidhwa at the semantic level also. Semantics is the study of 'meaning' in language. This level is significant. Meaning or sense of a word may differ according to context and situations. An English word may have varied interpretations when it is used in Indian English, because culture, customs, and other factors affect the different uses of a word. According to B.B. Kachru (1983: 82),

> "At the level of semantics Indians English is characterised by semantic extension of English words and contextual redefinition of lexical items besides a few other distinguishing semantic features."[6]

At the level of semantics, it is mainly through symbolism that we find Sidhwa trying to introduce Indianness into her novel *Ice Candy Man.*

Metaphor:

1. "She weigh less than this phulka." (50)
2. "Arrey baba, You're a Hitler! I'll take her." (50)

Similies:

1. "..........Jinnah, Who for a decade was known as Ambassador of Hindu Muslim unity is caricatured, and portrayed as a monster." (p. 160)
2. "Mr. Bankwalla, precise as the crisp new rupee notes he handles at the bank...." (p. 40)

Symbolism:

1. "No one knows which way the wind will blow, thunders the colonel, silence everyone with his admirable rhetoric." (p. 37)
2. "They're like the three bloody monkeys." (p. 62)

Imagery:

1. "The sun is up, dispelling the mist, filthy with dust, exhausted, we roll into Wagah, a village halfway to Amritsar."

2. "He drums his chest, flexes his muscles and emits the fierce barruk cries with which the Punjabi Village warriors bluff, intimidate and challenge each other".

In *Tamarind Mem* (1996), Anita Rau Badami tries to create special effect by code switching and code mixing. Kali-Kaluti—Black pepper, Coca cola, Total chutney, 'Thief-goonda Rascals' are the expressions used for a girl of black complexion, the poor man and anti social element respectively. Some other expressions used by her are: Jamun-fruit, besharam plants, wind Pretha (ghost), Ganji-bhaath (food item), Bauni (the amount received from the first buyer).

Raja Rao in *Kanthapura* (1969) and Arundhati Roy in *The God of Small Things* have used English modified to South Indian conditions to reflect Kannada and Malayalam speech rhythms respectively.

Raja Rao has used typical proverbs villagers often use in their daily conversation e.g. (1) The policemen are not your uncle's sons, (2) the first daughter milks the cow when the mother is ill, (3) saw you like a rat on your mother's lap, (4) there is neither man nor mosquito in Kanthapura (5) you cannot straighten a dog's tail, (6) land, lust and wifely loyalty go badly together (6) Every squirrel has his day, (7) our hearts beat like the wings of bats, (8) and yet he was as honest as an elephant, (9) the youngest is always the holy bull, (10) does a boar stand before a lion or a jackal before an elephant?

In regional novels, we come across many typical expressions which may dry up the translator's nerves. Here are a few examples:

> "Suna hai yahan ek koi ladki hai jo jadoo jaanti hai.Vah maaldar bakron ki eisi mehmaandari karti hai ki ve apni kaleji tak kaad aur bhoon kar uske upyog ke liye rakh dete hain."
>
> (*Juhu*, 45)
>
> "Mujhe apne sparshsukh se anandit karo, jis se main prasanna ho kar nayi sristi rachoon."
>
> (*Amritlal Nagar: Boond aur Samudra*, p. 140)

"Kalakar voh kampass hai jo toophan mein thik uttar disha ki or sanket karta hain."

(*Ila Chandra Joshi: Sanyasi*, p. 78)

"Aapni khudgarji ke liye mard aurat ki javani ka bhikhari banker usse dan pane ke liye uski nikammi tariphen kiya karta hai."

(*Amritlal Nagar: Boond aur Samudra*, p. 355)

"Naari ne kaha-tume sundar rachnayen ki hain nar parantu inme se ek bhi vastu meri srasti ka mukabla naahi kar sakti. Kah kar usne apne bachche ko pyar kar liya."

(*Amritlal Nagar: Boond aur Samudra*, p. 139)

"Sabji lekar lauti aa rahi thi, dekha to khadi didi ki sadi peeche se ek dam bhubhukka. Maine turant aad kar liya aur haramiyon ki gaali dekar bhagaya."

(*Phanishwar Nath Renu: Deerghtapa*, p. 95)

"ve jab-tab Angreji shabdon ka prayog isliye kar dete the taki log yeh na samajhlen ki ve angreji jante hi nahin. Shrimati Anand pray sabhi bhashaon ke ekadh kahavat, ashleel shabd aur ashleel ashay ke vakya janti hain aur avsar dekh kar unka prayog bhi karti hain."

(*Phanishwar Nath Renu: Deerghtapa*, p. 22)

"Mere tan, man aur dhan par unhone is majbooti se kabja kiya hai ki uski fariyad kisi bhi rastra sangh main nahi ho sakti."

(*Gopal Prasad Vyas: Kuch sach kuchh Jooth*, p. 35)

Figures of Speech: Translating the Untranslatable

Figures of Speech are virtually untranslatable because the phonological resemblance between sense segments whose referents are unconnected is unlikely to be reflected in another language. These, therefore, pose a formidable obstacle to the translator, who will probably have little choice other than to either ignore them or to add his own comment on the text. The translator may also struggle when the source language offers several distinct lexical items where only one exists in English. As Newmark (1988: xi) wryly observes,

> "You only deviate from literal translation when there are good semantic and pragmatic reasons to do so, which is more often than not." In reality, the translator will normally be forced to settle for accounting for only those meanings in the original that can be considered most relevant to his readers, as to do any more than this may place an unacceptable burden of mental processing on the reader."[7]

Gutt (1985) in Venuti (2000: 386) explains:

> "Sometimes it is possible to achieve a higher degree of resemblance but only at the cost of a decrease in overall relevance because it involves an increase in processing effort that is not outweighed by gains in contextual effects."[8]

ANTITHESIS—in which things mutually opposed in some particular idea or phrase are set over against each other.

Example: Aunt Jennifer's tigers prance across the screen.

While greedy good-doers, beneficent beasts of prey.

HAIKU is a major form of Japanese verse, written in 17 syllables divided into 3 lines of 5, 7, and 5 syllables, and employing highly evocative allusions and comparisons. This form of poetry influences Indian poetry as well. Some Hindi poets have experimented with this form.

Examples:

In the cicada's cry
No sign can foretell
How soon it must die.
No one travels
Along this way but I,
This autumn evening.

HYPERBOLE—an obvious exaggeration.

Example: His hands dangled a mile out of his sleeves.

IMAGERY—the use of evocative and figurative language to form vivid mental images.

Example:

"He leaped upon the rail and balanced himself there, to get greater elevation; his pipe, striking a rope, was knocked from his mouth. He lunged for it; a short, hoarse cry came from his lips as he realized he had reached too far and had lost his balance. The cry was pinched off short as the blood-warm waters of the Caribbean Sea closed over his head." (Richard Connell: *The Most Dangerous Game)*

PERSONIFICATION gives to animals, to inanimate objects or to abstract ideas the characteristic of a person.

Example: Then she turns to those liars, the candles or the moon; wind yells while blowing; the night is my friend.

PHRASES BORROWED BY ENGLISH FROM FOREIGN LANGUAGES

(1) Ad nauseam—[Latin]: to a sickening degree. "The politician uttered one platitude after another ad nauseam."

(2) In medias res—[Latin]: in the middle of a sequence of occurrences. "The film begins in medias res, with a panting, terrified man running through the night."

(3) Pro bono—[Latin]: work done or donated without charge; free. *"The doctor's pro bono work gave him a great sense of satisfaction."*

(4) Art nouveau—[French]: A style of decoration and architecture of the late 19th and early 20th centuries, characterized by flowers, leaves, and flowing lines. *"The architect's work has traces art nouveau."*

(5) Bête noire—[French]: literally means black beast; something that is particularly distasteful or difficult and to be avoided. *"Reservations have always been the bête noire of real reformers."*

(6) Cliché—[French]: overused or stereotypical. *"The depiction of women in that film is clichéd.*

(7) Crème de la crème—[French]: best of the best, 'cream of the cream'. *"Her parties always have the crème de la crème of Bollywood present."*

(8) Deus ex machina—[Latin]: a contrived device to resolve a situation. "The movie ended with a deus ex machina through which everyone was rescued at the last minute."

(9) Hors de oeuvre—[French]: starters or appetizers. "The hors de oeuvres were so tasty that we filled our stomachs on them."

SLANGS/LOLS

Commenting upon the use of slang/lol in literature S.T. Coleridge has said:

> The source of any bad writing is the desire to be something more than a person of sense—the straining to be thought a genius. If people would say what they have to say in plain terms, how much eloquent they would be

James Joyce has taken a defensive view and has justified their use on the ground that they capture the historical time and place of the drama and therefore they can be used frequently. Anthony Burgess has used certain slangs in *A Clockwork Orange* to immerse the readers quite well into the characters mind and gives a feel of the world the story is taking place. Dante clearly wrote in a language that was dismissed by many at the time as the "vulgar tongue". Shakespeare, Goethe, and many others coined endless words and phrases...and drew others from usage by the "common folk". The English language as a whole is made of endless terms that were borrowed from other languages...that were taken from specific regional dialects (compare Chaucer with Langland, for example), etc... Mark Twain wrote in colloquial vernacular style and overused slang. According to Lodge (1992, p. 18)

> Twain's masterstroke was to unite a vernacular colloquial style with a naive, immature narrator, an adolescent boy who is wiser than he knows, whose vision of the adult world has a devastating freshness and honesty.[9]

We find several slangy expressions in J.D. Salinger's *The Catcher in the Rye*. Examples:

"So I got the ax [from school]." (to get the ax = to get expelled)

"So I shot the bull for a while." (to shoot the bull = either to lie and exaggerate or to chat amiably)

"Boy, was he sore." (sore = angry, irritated)

"What really knocks me out is..." (to knock someone out = to delight or impress someone extremely)

"...so I went down to the can and chewed the rag with him..." (can=toilet; to chew the rag = to converse)

"I'll be up the creek if I don't get the goddamn thing in by Monday,..." (up the creek = in trouble)

"I got a big bang out of that." (to get a bang out of something = to enjoy something especially)

"Some of the ones he said were flits were even married, for God's sake" (flit = male homosexual)

"I mean he didn't hit the ceiling or anything." (to hit the ceiling = to become violently angry)

"...I was pretty loaded." (loaded = here: very rich, affluent)

"She had very big knockers."[10] (knockers = woman's breasts)

Nickname [rational discrimination]:

Henry Louis Gates JR. quotes Trey Ellis's essay '*Remember My Name*' in his essay '*What's In a Name?*':

...blood, darky, Tar Baby, Kaffir, shine... moor, Jim Crow, spook...quadroon, meriney, red bone, high yellow...Mammy, porch monkey, home, homeboy, George... spearchucker, schwarze, Leroy, smokey... mouli, buck, Ethiopian, brother, Sistah....[11]

"He calls all coloured people George." [12]

Maya Angelou in her Autobiography *I know why the caged bird sings* writes about the expressions people used to insult the Black:

> It was dangerous practice to call a Negro anything that could loosely constructed as insulting because of the centuries of their having been called niggers, jigs, dinges, blackbirds, crows, boots, and spooks[13]. (The word nigger is listed in the profanities in order of decreasing severity, the top ten being cunt, motherfucker, fack, wanker, *nigger,* bastard, prick, bollocks, arsehole and paki in that order.)

It is interesting to note that several writers including Shakespeare have used such expressions in their writings. Shakespearean terms with sexual meanings—an extraordinary number of terms-over 1500—with direct or implied meanings occur in the works of the greatest author of the English language. In *Romeo and Juliet* (II, iv, lines 93-115) the Bard includes no fewer than 12 different sexual terms, mainly for male and female genitalia and for intercourse. In regional novels too there are many instances. Hindi novelist Rahi Masoom Raza for example uses abusive language very often in *Aadha Gaon.*

Similies, metaphors, imagery (especially conceptual, emotional and compound images) also are the stumbling blocks for the translator. MacLeish (1965: 140-41)

> Poetry seems sometimes to regard itself not as an orderer of life but as life's opposite and anti-end, and the deepest human need in certain generations has appeared to be a need not to make sense of our human lives, but to make nonsense of them.... There is undoubtedly a human hunger for the anti-world and there is a poetry which serves it and no conception of the art can be complete which does not somehow keep in view the dark dimension.[14]

Similies:

> "Choices thin as shaved ice.
> Notes shredded
> drift like snow
> on my broken body,
> cover me like whispers

of sorries
sorries."[15]

"How many notes written
Ink smeared like bird prints
In snow."[16]

"Drawing praises to me
Like currents in the bed of wind,
Virile with confidence."[17]

"My doctrine shall drop as the rain,
And my speech shall distil as the dew."[18]

"Pleasures are like poppies spread,
You seize the flower, its bloom is shed."[19]

"He is as lively as a monkey;
The stars floated like lilies in a
calm, clear lake."[20]

Metaphor:

"Stars are daisies that adorn
The blue fields of the sky."[21]

Athens, the eye of Greece, mother
"of arts and eloquence."[22]

"Sleep that knits up the raveled sleeve of care,
The death of each day's life, sore labour's both,
Balm of hurt minds, great nature's second course,
Chief Minister in life's feast."[23]

"Hope, the balm life, of darts a ray of light through the thickest gloom." [24]

"He is a snail: I speared him with a jest."[25]

"Her eyes are hidden pools
Where my soul lies
Glimmering in their waters
Like faint and trouble skies."[26]

Imagery:

"It is half the planet
This dome, this half globe, 'tis bulging
Eyeball of water, arched over to Asia,

Australia and white Antarctica: those are the eyelids that never
Close; this is the starting unsleeping
Eye of the earth."[27]

(Robinson Jefferes: The Eye)

"This sea that bares her bosom to the moon
the winds that will be howling at bal hours,
and are up-gathered now like sleeping flowers."[28]

(Wordsworth: The World is too much with us)

"Hermes, hermes
The great sea foamed,
Gnashed its teeth about me;
But you have waited,
Where sea grass tangles with shore-grass."[29]

Personification:

"The gray-eyed morn smiles on the frowning night,
Chequerin the eastern clouds with streaks of light."[30]

(William Shakespeare)

"And every wave with dimpled face,
that leaped upon the air,
had caught a star in its embrace,
And held it trembling there."[31]

(William Shakespeare)

"I am silver and exact. I have no preconceptions.
Whatever I see, I swallow immediately.
Just as it is, unmisted by love or dislike
I am not cruel, only truthful."[32]

(Sylvia Plath: Mirror)

Hyperbole:

"So frowned the mighty combatants that hell
Grew darker at their frown."[33]

(Milton)

"The sky shrank upwards with unusual dread,
And trembling timber dived beneath his bed."[34]

(Dryden)

"I froze to death out in the storm."[35]

"Senior year passed by in a second."[36]

Clichés:

"I felt a lump in my throat and butterflies in my stomach."[37]

"The good die young."[38]

Exemplification:

"Waitresses are called orderlies, secretaries are called clerk-typists, nurses are called medics, assistants are called adjutants, and cleaning up an area is called policing the area."[39]

Euphemism:

"He 'moonlighted' as a janitor in the evenings for the telephone company."[40]

Parallelism:

"I like hiking, skiing and to cook"[41]
"Walk groundly, talk profoundly,
Drink roundly, sleep soundly."[42]

Apostrophe:

"'O' liberty, what crimes have been committed in thy name?"[43]

Transferred epithet:

"The ploughman homewards plods his weary way."[44]

Hypallage:

"The merry bugles rang out their peal."[45]

Irony:

"You are a wise man! Cry aloud: for he is a God."[46]

Ambiguity:

"The opening lines of Jabberwocky, here slithy means 'lithe and slimy': "Twas brillig, and the slithy toves Did gyre and gimble in the wabe."[47]

Malapropisms:

"...promise to forget this fellow—to *illiterate* him, I say, quite from your memory." (i.e. *obliterate*; Sheridan: *The Rivals*, Act I, Scene II, Line 178)

"...she might *reprehend* the true meaning of what she is saying." (i.e. *comprehend*; Act I, Scene II, Line 258)

"...she's as headstrong as an *allegory* on the banks of Nile." (i.e. *alligator*; Act III, Scene III, Line 195)

"Sure, if I *reprehend* any thing in this world it is the use of my *oracular* tongue, and a nice *derangement* of *epitaphs* !" i.e. *apprehend*, *vernacular*, *arrangement*, *epithets*)

"Our watch, sir, have indeed *comprehended* two *auspicious* persons." (i.e., *apprehended*, *suspicious*; Shakespeare, *Much Ado about Nothing*. Act 3, Scene V)

"If you be he, sir, I desire some *confidence* with you." Benvolio then responds "She will *indite* him to some supper." (i.e., *conference*, *invite*; Shakespeare, *Romeo and Juliet*, Act 2, Scene IV)

"Bottom (*Mid Summer Night's Dream*) says he will "aggravate" his voice when he really means he will "moderate" it." (Act 1, Scene II)

"Bottom says "deflowered" when he means "devoured". (Act 5, Scene I)

Allusion:

In 'Wasteland' Eliot depicts how a woman sat at her modern dressing table:

"The chair she sat in, like a burnished throne,
Glowed on the marble,"[48]

Bombast:

Marlowe in *Dr. Faustus* describes what Faustus declares:

"now by the kingdom's infexnal rule
of styx, acheron, and the fiery lake of
ever burning phlegethon i swer that i

do long to see the monuments and
sitiuation of briht splendent Rome...."

[*Dr. Faustus* 1604; 3rd.i.47][49]

Adjectives:

"All potilical parties die at last of swallowing their own lies."[50]

Alliteration:

"Gay goes Grammar with gold and glamour."[51]
"Aload of learning lumbering in his head."[52]
"His heavy shotted hammock shroud."[53]

Archaism:

"A-list'nin' to the witch tales 'at Annie tells about
An' the gobble-uns 'at gits you
Ef you
Don't
Watch
Out!" [J.W. Riley][54]

Concrete Noun:

"Give me a lever long enough,
And a prop strong enough,
I can single-handed move the world." [Archimedes][55]

"The philosopher is Nature's pilot. And there you have our difference: to be in heaven is to steer." [George Bernard Shaw: *Man and Superman*][56]

Dative of Interest:

"The Jew ate me a whole ham of bacon". [Addison][57]

Dialect:

"Oh, wad some power the giftie gie us
To see oursel's as ithers see us!
It wad frae monie a blunder free us,
And foolish notion." [Burns][58]

Epigrams:

"Affected simplicity in refined artfulness."[59]

Indian Idioms

Hundreds of idioms which frequently occur in the narratives of Indian languages cannot be translated into English. E.g. *paise khana* in Hindi or its equivalent *dabulu tinuta* in Tamil will be rendered in English as "to eat money"[60] which will be a ridiculous translation.

Conclusion

As stated earlier, the translation of literature has often been regarded as "a subtle form of torture, an arduous job that mortifies and puts in a state of despair at times" due to the afore-listed impediments. In such cases, it is obvious that a faithful translation is a remote possibility. Taking faithfulness, naturalness, expected effects and fluency as judging criteria for comparing two versions, the translator finds that in place of faithful translation, the most appropriate may be the 'adaptation' procedure to avoid causing confusion due to the target user's lack of background knowledge. It may be observed here that due to the uniqueness of the source language and culture, sometimes there is no "equivalence" in the target language and its culture for the translator to adapt to. To fill the gaps or "lacunae" in the target language by use of the corresponding elements, so that the overall impression is the same for the two messages, the translator of a literary text has to decide on the importance given to certain cultural aspects. Keeping in view the intended readership, he/she has to figure out to what extent it is necessary or desirable to translate them into the TL. The fundamental strategy is to let the readers fully comprehend the content. So the translator must often exercise freedom to eliminate the alien and untranslatable/colloquial parts which would cause obstacles to comprehension. He may use adaptation procedure most of the time to let the readers not feel confused and lost when encountering unfamiliar colloquialisms and other items, so that his/her reader is able to fully enjoy the translation and almost imagine that he/she is reading the text in its original language.

References

1. Nida, E. & Taber Ch. 1974. *The Theory and Practice of Translating*. Brill, Leiden.
2. Kussmaul, Paul. 1995. *Training the Translator*. John Benjamins Publishing Co.
3. Joseph H. Greenberg, "Some Universals of Grammar with Particular Reference to the Order of Meaningful Elements," in *Universals of Language,* ed. Joseph H. Greenberg (Cambridge: M.I.T. Press, 1966), pp. 108-109.
4. Heilbron: *Towards a Sociology of Translation*, European Journal of Social Theory 2 (1999), no. 4.
5. Katie Wales, *Dictionary of Stylistics*, Longman, 1989.
6. Kachru, B: *The Indianization of English*, OUP, 1983.
7. Newmark, P. (1988). *A Textbook of Translation.* Hemel Hempstead: Prentice Hall.
8. Gutt, A. (1991). 'Translation as Interlingual Interpretive Use.' Chapter 5 in *Translation and Relevance: Cognition and Context.* Oxford: Blackwell. Reproduced in Venuti, L. (ed.) (2000), pp. 377-396.
9. Lodge, D. 1992, *The Art of Fiction*, Penguin, London.
10. Salinger, J.D. *The Catcher* in the Rye Penguin Books, London. London: Penguin Books Ltd., 1994.
11. Laurie G. Kirszner, Stephen R. Mandell, *Patterns for College Writing: A Rhetorical Reader and Guide*, Boston, New York, 2001, p. 5.
12. *Ibid.*
13. Maya Angelou, *I know why the Caged bird sings.*, New York, Random House, 1969.
14. Archibald MacLeish, *Poetry and Experience* (Harmondsworth: Penguin Books, 1965), pp. 140-141.
15. Laurie G. Kirszner, Stephen R. Mandell, *Patterns for College Writing: A Rhetorical Reader and Guide,* Boston, New York, 2001, p. 316.
16. *Ibid.*
17. *Ibid.*
18. The Christian Literature Society: *New Manual of English Grammar*. Rev. Ed. London, 1917, p. 200.

19. *Ibid.*
20. S.D. Kothare, Y.G. Talpade, *English Composition for Indian Students*, Macmillan and Co. Limited, Bombay, 1934, p. 243.
21. The Christian Literature Society, *op. cit.* p. 201.
22. *Ibid.*
23. *Ibid.*
24. *Ibid.*
25. S.D. Kothare, Y.G. Talpade, *op. cit.* p. 243.
26. Dodsworth, Martin Ed. *The Penguin History of Literature: The Twentieth Century*, Vol. 7, Penguin Books. 1994, p. 119.
27. Naresh Chandra, *The Practice of Criticism*: part 1, Poetry, Ram Lal Pury, 1975, p. 121.
28. *Ibid.*
29. The Penguin History of Literature, *op. cit.* p. 209.
30. The Christian Literature Society, *op. cit.* p. 202.
31. *Ibid.*
32. Sylvia Plath: *Mirror* in http://vmlinux.org/ilse/lit/plath.htm
33. The Christian Literature Society, *op. cit.* p. 203.
34. *Ibid.*
35. Laurie G. Kirszner, *op. cit.* p. 695.
36. *Ibid.*
37. *Ibid.*
38. *Ibid.*
39. *Ibid.*, p. 169.
40. Geofferey N. Leech, *A Linguistic Guide to Poetry*, London and Harlow, Longman, 1969, p. 62.
41. Laurie G. Kirszner, *op. cit.* p. 697.
42. *Ibid.*
43. The Christian Literature Society, *op. cit.* p. 202.
44. S.D. Kothare, Y.G. Talpade, *op. cit.* p. 245.
45. *Ibid.*
46. M.H. Abrams, *A Glossary of Literary Terms*, Seventh Edition, Bangalore, Prism Books, 2004, p. 10.
47. *Ibid.*
48. *Ibid.*

49. M.H. Abrams, *op. cit.* p. 25.
50. Jagat. S. Bright, *Dictionary of English Grammar*, New Delhi, Atma Ram and Sons, 1961, p. 4.
51. *Ibid.*
52. *Ibid.*
53. *Ibid.*
54. *Ibid.*
55. *Ibid.*
56. *Ibid.*
57. *Ibid.*
58. *Ibid.*
59. *Ibid.*
60. Nageswara Rao: "Indian English Idioms" in Laxmi Shanker Ed. *Synthesis: Journal of English Literature & Language*, Vol. 2, No. 2, p. 158.

9

Challenges and Strategies in Translation

Satyendra Singh

Translation is considered to be an act of rendering a text written in one language into a different language. What are the challenges involved in translating a text? What are the strategies a translator uses when he attempts at translating a particular text? To answer such questions and others this paper will focus on the attempts at studying the challenges and strategies in translating texts from one language to another.

Generally, there are four categories of translation:

(1) all purely informative statements like announcements at railway stations;

(2) ordinary readable prose that has no outstanding characteristics;

(3) poetry and prose having an enjoyable content, in other words, literature;

(4) learned, scientific, technical and practical writings.

A perfect translation of the first category is possible. Adequate translation of the second and fourth categories is also possible in any cultivated language. However, in the third category, translation is an extremely difficult occupation. In a piece of literature, generally speaking, form is more important than content. As a matter of fact, the other three categories can be grouped together because adequate rendering of such writing where content is more important does not involve such a difficult problem.

In literature itself a similar categorization is not only possible, but natural. The division of literature into (1) the literature of language, where form is more important than content, and (2) the literature of power, where the emotional aspect is dominant is well-known. Poetry, drama and fiction belong to the latter category and creative element in these makes them more difficult for translation. What is most difficult for rendering in a new language is the aesthetic experience of the original author which he has successfully communicated to his readers in his own language. The expression of this experience is inextricably connected with idioms, images and nuances of the source language that it becomes a challenge to find exact equivalents in the receptor language to convey the same experience. It is the critics who have realized this difficulty and challenged the translatability of literature in such terse expressions as the following:

> 'Poetry cannot be translated'; 'No translation is exact translation' (Dr. Johnson); 'All translation seems to simply an attempt to solve an insoluble problem' (Humboldt); 'Translations can offer us but a vague equivalent' (Virginia Woolf).

As far as the Italian proverb 'Translators are traitors' and its truth is concerned, there is more truth and less parody. 'Translators are traitors', because they cut and join to fit a new entity.

Robert Frost's provocative and sharp remark, 'Poetry is that which is lost in translation' is evidently not a definition of poetry; but a pointer to the fact that the five elements of aesthetic appeal in poetry, or in literature refuse to be transferred to a new medium. We can therefore generalize and say that the more creative a work of literature is, the more difficult it is for translation.

All these observations are useful as they make us aware of the difficulties of translating literary materials faithfully and adequately. As is well known, translation is an activity that belongs to the domain of art. It has evolved independent of formal training. While theories and textbooks provide an important knowledge it is the insight acquired in practice that sharpens skills.

Talking generally about translation one would do well to begin with some basics. The basic questions a translator has to answer before embarking on the practice are:

1. Which is the text being translated genre wise: prose, poetry, fiction or drama?
2. What is the purpose of translation: transferring information from one language to another or carrying a literary text from one language to another?
3. Is it translating instructions, etc. from a manual in one language to another?
4. What is the type of text in terms of its original composition, contemporary, classical, medieval or ancient?
5. What is the target reader: the elite, the neo literate, the general public or the student with a specific purpose?
6. Is the translation a rendering into the same genre or another?

Translations vary according to the need, and according to the target reader the translator has in mind. For example, translations may be intended to be used for learning a language and cultivating literary appreciation in the target language. This demands extensive notes not only in lexical, semantic, and syntactic items but also in expressive literary devices. If the translator does not know for certain the perspective use of his work, he would not be able to give what the reader may deem essential. Pedagogic translations ought to be different from translations for the general reader.

Interactive translation is possible only when the original writer and the translator can exchange notes on the translated texts at every stage so that the translation is evaluated by the original writer himself. This kind of translation ensures credibility and authenticity. The writer and the translator confer, and the translator's task becomes easier.

Then, there is collective, co-operative translation. This is undertaken by institutions like Sahitya Akademi. A number of translators gather. Works are discussed and assigned to different hands. Drafts are discussed, revised and edited. Some kind of uniformity is assured when different translators translate different parts under the guidance and supervision of a general editor. The object is to communicate the very best of a literary text with collective, co-operative efforts.

If we are concerned with literary translation, it should be our aim to take as much of the beauty and significance of the source text into the target text. One of the main challenges in translating one text into another is its cultural linguistic layering. How can one transfer one linguistic code into another? Can the dynamics present in the original text be carried into another? As the idea of a translation, by and large, is to present the original work to a reader from another language known to him, it is obvious that every item of beauty in the text of the original language is to be incorporated in the target language. This brings us to the question of fidelity. Does translation focus on the question of fidelity to, or betrayal of, the original? In fact, fidelity can be obtained when some affinity of historical situations, underlies the translator's ability to confront the theme his author confronted and wrote, as if for the first time. A great deal depends on what the translator regards as the main strand of the original, and what he is willing to modify or abandon.

Notwithstanding the innumerable inherent limitations of translation, every effort has to be made to convey as much as possible. The reader of a translated text does not fully comprehend the grandeur of the original but conveying not meant, not intended, and supposed to be intended, would be unfair both to the reader and the writer. It would be fairly satisfactory on the part of the translator to give some idea of the eminence in the writing to the extent the reader would not be disappointed.

Social markers, markers of cultural levels, registers, and technical words, need to be carried into the target language. The ideal thing is to be inviting, enthusing and encouraging the reader to get the feel of the original text. It is also useful to retain some words of the original especially terms of kinship, items of dress, words of address, interjections, expletives, items of food, clothing, etc. not only in unrelated but even in cognate receptor languages. The receptor language stands to gain borrowings from the original, when they eventually become familiar and popular. This is evident from the works of many Indian writers who have used English, a non native language and who have successfully conveyed native feelings and thoughts in the form of translations of idioms and phrases from mother tongue into English and with retention of some of the original words. Here are a few examples:

Retention of original words: Kala naag, Phannyar for black Cobra and hooded (in the story of the *Mark of Vishnu* by Khushwant Singh); The Great Maharatta Hotel, Biryani aur pulao (in the story *Sweets for Angels* by R.K. Narayan); Baap re Baap, Gulabjamun, Rasgulla, barfi, Jalebi, Gulmohar, Dupatta, Maina, Gurkha, Sarpanch, etc. in the various stories of Mulk Raj Anand. All this displays the author's remarkable felicity to weave Indian words into the texture which gives a local flavor to their translations. It is important to note that while translating one text into another the goal is often to help create a sensibility among the target language reader. A good translator does this not by mechanical means of a literal translation but by the deployment of an existing diction in order to prepare readers to welcome a new style as in the case of almost all Indian authors writing in English. Especially Anand's works illuminate the working of deeper cultural and ideological factors in the act of translation. Some more examples will suffice:

> Spoiler of my salt (*untouchable*); bow my forehead, The eater of your masters, face at your face (*Coolie:* p. 18, 60); A dog is a lion in his own street (*Across the black waters:* p. 71). Abuses and curses: You eaters of your masters, You of evil starts, May the vessel of your life never float in the sea of existence (*Coolie*: p. 18, 16, 78); You lock–id son of a bow-legged scorpion, You son of a pig (*Untouchable*: p. 13, 38). Greetings: Bow at my

forehead, Fall at your feet (*Coolie:* p. 14, 10). Blessings and flattery: Draw a hundred lines on the earth with the tip of my nose (*Coolie*), Your shoe and my foot (*Untouchable*). Modes of address and reference: Mother of my daughter (*Coolie*), Baba Bibi Ji, etc. Use of swear words from Punjabi or Hindi into English: May I be your sacrifice, Is this any talk, After eating seventy mice the cat is going on a pilgrimage. Use of Expletives: Ari, Hey, Wahh, Ohe, Achhaa, hai, Bas! Bas! Honorifics: huzoor, Sarkar, Maharaj, Sahib, etc. Literal translations of Hindi and Punjabi idioms abound. Some very interesting examples are: 'He was dead over her' for 'he was madly in love with her', 'Why do you eat my head?' for 'Why do you pester me?', 'Come on my head, Come on my eye' for 'you are right welcome'. All these examples prove how language and culture cannot be separated as both are inextricably interwoven with each other.

Having discussed the various facets of challenges and strategies involved in the process of translating texts it is worth enumerating to recount the misunderstandings that make for bad translations and it is with this that we hope to end this paper. As is evident any inadequate acquaintance with the original will naturally lead to mistakes, but what prevents an inferior translation from holding the reader's interest is less likely to be inaccuracy than incompetence in managing the new language, or in an imperfect idea of its resources. Though a translator cannot know his language too well it is easy for the scholarly translator to be too familiar with it. A translation so far as the reader is concerned is a work written in his own language. He cannot be expected to take an interest in the translator since off duty towards the original, though this commonly accounts for dead passages. The first mistake of an Inept Translator is unwillingness to leave anything out, though reflection will show the wisdom of not admitting into the new work what one cannot cause to function within it. The second cause of failure is uncertainty about why the original is worth translating. Why it has some claim on the attention of a specialist, but why it is needed in the economy of the new language. The third is unsuitable choice of diction. To this is related the most uncommon supposition that an idiom once chosen is simpler to sustain than it is. Having said all this, one can safely submit that the ideal translation is that which successfully recaptures the tone and texture of the original, which in many cases amount to transcreation of the original. This means that a good translator must have gifts which are comparable to those of the original author he wants to translate.

References

Choudhary, Kiran. 'Translating Hybrid Text in/on Cosmopolitan Spaces' in GJV Prasad (ed.) *JSL,* New Series, 10, Autumn 2008. p. 7.

Nayak, MR (ed.) 1977. *Selected Short Stories of Mulk Raj Anand.* New Delhi: Arnold Heinemann. pp. 44-46.

Preminger, Alex (ed.) 1974. *Princeton Encyclopedia of Poetry and Poetics.* London: Macmillan. pp. 866-67.

Rao, VVB Rama 2009. Insights into Literary Translation and Language in Distinctive Use. Delhi: Author's Press. pp. 6-7.

Singh, S.K. 'The Problem of Style in Indian Writing in English and the Indianism of the English of Mulk Raj Anand' in Dr. Laxmi Shankar (ed.) *Punya Bhoomi*, Vol. 1, No. 1, Jan. 2010, pp. 30-31.

10

Cultural Constraints in Translation

B.O. Satyanarayana Reddy

The act of translation as such is based on the level of culture of a translator. A translator's desire to share the sweet aesthetic experiences he gets while going through a literary text reflects his appreciable culture. If the translator's desire is just getting name and fame as a translator, then his act of translation does not possess the vibrating spirit of good culture which guides the translator and helps him to get through any kind of barriers in the process of translation. There are two types of major problems faced by a translator. Both are related to culture. One is the culture of the translator and the other is the culture of the text. The two kinds of culture influence the culture of the translated text. In this paper, different constraints of culture faced by a translator in the process of translating a text from one language to another are discussed at length with some illustrations from the texts translated from Telugu and Kannada into English.

The first and foremost question that arises in the direction of culture-oriented translational problems is whether translation is a mechanical and masterable art or is it a subjective and mood related art. From one point of view it is only subjective. From scientific point of view, it is a skill that can be cultivated and mastered by any person. Language is a scientific and systematic arrangement of words to form meaningful and understandable sentences whereas the spirit, meanings and culture of a text are incorporated and hidden in behind the syntactical structures of sentences. The hidden things cannot easily be grasped by the mere technical approach to a text. A text, therefore, is not just the language which constitutes the body and shape of a text. A text is to be taken into consideration and understood by the implied spirit and culture like the flesh and blood of a person. The nature of flesh and blood with its responses in various contexts decides the culture of a person. So, either for translating or for understanding a text, the culture of the translator is more important rather than the culture of a text. It is because the culture of the translator influences the quality of the translation in terms of diction, syntax and semantics of the language of the text.

The culture of a translator decides the point of view of the translator towards the source language text and the target language text. For instance, the great Indian epic *The Ramayana* has been translated into many Indian languages from the original text in Sanskrit language. In a single language like Telugu, there appeared many translations by different writers like *Bhaskara Ramayanam* by Bhaskarudu, *Nirvachanottara Ramayanam* by Tikkana, *Uttara Rama Charita* by Kankanti Papa Raju, *Molla Ramayanam* by poetess Molla, *Ramayana Kalpa Vriksham* by Viswanatha Satyanarayana, *Ranganatha Ramayanam* by Gona Buddha Reddy and others at different times. The translations of all these writers express their intensity of devotion and positive approach towards the text. A translator is also likely to fall a prey to the critical interpretations of the texts by the critics. The translator's point of view is probable to change by the critical works. The same *Ramayana* which was considered to be the cultural asset and great epic by Indians was interpreted critically in Telugu by a recent Feminist and Marxist writer Muppalla Ranganayakamma from a Marxist and feminist point of view. She entitled the novel *Ramayana Visha Vriksham* (*Ramayana: a Poisonous Tree*). A modern translator is likely to be influenced by this work and thereby his translation may get a sea change. This change can affect the health and welfare of the society. So, this point illustrates a fact that the culture and point of view of a translator plays key role either in protecting and developing, or in disturbing and destroying, the harmony of society.

As literature is mirror of society, we can also observe how the culture of a society gets reflected in translations through the translators who are part and parcel of society. In olden days when cultural and moral values were given high regard in social life and when discipline and decency were the order of the day, we can notice the same characteristics in translations and creative works. The translators used to do translations as divine duties, not allowing their self or personality to come in the way. The best example for this is the translation of the great Indian epic *The Mahabharata* into Telugu language by the great and famous poets Nannaiah, Tikkana and Yerrapragada. These poets have carved niches in the hearts of the Telugu people with their laudable work of translating *the Mahabharata* as a grand, sublime and sacred work. The towering example for translating or rather transcreating *The Mahabhagavata* (the text with the stories of great devotees) by nullifying the self is Sri Bammera Potana. Look at his point of view of himself as a translator and the text:

> Palakedidi Bhagavatamata
> Palikinchedivadu Ramabhadrudata, ne
> Palikina bhavahara magunata
> Palikeda verondu gatha palukaganela.

The above telugu poem means that the story that is spoken is called Bhagavata. The one who speaks through is called Ramabhadra. If I (the poet) speak, my sin will be annihilated. Therefore, why should I speak any other story? I will speak only Bhagavata. The poet translator Sri Potana thus expresses his will of translating the work as divine will.

Similarly, we can observe in today's creative and translated works the kind of society we are living in. As we have integratedly disintegrated, loosely knit, western influenced free society, we can notice the same characteristics in today's translations in the form of loosely knit disintegrated sentences. These sentences can be mainly noticed in the texts of those translators who are under the mixed influence of western and Indian cultures. Tracing out such sentences demands keen observation from us, just like we need keen observation to distinguish foreign culture from our own because it is inextricably interwoven in our culture. Of course, it is not the fault of the translator because he is the product and representative of the cultural society. Even if the translator is not under the influence of the culture of society he lives in, still he would have to select for his target language text only that kind of language which readers can easily understand. But one plausible question that arises here is: should the translator give so much importance to readers in selecting the language? If he gives importance to the language, does he not fail to do justice in translating the text in a befitting manner? It is because if the text has grand and sublime language, then which language should the translator should select for translation? If he selects the ordinary language so as to be understood easily by the readers, definitely the grandeur of the source language is spoiled in target language. So, the translator should neither be the text-favoured nor the reader-favoured, nor the language-favoured one. He should be an arbitrator in protecting the propriety and originality of the source language text, the target language and the interests of the reader. It means that he has to keep up the cultural integrity of the three.

Generally, the job of a translator is not such an easy one. It is an onerous one. Learning the mechanism of translation does not make one a successful, perfect and ideal translator; just as learning the grammatical mechanism of a language does not entitle a person either to speak or write language perfectly, unless he develops personal interest and involvement in those activities. So, the act of translation is an art of combining both the skill of mastery over languages and the spirit of interest in the content and culture of the source language text. The translator has to keep up the same kind and amount of interest, inspiration and motivation which push a person into act of translation all through the period until the text is completed. Some fail at some or other point. Paradoxically, if the translator happens to be a creative artist too, while translating his own text into another, there appears a perceptible difference between the two texts. For example in

S.L. Bhyrappa's Kannada novel *Vamshavriksha* (*Family tree*) which has been translated into English by himself and Sushma Chandrasekhar, we can notice some slight differences in the following sentences:

> "It is true that *we* and *we* alone must carry the burden of our anguish."[2]
>
> "The repetition of the pronoun for emphasis sake is a mother tongue influence (M.T.I)."
>
> "You must excuse me. I *seem* to have kept you waiting."[3]
>
> "The word 'seem' is also an Indian expression. In English, simply it would be "I have kept you waiting."
>
> "I have no other *pressing* work."[4]
>
> "The word 'pressing' is an Indian usage. It is also an effect of MTI."
>
> "If you refuse my gift, you will be guilty of breaking the code of *dharma*, guilty of *adharma*."[5]

The cultural constraint really crops up in translating the words like *dharma* and *adharma* which are neither so easy for the translator to translate with exact equivalent words in English, nor is it so easy for other than Indians to understand. It is because both the words mean different meanings in different contexts. For instance *dharma* in ordinary parlance is used in the sense of 'duty'. But this duty is different from person to person, according to his profession and context to context and place to place. The same word in spiritual field gives a different meaning with reference to soul. There are different kinds of dharma like individual *dharma*, *human dharma*, *Atma dharma*, *prana dharma* and so on and so forth. The word *adharma* is also as complicated as the word dharma to be translated.

Another difficult pair of words used by Bhyrappa which is hard nut to crack for translators and readers is "*dharma* and *karma*."[6] One means duty and the other means action or work. But the Indian cultural shades of meanings of these words cannot be understood so easily by the readers of English language. According to the Indian cultural shades of meanings, karma does not mean just the physical activity but also the mental activity like thinking. In Indian culture the mental activity of thinking is given as much and equal importance as the physical activity. So, if these words are translated in a casual way, they lead to misunderstanding of the text.

This kind of multi-layered, cultural connotations enshrouded words are found plenty in another Kannada writer U.R. Ananta Murty's novel *Samskara*. The very title 'Samskara' itself has got nine meanings as the novelist himself quotes in the beginning of the novel. Though A.K. Ramanujan has translated it in an appreciable way, still one can observe, with dissatisfaction, some words and metaphors which do not yield their complete sense to the translator or rather in other words, we can say the target language does not have proper equivalents. One reason for this problem is the cultural dichotomy between the source language and the target language of translation. The examples of some such words are given here with meanings provided in text to demonstrate the difficulties and disabilities of the translator to overcome the cultural constraints:

> *Panchamrita*: *five-fold nectar*. The five nectarious substances: milk, curd, ghee, honey and sugar, and a compound ade of them, offered to gods and distributed to devotees on special days.[7]

Though, here, the meaning of combination of *panchamrita* is given, the meaning of the word *amrita* is not given properly. Actually *amrita* in Indian culture means the drink of the gods which makes one who drinks it deathless and immortal. This *panchamrita* is taken by the devotees with the faith of getting their immortal state. But this cultural connotation is missing in the translation because the word 'nectar' according to the *Oxford Advanced Learner's Dictionary*, means:

> Nectar: 1. a sweet liquid that is produced by flowers and collected by BEES for making HONEY. 2. The thick juice of some fruits as a drink.

Nowhere the Indian cultural meaning of immortality is mentioned here.

With regard to the word *dharma*, we have to appreciate the translator because in notes he mentions its nature as untranslatable.

Dharma: a central word in Hinduism, therefore, multi-vocal, untranslatable; usually glossed 'law', righteousness, duty, code, etc.[8]

Wedding-string: tali, ceremonially tied by the bridegroom around the bride's neck, as part of the wedding-ritual.[9]

The meaning of 'tali' to an Indian means more than the meaning provided here. The concept and culture of 'tali' cannot easily be translated or understood.

Achari: a vulgar disrespectful form of Acharya.[10]

Here the proper meaning of the word's culture is missing. Actually 'Acharya' is the one who practices first and then preaches others to follow.

Five-fold breath of life: pancha prana; Tradition lists five such vital breaths (the soul vital power).[11]

Here also the right meaning cannot be suggested through translation because of the culturally deeper meanings of *panchaprana*. Unless one knows their specific functions in human body one understands the word in incomplete way.

We have, thus, some expressions like "A hundred and one dreams"[12] (noora ondu kanasugalu) in another famous Kannada writer Kuvempu's novel. This cannot give us proper idea of the expression to the target language readers. There are no English equivalents to this type of expressions.

All the above constraints in translation remind us the fact that a word is not a mere word made up of some symbols, syllables and sounds; just like a sentence is not a mere sentence made up of some words and punctuation marks. They denote and connote more than what they appear to mean for our casual reading. So, the cultural standard of a reader is also equally important as the cultural standard of a translator to understand the text translated.

Translation in society has a second place after creation. But when we observe all the above problems faced by a translator, his effort is more than the creator's. it is because the creator when gets mood creates easily, whereas the translator has to get mood as well as industrious nature to give keen attention to minute and negligible things of the original text. So, a translator has to be understood with a right perspective.

Notes

1. P. Rajeswara Rao, *Prasidha Telugu Padyalu* (*Famous Telugu Poems*) Hyderabad: Pratibha Publications. 2001, p. 16.
2. S.L. Bhyrappa and Sushuma Chandrasekhar trans. *Vamshvriksha,* Madras: Manas affiliated East-west Press PVT. Ltd., 1995, p. 13.
3. *Ibid.*, p. 14.
4. *Ibid.*
5. *Ibid.*, p. 18.
6. *Ibid.*, p. 79.
7. A.K. Ramanujan, trans. *Samskara: A rite for a dead man*, Delhi: Oxford University Press, 1995, p. 149.
8. *Ibid.*, p. 150.
9. *Ibid.*
10. *Ibid.*, p. 152.
11. *Ibid.*, pp. 156-56.
12. Ramachandra Sharma and Padma Ramachandra Sharma, trans, *The House of Kanooru*, New Delhi: Penguin Books, 1999, p. 211.

11

The Problems of Translation in English

B.N. Gaikwad

Greek philosopher Aristotle in his significant work *Treatise on Poetry* stated that poetry is not mere copying or imitation but a recreation. It is also true about the act of translation. Translation, according to Dante, is reinvention, verse making, or a project of recreation. Translation is the wandering existence of a text in a perpetual exile, says J.H. Miller.[1] As English becomes an increasingly global language, more people become multilingual and translation becomes a crucial communication activity. Traditional thinking about translation saw it as a poor copy of invention that produces a new original in another language. Of late translation studies have challenged the long standing notion of translation as inferior to the original.

Etymologically, "translation" is "carrying across" or "bringing across." The word translation is derived from the Latin word "translatio". Additionally, the Greek term "metaphrasis" ("a speaking across"), has supplied English with "metaphrase" (a "literal translation," or "word-for-word" translation)—as contrasted with "paraphrase".[2]

An American writer Octavio Paz says, translation is the "principal means of understanding this world." To him "each text is unique yet it is translation of another text. No text can be completely original because language itself in its very essence is already a translation—first from nonverbal world, and then, another phase, because each sign and each phrase is a translation of another sign.[3]

Throughout the 18th century, the watchword of translators was ease of reading. Whatever was not understood in a text, or thought might bore readers, translators avoided it. They cheerfully assumed that their own style of expression was the best, and that texts should be made to conform to it in translation. For scholarship they cared no more than had their predecessors and they did not shrink from making translations from translations in third languages, or from languages that they hardly knew or—as in the case of James Macpherson's "translations" of Ossian—from texts that were actually the "translator's" own composition.[4]

The 19th century brought new standards of preciseness, accuracy and style. Regarding accuracy J.M. Cohen observes that the policy became "the text, the whole text, and nothing but the text," except for any coarse passages and the addition of numerous explanatory footnotes. As far as style is concerned, the Victorians' aim, achieved through far-reaching metaphrase (literality) or pseudo-metaphrase, was to constantly remind readers that they were reading a foreign classic. An exception was Edward Fitzgerald's *Rubaiyat of Omar Khayyam* (1859), which achieved its Oriental flavor largely by using Persian names and discreet Biblical echoes and actually drew little of its material from the Persian original.[5]

In advance of the 20th century, a new pattern was set in 1871 by Benjamin Jowett, who translated Plato into simple, straightforward language. Jowett's example was not followed, however, until well into the new century, when accuracy rather than style became the principal criterion.[6]

As the world is changing with the highest speed never before, the transmission of knowledge also is speeded up. Knowledge is being shared all over the world and translation is the vehicle of the process. The translation movement is now a worldwide phenomenon and catching considerable attention of the literature lovers, readers, critics, and the translators. As translation is a global literary phenomenon it is widely seen in Indian literary world too. In fact the translation practices have long tradition in India: Sir William Jone's (1746-96) *Sacontala* or *Fatal Ring* is a translation of the Sanskrit romantic play *Abhijanshakuntalam*. Omar Khayyam's *Rubaiyat* is also translated in Hindi. Hariwanshrai Bachchan's *Madhushala* is also translated into English as *The House of Wine* (1935). Tulsi Das (1532-1623), the greatest poet ever in Hindi, has rewritten the *Ramayana* in Hindi. The translation within Indian languages is now a popular tendency. The Indian literature written in Marathi, Hindi, Bengali, Oriya, Malyalam, Telgu possesses colossal store of knowledge. Hence it demands translation so that it can be exchanged, shared within and outside India.

But the act of translation is not an easy literary endeavor. It faces many theoretical and practical problems. One may confront the problem of understanding the relationship between the original, the source and the translation of that original. The problem of owning the text is also significant, for example if a printer or author owned a text, what rights did the translator have? The problem of cultural context and its understanding, particularly when the writer and translator belong to varied cultures, is the major problem in translation practices. Translation was a key to the other language and, above all, its literature. Some people come from families where several languages are either inbred or thrust upon them by dire necessity. For them the problem is entirely different. They may even be inclined to believe that there is no problem. But it does not mean that they are good translators when put to the test.

"A text produced by a human being and rendered into another language by someone who is not its author. Substitute 'fathered' for 'produced' and Dr Freud comes in handy with a few suggestions. For, indeed, producing words is a function of the body as well as of the mind. Is the process as essential and ominous as killing a father? Is not the text bastardized in the process? Such questions will remain unanswered for the meantime", says Jean Migrenne.[7]

Translating Prose

No poem, drama, novel, short story, or essay would ever be read, without translation, in countries whose language is different from the author's. It is unthinkable. Translation is as old as the world. Problems occur with the first attempts and have kept cropping up as conditions changed. Among the main ones is the quality of the original texts, the in/capacity of those who translate to have access to them and read them properly. It often was a matter of remote translation, i.e. translating from translations. Bible scholars are familiar with such problems. These days the problems of translation are different. A third party occupies pride of place: the publisher. And that means money and deadlines. In most cases translators cannot submit their work to a publisher and authors cannot impose their translators, if they ever care to have their own. The system is one-way: publishers have their own firms. They buy rights and are intent on making quick profit. Paying the translator is not their main concern. Long translations may also be subcontracted by the main translator, resulting in patchwork-like books. Translators can be friends, friends of friends, well-paid relatives or exploited hacks. In such cases quality is not on the agenda. The publisher thinks that the translator is competent or does not care; does not read the translation, or does not see any point in firing the incompetent go-between. Ordinary readers are not aware of it; they buy the stuff, and that is what matters. If they read the whole book, they have a good enough idea of what the author actually wrote. Mistranslations are diluted in the sheer mass of words.

With translation there is the problem of time. Translations do grow old. Nobody could write, today, in the language of yesterday. And few would be able to read that prose anyway. To this one should add the problem of rights, once again. Translations are protected by copyright and in some cases, in some countries; the rights extend far too long or are systematically exclusive. Even GOOD translations, signed by famous names, need some dusting. Even not having wide readers for the works like some classics is the problem with translation.

Translating Drama and Poetry

Novels or short stories are no mere catalogues of words. There is at all times the author's experience lurking behind the words, there is style, slang, humor and wit, there is imagery and there are metaphors. This juggling with words, transfer of feelings and experience onto a sheet of printed paper takes one away from plain fact and into drama and poetry, where it becomes essential. Drama, besides, implies time and space requirements either intended by the author or introduced by the successive directors who stage the play. Translations rarely age well. Translation then, becomes version, especially for the screen, where dubbing or subtitles impose limits that have little to do with translation any more; and to say that wit and puns and double-entendre, especially in titles must make us pause. There are considerable translators of poetry as well, whether the poesy is found in prose, dialogues or poems. For the poets of the past, there is enough research, criticism and translation on library shelves for translators to find what they need if they wish to produce something new, and supposedly better, different or updated. The new translator, then, thinks that he/she can improve, and their learned, limited public will publish reviews, praising or savaging the improvement. It is an insider's job. Praising is less frequent than savaging. "Lack of competence is suicidal. And, if there is no improving a given translation, any attempt at doing so is doomed from the start. If translation is not done for money, it is done for pleasure, for culture's or friendship's sake. It may even be a climactic experience. If it is so, why should not the translator overdo it? Addicts will know no limits, particularly those arising from supposedly untranslatable works."[8]

But in any genres of literature translating feelings and sensations is complicated work. Humor, wit, jokes, puns are also obstacles that sometimes turn out to be insuperable. Not that one lacks words, but when background references are specific to one civilization those who were not born into it must do without the original. Translation is not a mere act of translation or transfer but bringing in the right feeling. There are abundance of problems in translation in general. Bringing in exact historical and social context in translated work is also the significant problem. The translation work is a subjective work missing subjective experience or involvement; hence creation of the similar ambiance in translated work may not be reproduced. It is also difficult to decipher the motive or intention of the creator; hence the translator may misunderstand and misinterpret the work. Due to the absence of writer, especially in translation of posthumous work the problem of maintaining accuracy is high. In the act of translation understanding diction is the biggest problem. One need to be perfect bilingual or else the translator sometimes can be helpless to get the exact words and to bring natural beauty of language in the original text. All languages have their own culture and social background which is vital in translation. For example Mirza Galib, Rumi, Khalil Zibran are Arabic poets and their poems are translated without understanding the poets; the society in which they are brought up, the language and the then mental conditions of the poets. The knowledge of Persian language becomes pre-requisite to translate their work.

There are some particular problems in the translation process: problems of ambiguity, problems that originate from structural and lexical differences between languages and multiword units like idioms and collocations. Another problem would be the grammar because there are several constructions of grammar poorly understood, in the sense that it isn't clear how they should be represented, or what rules should be used to describe them. The words that are really hard to translate are frequently small, common words, whose precise meaning depends heavily on context. Besides, some words are untranslatable when one wishes to remain in the same grammatical category. The question of whether particular words are untranslatable is frequently debated. For example, it isn't easy to translate poetry because you need to examine the words and meaning and after the flow and rhythm (or rhyme). Most translations of poetry are bad. This is principally because the translator knows the foreign language too well and his or her native language too poorly. In language understanding certain idioms, terms and neologisms, unsolved acronyms and abbreviations, proper names of people, organizations, and places, slangs and sometimes even punctuations in a language can be a problem. As the genre changes the literary translation techniques and devices demand change. The difficulty of translating poetry is also twofold: the words and meaning on the one hand, the flow and rhythm (or rhyme) on the other.

In spite of the above-mentioned facts about translation we have to accept that translation is creation of different territory, new awareness, wider readership, creation of appreciation and creating accessibility.

Notes

1. Quoted from the Professor J.H. Miller's lecture given at the ninth Centenary Celebration symposium of the University of Bologana, Italy, 1988.
2. Paz, O. Trans. Irene del Correl. 1992. "Translations of Literature and Letters" in R. Schlte and J. Biguenet (eds.) *Theories of Translation from Dryden to Derrida* Chicago: University of Chicago Press, pp. 152-63.
3. J.M. Cohen, "Translation," Encyclopedia Americana, 1986, Vol. 27, 12.
4. *Ibid.*, p. 21.
5. *Ibid.*, p. 38.
6. *Ibid.*, p. 45.
7. Migrenne, Jean. "On Translation," http://www.cosmoetica.com/B43-JM1.htm Migrenne, 4/5/02.
8. *Ibid.*

12

The Basics of Translation

Mallikarjun Patil

The word translation is derived from a Latin word 'translatus.' The prefix 'tran' means 'passing something' and the stem 'stale' means 'cover.' The generic term 'translation' has several implications such as alteration, change, conversion, interpretation, paraphrasing, rendering, rephrasing, rewording, transcription, transformation and transliteration. Translation specifically means translating, rephrasing, interpretation, rendering and decoding.

The Oxford English Dictionary defines translation as "an act of turning from one language to another."[1] New Standard Encyclopedia says, "Translation is rendering of meaning, especially in writing from one language into another."[2]

Translation is an art, a science, a craft, a creation. It is a linguistic and cultural activity. It is interlingual. Translation is concerned with the business of meaning. It is an understanding process. It is reporting, sometimes, an explanation, an analysis. Translation is a means for acquiring knowledge apart from being oral communication.

Translation is a means for understanding the other and otherness. It is a means for updating knowledge. Translation helps for establishing a link with other languages and literatures. Translation helps for a national and international rapport. Octavia Paz says all knowledge is translation. Collingwood says translation is a dislocation. Wilmowitz says translation is a process of signification. Wittgenstein says translation is a mathematical problem. Heidegger says translation helps for more knowledge. Sujit Mukherjee says translation is a discovery.

Translation is transference of meaning of a text from one language into another. Here two languages come into focus. One—the language from which a text is translated into another language. This language is known as Source Language or SL for short. Such a text translated is called Source Text or ST. Likewise, the language in which the source language text is translated is called Target Language or TL. Such text rendered into other language is called Target Text or TT. When one translates a text he should have command over both the languages. That is to say words should obey his call. He should have both the sense and feel of language. Besides, he needs to be familiar with the socio-cultural matrix.

Translation should be faithful and idiomatic. Nothing should be added or omitted. A translator should accord in all parts, even length, with its original. Through his dynamic encounter between two languages he should follow closely the syntax, cadence and sound of the other language into his own. He must know translation is neither transliteration nor transcreation. It is rather a tight-rope walking between two languages. Samuel Butler says, "You must not skin him, stuff him and set him up in a case."[3]

Lord Roscommon, Dryden's contemporary insists upon fidelity in translation:

> Your author always will be the best advise
> Fall when he falls and when he rises, rise.[4]

Alexander Pope says:

> Know well each ancient's proper character:
> His fable, subject, scope in every page;
> Religion, country, genius of the age...
> Thence form your judgment, thence
> Your maxims bring
> And trace the muses upward to their spring.[5]

But it does not mean the process of translation is mechanical, exact and artificial. There should be a compromise between the original author and the translator. This is to make the original relevant and readable. Otherwise the translated work loses its flavour. Therefore Benjamin Jovit says, "All translation is a compromise, the effort to be literal and the effort to be idiomatic."[6] Indeed, to preserve the original in reworded version, the process requires translator's complete involvement in the life and idiom of one's own age.

There are debates and discussions on the possibility and impossibility of translation. Scholars ask whether translation is possible. In Shakespeare's play *A Midsummer Night's Dream*, when Quince says, "Bless thee Bottom, bless thee, thou art translated," Bottom sharply reacts: "I see the knavery, this is to make an ass of me."[7] Bottom's reaction, in a way, sums up the popular attitude to the translator, that the translator is a traitor. There is a feeling that translation can result into perversion. There is a saying that total translation is a myth. The reason for this, Roland Barthes says, "a text has many meanings."[8] Roger Bacon, of 12th century, thinks every language is indivisible, unitary and single. According to him, a journey from one text into another is difficult. American linguist Edward Sapir says," No two languages are ever sufficiently similar to be considered as representing the same social reality. The worlds in which different societies live are distinct worlds not merely the same world with different labels attached."[9] Anatole France adds, "There are perhaps some good translations, there are not many faithful ones."[10]

People doubt whether translation is possible. According to them, when we think language is God-given, or something that comes to us by birth, this doubt becomes stronger. Some religious people think men should not take up translation. For example, Koranic translation is not encouraged. But Christian missionaries encourage it. Some people hold the view that translation degenerates the original.

Those people who hold the view translation is impossible further the case of poetry translation. Usually a poem is untranslatable as it is an organic whole in which music and meaning, sound and sense, image and metaphor, in fact, all poetic elements are inextricably combined. There to change the sound pattern is to mutilate the poem. There is an asking can dancer be separated from dance? Likewise, we can ask: can poetry be separated from words? Robert Frost says, "Poetry is that which is lost in translation."[11] Here sets of meanings for words create problems. So K.R.S. Iyengar says poetry translation is impossible.

Reacting to theorists like Edward Sapir, Noam Chomsky thinks there is a universal grammar behind all languages which can help us understand others' language. This he calls Transformative Generative Grammar. George Steiner thinks "translation is realizable precisely, because those deep-seated universal genetic, historical, social elements from which all grammars derive can be located and recognized as operative in every human idiom, however singular or bizarre its superficial forms...."[12] That means translation is possible. Even poetry translation. Sri Aurobindo is of the opinion that there are two ways for the translation of poetry: "One to keep it strictly to the manner and turn of the original, (and) the other is to take its spirit, sense and imagery and produce them freely so as to suit the new language."[13] Goethe in his letter to Carlyle writes that whatever might be limitations in translation, translation is necessary for understanding the world. Able translators can do justice to the original and enrich both the languages. Accordingly translation rejuvenates the original. The argument that translation is not possible stems from the people who are local and narrow-minded.

Poetry translation is difficult because poetry is abstract. A poem is not a concrete thing. Since it is created by the esemplastic power of imagination, it cannot be captured easily. Great poetry translators like Dryden, Pope, Shelley, Arnold and Tagore have much thought over it. According to them, only a poet can translate poetry. As we know Tagore translated his poetry *Geetanjali* and he got Noble prize for it. Still the point is that much of Tagore's poetry is transcreation. It is transposition in Jacobson's words. Even drama translation poses problems. The dialogues, stagecraft, intonation, etc. cannot be translated easily. As well as certain philosophical and abstract concepts cannot be rendered satisfactorily.

People think translation is a secondary activity. It is a mechanical work. They say it is not creative. It is not worthy of critical attention. It is not of general interest. Some think what we get by way of translation is not a real thing, but a pale shadow or a faint echo which can give only a rough idea of what the source text is like. Belloc says, "The art of translation is a subsidiary art and derivative."[14] Matthew Arnold says translation is an inferior activity.

The act of translation has several besetting problems. First language problems, then culture problems and then difficulty in understanding the text and its meta meanings. The problem of maintaining fidelity, avoiding repetitions, using stylistic devices, etc. worries anybody.

Once upon a time, translation meant just rendering of knowledge without bothering about accuracy, exuberance, content and style. So Friedrich Nietzsche says ancient Romans translated Greek texts as they wished. Europeans did the same later. This continues still. So translators either did a free translation or adapted originals to suit their taste. Sometimes they paraphrased or summed up, or transliterated or transcreated.

There are many types of translations. Machine or manual translation is rather artificial. More familiar translations include literal (metaphrasing) translation, free translation and transcreation. Adaptation is another one.

1. Literal (metaphrasing) translation has word for word rendering. Here exactness is important.
2. Free translation involves the liberty of translator. This is meant for information and exuberance. Here fidelity to the original is less important. The aim of translator is less to make an accurate rendering than to make the substance of foreign work thoroughly intelligible to the spirit of Target Language. That is to say "the character of the translation precedes as much from the mind of the translator as from the mind of the original writer."[15] Free translation was done in medieval times. King Alfred and poet Chaucer translated Latin works into English freely. Malory's

Morte d' Arthur is partly a free translation. Here is a tendency to make a foreign work express essentially Target Language spirit.

3. Transcreation is another mode where a translator makes use of the original for creating something of his own. He adds his own and deletes certain things which is not necessary, or relevant. He takes liberty with the work. For example, Tagore made use of transcreation when he translated his *Geetanjali* into English. This is more a creative activity.
4. Adaptation is an adjustment of a text according to one's tastes. It is called bawdlirization. This is done when the original text is cumbersome. For example, Romesh Chunder Dutt bowdlirised the *Ramayana* from 48,000 lines to 4000 lines and the *Mahabharat* from 2,00,000 lines to 8000 lines. Dryden's *All for Love* is an adaptation of Shakespeare's *Antony and Cleopatra.* So is Tom Stoppard's *Rosencrantz and Guildernstern are Dead* as an example of Shakespeare's *Hamlet.*

Translation has a long history to speak of. There have been translations right from the time of Christian era. Scholars like Quintilian, Cicero, Horace, Catallus and Pliny considered translation seriously. They heralded the concepts 'word for word' and 'sense for sense.'

Romans translated many Greek works into Latin. Later Europeans translated Greek and Latin works into their languages. In medieval times Europeans translated eastern knowledge into their languages.

The means of translation was extremely significant until the time of renaissance for rendering human knowledge into English. It is said the aim of translator was then less to make an accurate rendering than to make the substance of foreign work thoroughly intelligible to the English spirit; the character of the translation thus preceding as much from the mind of the translator as from the mind of the original writer. Much translation was done in medieval times. King Alfred and poet Chaucer translated/adapted foreign works into English freely.

Malory's *Morte d' Arthur* is a translation. Printing, Renaissance and the rise of new educated classes expanded translation in the 16th century. The first important translation in English is Gavin Douglas's Virgil's *Aeneid* in 1553. Spenser, Chapman, Philomon Holland, John Florio, Dryden and Pope were great translators.

The 16th century was marked by a serious theory of translation. Etienne Dolet advocated 'sense for sense' translation. Contemporary idiom and style were used to add immediacy. Martin Luther used modern English in translation. Renaissance Europe used the art of translation richly.

The 17th century saw a lot of French texts getting translated. Abraham Cowley viewed imitation as a branch of translation. John Dryden used translation for updating ancient texts. His preface to Ovid's *Epistles* consists of good ideas on the art.

The 18th century translators held the view that translators should think of their contemporary readers when they translate. They said that they should convey the authors' spirit and manner in a natural way. Friedrich Schleiermacher suggested a separate sub-language for translation. Victorians valued literalness. Arnold translated Homer literally and laughed at.

After 1850 translation became a kind of net for hauling in exotic writings and its field became very wide. Fitzerald translated *The Rubaiyat* of Omar Khayyam (1859), Richard Burton, *Arabian Nights*, William Morris, *Icelandic Sagas*. The vice of the period was to make a foreign work express essentially English. This helped them create an air of authenticity—a fault which Matthew Arnold criticized in his essay *On Translating Homer*.

Tolstoy's works in English translation became extremely popular. Ibsen, Proust, Ezra Pound and Kafka's works were brought into English during the 20th century.

Today translation is popularly cultivated. The art has become more widespread, making texts in many languages readily available.

The development of communication, the expansion of the field of structural linguistics and application of it to the study of translation affected significant changes in translation.

George Steiner divides the history of translation into four divisions. According to him the first division covers Cicero and Horace. This is ancient age. The second division covers Valery, a French translator involving hermeneutic methodology. This is medieval period. The third division is the late 20th century when structural linguistics and communication theories influenced translation. The fourth division began in the 1960s with hermeneutic methodology being revived again. Hermeneutic methodology is related to the process of interpretation. Accordingly there is only one truth in interpretation.

The Bible played an important role in translation business. It is the most translated work. The Hebrew of Old Testament was translated into English before the Christian era. Chrstian missionaries enhanced the art of translation. St Jerome, John Wycliffe and William Tyndale did Bible translation. Arabs translated many Sanskrit works. William Jones and Max Mueller were great translators. Indeed, it is because of translation all the knowledge of the world is available to us today.

There are certain translation theories. The ancient translators held the view that translation should be done either 'word for word' or 'sense for sense.' Cicero (46 BC) said that a translator must care for the meaning of the text. Dryden said that there exist three types of translations i.e., (a) metaphrasing (literal), (b) paraphrasing and (c) free translation. A French writer Etienne Dole devised five rules for healthy translation:

1. The translator should clearly know the author and his work while translating.
2. He should have known his language and the language of the work to be translated by him.
3. He must conform to the meaning of a sentence instead to the series of words in the translation.

4. His aim should be translating in a simple language, and,
5. He should achieve a rhythm that smoothes the ear and heart of his readers.[16]

Lawrence Humphrey suggests a middle path. According to him a translator must combine the elements of simplicity, scholarship, beauty, dedication, sensitivity and boldness. This is an aptitude. Purity and propriety may be achieved at the same time. Modern thinkers like Herder, Humboldt, A.W. Schlegal have thought over the issue. There was much discussion about language distance in Germany. Still the ideal situation is one where translation is like the transfer of an employee from one department to another. Unfortunately we do not have any book on translation. Books like Aristotle's *Poetics* or Bharat's *Natyashastra* do not exist on translation. Hillarie Belloc says the translator must render unit by unit, idiom by idiom and intention by intention. He says "the essence of translating is resurrection of an alien thing in a native body."[17] He gives moral responsibility to the translator but at the same time the liberty to change the text to suit the needs of the TL text is curtailed.

J.C. Catford, a modern theorist, defines translation as "the replacement of source language text material by equivalent target language material."[18] He considers it a branch of comparative linguistics. He introduced the concepts 'Total Translation' and 'Restricted Translation.' Like Dolet, Catford values meaning in translation. He speaks of linguistic translatability and cultural translatability. He says when certain words are not understood, there will be some ambiguity. Likewise, certain culture-bound words create vagueness. Another translation theorist Nida speaks of direct and analytical methods in translation. Peter Newmark focuses on semantic and communicative translations. He says there are three levels of translation—referential, textual and subjective. These theories prove that translation needs much original genius to recreate a text in target language.

Prague school linguists view translation as a linguistic process involving the transfer of a message from SL to TL.

Modern translation theorists like Susan Bassnett and Andre Lefevere say that translation has been a major shaping force in the development of world culture, and no study of comparative literature can take place without any regard to translation. Translation theories involve the concept of hermeneutics in the 20th century. This is related to the science of interpretation as opposed to commentary. It is about determining meaning. Accordingly there is one linguistic truth but not many as pluralism says (for example deconstruction).

There is an effort to understand the art of translation differently in modern times. Russian formalism, linguistics, stylistics, structuralism, information science, etc. have influenced human understanding of translation. Logic, semantics and literature have their own impact. In fact, translation has become a multi-disciplinary area. Anthropology, sociology, philology, poetics, grammar, etc. are studied for understanding translation.

Notes

1. *Oxford English Dictionary*, New Delhi, 1992, p. 1297.
2. *New Standard Encyclopedia*, Vol. 13. pp. 360-61.
3. Samuel Butler, quoted by Mallikarjun Patil, "Literary Translation," *Studies in Translation*, Atlantic Publishers, New Delhi, 2002, p. 11.
4. Lord Roscommon, quoted by Mallikarjun Patil, "Literary Translation," *Studies in Translation*, Atlantic Publishers, New Delhi, 2002, p. 13.
5. Alexander Pope, quoted by Mallikarjun Patil, "Literary Translation," *Studies in Translation*, Atlantic Publishers, New Delhi, 2002, p. 14.
6. Benjamin Jovit, quoted by Mallikarjun Patil, "Literary Translation," *Studies in Translation*, Atlantic Publishers, New Delhi, 2002, p. 13.
7. Shakespeare, quoted by Mallikarjun Patil, "Literary Translation," *Studies in Translation*, Atlantic Publishers, New Delhi, 2002, p. 14.
8. Ronald Barthes, quoted by Mallikarjun Patil, "Literary Translation," *Studies in Translation*, Atlantic Publishers, New Delhi, 2002, p. 14.

9. Edward Sapir, quoted by George Steiner, After Babel, Oxford: OUP, p. 87.
10. Anatole France, quoted by Mallikarjun Patil, "Literary Translation," *Studies in Translation*, Atlantic Publishers, New Delhi, 2002, p. 16.
11. Robert Frost, quoted by Mallikarjun Patil, "Literary Translation," *Studies in Translation*, Atlantic Publishers, New Delhi, 2002, p. 17.
12. George Steiner, After Babel, Oxford: OUP, p. 87.
13. Rama Kundu, quoted by Mallikarjun Patil, "Literary Translation," *Studies in Translation*, Atlantic Publishers, New Delhi, 2002, p. 18.
14. Hilaire Belloc, *On Translation*, Oxford: Clarendon Press, 1931, p. 23.
15. Rama Kundu, quoted by Mallikarjun Patil, "Literary Translation," *Studies in Translation*, Atlantic Publishers, New Delhi, 2002, p. 18.
16. Atini Dole, quoted by Mallikarjun Patil, "Literary Translation," *Studies in Translation*, Atlantic Publishers, New Delhi, 2002, p. 15.
17. Hilaire Belloc, *On Translation*, Oxford: Clarendon Press, 1931, p. 24.
18. J.C. Catford, quoted by Suka Joshua, "Translation: Its Brief History and Theory," *Studies in Translation*, Atlantic Publishers, New Delhi, 2002, p. 5.

13

"The Better a Writer is in a Regional Language, the Harder He is to Translate": A Critical Study of Two Marathi Dalit Autobiographies Translated into English

Vandana Pathak

> It is half English, half
> Indian, funny perhaps but it is honest,
> It is as human as I am human, don't you
> see ? It voices my joys, my longings, my
> Hopes, and it is useful to me as cawing.
> Is to crows or roaring to the lions.... (Kamla Das)

Many Marathi Dalit autobiographies have been translated into English. Laxman mane's *Upara* has been translated into English as *An Outsider*. Laxman Gaikwad's *Uchalya* has been translated into English as *The Branded*. Kishore Shantabai Kale's *Kolhatyache Por* is entitled *Against All Odds* in the English translation. Dr. Sharankumar Limbale's *Akkarmashi* is translated as *The Outcaste* and Dr. Narendra Jadhav's *Aamacha Baap ani Amhi* is well known as *Outcaste: A Memoir*. Vasant Moon's *Vasti* has been translated as *Growing up Untouchable in India*. Urmila Pawar's *Aaydan* has been translated into English as *The Weave of My Life—A Dalit*

Woman's Memoir. Dalit autobiographers have written self-narratives in profusion. Their autobiographies are documents of their agony and protest. The very titles of their autobiographies in original Marathi versions are metaphorical and possess varied nuances of meaning, gradually unfolded through the narrative.

In the translated autobiographies selected for the purpose of this study, Laxman Mane's *An Outsider* is the autobiography of a writer from a nomadic tribe and Laxman Gaikwad's *The Branded*, of a person from a criminal tribe. Daya Pawar's *Baluta,* widely acclaimed as the first Dalit autobiography in Marathi, Laxman Mane has employed the technique of *Baluta* in his *An Outsider*. Yet it is written almost like a novel, but the method of writing used by both these writers is different. Both have described their individual and communal experiences in the autobiographies. Laxman Mane's An Outsider is written almost like a novel, the technique used in Daya Pawar's Baluta acclaimed as the first Dalit autobiography aimed at social transformation. Laxman Gaikwad's *The Branded* is more episodic in nature. Hence it appears disorganized.

Dalit literature deals mainly with life in villages or rather outside the village bounds. Naturally the language used by the autobiographer is rural language (*gramin bhasha*). Three factors, society, period, and place influence a language. The language of the Dalit autobiographer depends upon the geographical locale of the writer and his community. Nagnath Kotapalle comments,

> A plane of rural society is felt here. In this society are seen the scattered islands of exploited Dalits. A different life style and dialect of that society is observed here. As the generation in this society goes on acquiring education, the pictures of that life along with its background will appear in literature.

These writers resided outside the village. So they were unacquainted with the language and culture of the *Savarnas* and the middle class people. They used the language of their community, the language of their every day life, to share their experiences with others. The language was used along with all its distinctive features and regional flavour. Jyoti Lanjewar opines,

> The language of Dalit autobiographies is regional. The autobiographies reveal many strains of colloquial languages in Maharashtra and along with colliquiality, means of subsistence, village system, customs and economic system are also reflected.[2]

The colloquial language is used naturally and simply. It is not used as a deliberate strategy, spontaneity of expression is its main feature. Bhalchandra Phadke argues, "In reality Dalit autobiographies have enriched the vocabulary of Marathi language and they have also enhanced the grandeur of different colloquial languages."[3]

Laxman Mane's *An Outsider* is an autobiography of a person belonging to the Kaikadi tribe—a nomadic tribe in Maharashtra. Prior to writing this autobiography, he had published three to four articles in *Sadhana* and in *Purogami Satyashodhak*. He accepts very frankly, "A few years ago, if someone had even joked about my writing a book, I would have laughed heartily at the prospect, considering my standing in the field!" (*A.O.*, p. 5). The famous Dalit writers, Daya Pawar and Raosaheb Kasbe, had encouraged him to write about his experiences. Subsequently, at the insistence of Anil Awachat, he agreed to write. He knew well that according to the Kaikadi Panchayat, the writing of this autobiography was a crime and he would be punished for it. Yet he 'dared to write' *Upara*.[4] It is a record of all his varied experiences in life. While talking about it, he says,

> What shall I say about the book? Whatever I lived, experienced and saw, I poured into my writing. I lived it all again once more. I do not mean to blame anyone. It was a temptation I had to control. If I have changed certain names in this book, that is only because I could not do otherwise. Beyond this, there is no change or invention I can lay claim to (*A.O.*, p. 06).[5]

The Marathi *Upara* is dedicated to his parents who gave him a slate and to his wife who gave up all happiness to give him company in his stormy life and to the Samajvadi Yuvak Dal that developed his social consciousness. In the English edition of *An Outsider*, the dedication page is missing. An additional detailed note of Mane entitled '*Upara* and After' occurs in the English version (this is missing in *Upara*). The Marathi word *Upara* literally and figuratively means *An Outsider*. The author Laxman Mane, owing to his birth in the Kaikadi tribe, always remained an outsider in the Indian social order. He lived outside the village boundary and led a neglected, ostracized, marginalized existence. He could not, inspite of numerous attempts (sincere and genuine), become a part of the mainstream society. The titles (both, in the original Marathi and translated English) signify this peculiar plight of the narrator. The translator of the autobiography is A.K. Kamat, Professor of French in Bombay University. He has translated *Upara* into French too and the translation has received a good response in France. The original *Upara* in Marathi has been published by Granthali whereas the English translation is by Sahitya Akademi. The front side of the blurb of the English edition mentions it as a 'Sahitya Akademi award-winning autobiography in Marathi'. It has the name *Upara* written on it boldly followed by its English translation *An Outsider* mentioned below it. The huge fame and response to the identity of *Upara* has been retained in an effective manner by this strategy. On the cover page is the symbolic picture of a loaded donkey indicative of the nomadic life of the Kaikadi community. *Upara* proclaimed Laxman Mane's debut on the literary scenario. Due to the spontaneity, genuineness and sincerity of Laxman Mane's realistic emotional expression, the autobiography received an overwhelming response and bagged many coveted prestigious awards like Bando Gopal Mokadam Puraskar (1982), N.C. Kelkar Puraskar (1982), Bhartiya Vidyapeeth Puraskar (1982), Ford Foundation Fellowship (1981) and Homi Bhabha Fellowship (1985).

Upara has a total of 154 pages. These one hundred and fifty four pages have not been divided into chapters. The autobiography commences with Laxman's childhood and ends with his marriage to Shashi and acceptance by the Panchayat into the caste community. *An Outsider* begins and ends on the same note but here it is divided into parts. In the English edition, there are 212 pages. These many pages are divided into XIII chapters or parts. In the Marathi version, the end of one part and the beginning of another is indicated by space which is not so in the English translation. The kind of diction that a writer habitually uses can tell us a great deal about the quality of the writer's mind and style.[6] The writer has to choose his words according to the subject matter, occasion, purpose and audience. Usually, writers have an extensive vocabulary and wide range of styles to choose from. This statement is inapplicable to Dalit writers, especially autobiographers, as each of their autobiography is his or her first work of art. These autobiographies are without any literary pretensions or 'pseudo literary traditions'. Their vocabulary is also meager having been a product of their marginalized, inhuman, animal-like existence. It is picked up in childhood from family members and the community. As the circle of their social interaction is very restricted, the range of vocabulary also is limited. Laxman Mane, the writer of *Upara*, hails from Kaikadi community. It is a nomadic tribe wandering from place to place. "The language used in an autobiography is very significant as it throws light on the life of the writer. If the writer belongs to the nomadic tribe, then the language becomes the sum total of all the formative influences that shape and mould the life of the writer."[7]

The family of Laxman Mane moved from place to place incorporating various strains and nuances of the language and dialects used in the region of Nirgudi, Satara, Kolhapur and its vicinity. The famous Dalit writer Bama points out,

> The Dalits have different vocabulary and speech. They should deliberately overstep what they are permitted to write, by the rules of the 'dominant' grammar. The Dalit should write as a Dalit. The Dalit writing should be read like the Dalit's.[8]

Each writer has his own vocabulary, style and linguistic characteristics. These depend upon and are inherited from his family and social background (*Samskaras*). These peculiar expressions reflect upon the personality of the writer. Yashwant Manohar has suggested that these characteristics can be analyzed from the point of view of linguistics and statistics.[9] The words (language component) of *Upara* can be classified as follows:

- Words in the colloquial language
- Words used in the rural sector
- Words used by the nomadic tribes like Kaikadi, Wadar and Pitali
- Words used by the Dalits
- Words in the Kaikadi language
- Some English and other words

The Kaikadi language being difficult to understand, people could not comprehend the abuses and thus all their fights and quarrels remained unknown to outsiders. Of course, the Kaikadi fraternity understood everything and intervened on occasions. Thus, the Kaikadis possessed a distinct advantage due to their language. There are many sentences in the Kaikadi dialect in *Upara*. Laxman's parents, especially his father, switched over to Kaikadi language whenever he was angry or disturbed. This is quite natural. It is said that a man dreams in his mother tongue and in a similar manner, expresses his worst possible fears in the same language. These sentences in the Kaikadi language are immediately translated into Marathi and put into brackets for the comprehension of readers. There are 117-118 sentences in the Kaikadi dialect strewn all over the autobiography. These sentences add a unique flavour to the narrative and offer the readers a glimpse into a language and culture which is so unlike their own. The abusive language jolts the readers. Arati Kulkarni has pointed out as to why Laxman Mane has used such an abusive language. She says,

> In his dialogues, Mane has used many abuses of the rural sector. It is true that the author could have described them without using such abusive language. Mane must have used this language to describe the life of the folks and to express human emotions like anger and affection, etc.[10]

Many Kaikadi words, phrases and proverbs also figure in the text. These add a touch of reality, liveliness and raciness to the narration. These words seem to possess a natural spontaneity and rhythm. The use of Kaikadi dialect is more in the first part of the autobiography. The use of regional words in the language has added novelty. It has enriched Marathi literature too. Yet it has posed the problem of obscurity. Regional variation has resulted in variation in pronunciation of words in Marathi as well as in English translation. *Upara* has three different pronunciations of the word 'duty'. Later on for the purpose of education, Laxman lived all alone. Naturally, the Kaikadi language was not used. Laxman's language becomes more abusive and aggressive in the last part of the text when he has to grapple with the harsh reality of life. 'The thorns of life', 'fever and fret of the world' along with 'chill penury' have made him more cynical and hence his language is a mirror of his inner revolt and protest against the social system. There are many English words used in this autobiography. The use of English words is more in the second and third part of the autobiography when Laxman acquires the benefit of education. These English words occur with hackneyed pronunciations. In addition, there are few words from the Hindi language. Konakani dialect is used at one place to bestow a touch of reality and authenticity to the narrative (p. 43) and Wadari dialect has been used at another place.

Another remarkable feature of *Upara* is the change in the manner of speaking while talking to people belonging to higher, same or lower class people. When Dagdya Ramoshi accosted the family, Laxman's father folded his hands and offered him a hen. He touched Dagdya's feet and entreated him to keep an eye on them. The difference in the language due to pidgin made schooling a difficult exercise for Mane. The development of Laxman's personality is visible through the change in his language. Language acts as an index of culture and the rural Dalit language in the first part of the autobiography paves way for the refined, polished language in the third part of the autobiography.

Upara thus depicts "those experiences that did not find a place in literary representations."[11] It portrays the struggle of Laxman Mane to survive and struggle in this life of

> ...perpetual physical and mental persecution, and his transformation into a speaking subject and recorder the oppression and exploitation he endured, not only as an individual but also as a member of a stigmatized and oppressed community[12]....

Mane, thus, has broken new ground and mapped a new territory in this '*swakathan*'. In order to depict the harsh reality of Dalit life, Mane and with him other writers of Dalit autobiographies, used a language quite unfamiliar to Marathi literature. The world of suffering and exploitation painted in Dalit autobiographies is unknown to the mainstream readers. M.N. Wankhede states that high caste Marathi literature is artificial and false, 'like a paper flower'. He adds,

> A Marathi writer's understanding of life is restricted.... He has never seen that outside there is a vast world—a suffering, distressed, struggling, howling world, burning with anger from within like a prairie fire.[13]

Dalit literature is literature of protest. It is a manifesto for revolutionary transformation of society and human consciousness. It is an attempt to arouse Dalit awareness. Hence, it is written in the language of the Dalits. Rural colloquial language becomes an apt vehicle to reveal in all honesty agony, pain, exploitation, marginalization, poverty, anger and protest of the Dalits.

The translation of such a document into a foreign language is a tedious task. The translator of *Upara,* Prof. Kamat has made a worth while effort in translating it into English. The autobiography has been translated into simple, plain, unadorned prosaic English to reveal the stark reality of human life in *An Outsider*. The translator has remained faithful to the source text and through his literary maneuvering has succeeded to a great extent in depicting the essence of *Upara*. The translator has embarked upon voluntarily inculcated mode of code mixing and code switching with strong determination. He has gone a step further and introduced multiple lexical features from the vernaculars, Marathi and Kaikadi. *Upara* is an authentic socio-cultural document depicting Indian panorama of life via Indian ethos, people, customs and traditions, rites and rituals, etc. The translator has sometimes substituted English equivalents for words in the vernacular. The cultural associations have strong tie ups with the colloquial language and hence here the translated version (*An Outsider*) has suffered a loss. The author has attempted to incorporate many lexical items from the vernacular into the text corroborating Prestan's view of "Language shift to meet social demands."[14] There are many proper nouns used in this autobiographical narrative that are steeped in Indian culture and ethos. Laxman, the protagonist of the autobiography, is addressed as 'Laksha' or 'Lakshya'. It is used as a pet name, as a term of endearment, and at other times contemptuously. Most of the proper nouns are shortened by clipping their final constituents. This has a special significance as it is a means by which love, affection, tenderness, and proximity is expressed. The same is used to indicate anger, displeasure, irritation or mockery at other times. Sami, Lali, Pushpi, Kisnya, Jayshya, Mahadya, Khagya, Indya, Martya, Shardi, Aani, etc. usages in the autobiography substantiate this. ('Aani' is the shortened form of Aanwari (*A.O.*, p. 37), 'Ithalya' (*A.O.*, p. 96), 'Datya' (*A.O.*, p. 86), 'Chhabya' (*A.O.*, p. 87), 'Yadu' (*A.O.*, p. 80) can be cited as examples.) The higher caste people were addressed respectfully as Raosaheb Khalata, Anantrao Deshpande (*A.O.*, p. 123), Prof. Patgaonkar, Prof. Dabhole, Bapusaheb Deshpande (*A.O.*, p. 125), Dr. Dabholkar (*A.O.*, p. 139), etc. Some proper nouns like Laxman, Indya, Martya, Kisna, Radhi, Ratna, Shashi, etc. are well known to Indian readers. There are frequent references to gods and goddesses such as Khandoba, Kalubai, Yellamma, Saatasaraya, Mariai, Shiva, Lakshmibai, Hiruba, Mhasuba, Laman, Bhawani, Satyanarayan, Rama and Satwai. The names of the months are also the ones that occur in Hindu calender like 'Paush' (*A.O.*, p. 34), 'Chaitra' (*A.O.*, p. 48), 'Ashad' and 'Shravan' (*A.O.*, p. 68), 'Kartik' (*A.O.*, 87), 'Jeshta' (*A.O.*, p. 203), 'Falgoon' (*A.O.*, p. 90), and 'Vaishakh' (*A.O.*, p. 91). There are words depicting different relationships. In Marathi, the meaning of terms such as 'Kaka', 'Mama', 'Vahini', etc. is very clear whereas in English 'uncle' could be a 'kaka', a 'mama' or even any casual acquaintance. 'Vahini' is brother's wife and in English brother-in-law's wife is also called sister-in-law. In *Upara* many such terms are used.

In *Upara,* Laxman addresses his father as 'Ba' and his mother as 'Aai'. In *An Outsider,* father is addressed as 'father' and mother is called 'mother'. The common noun is used to address and refer to both the parents. In *Upara,* many words are used to call and address a person informally. These are repeated umpteen numbers of times. The names of the festivals are given in Marathi in both the versions. 'Dassera' (*A.O.*, p. 48), 'Navratra' (*A.O.*, p. 69), 'Diwali' and 'Ramnavami' (*A.O.*, p. 79), 'Vatpurnima'/'Vatsavitri' (*A.O.*, p. 203), etc. are used in *An Outsider*. These celebrations have many cultural associations familiar to Marathi readers and unknown to English readers especially outside India. Many other words for food items such as 'bhakri' (*A.O.*, p. 19), 'chapatis' (*A.O.*, p. 89), 'misal' (*A.O.*, p. 116), 'bhujeas' (*A.O.*, p. 130), 'bhel' (*A.O.*, p. 41), 'Biryani' (*A.O.*, p. 189), etc. are used. To this list can be added names of newspapers and periodicals such as *Kesari* (*A.O.*, p. 135), *Sakal*, *Sahyadri* (*A.O.*, p. 136), Pudhari (*A.O.*, p. 152), and *Sadhana* (*A.O.*, p. 168); names of musical instruments like '*Kalat*'—a flat drum (*A.O.*, p. 112), and '*padgham*' (*A.O.*, p. 149), etc. Various castes and tribes in Maharashtra have been named. This list includes 'Dhangar', 'Kaikadi', 'Makadwale', 'Joshi', 'Davri' (*A.O.*, p. 40), 'dombari' (*A.O.*, p. 41), 'Vaghyeas' (*A.O.*, p. 42), 'Kolati' (*A.O.*, p. 43), 'Mahar', 'Mang', 'Ramushi', 'Vallar', 'Sonar' (*A.O.*, p. 47), 'gondhalis', 'Mang-garudis', 'gosavis', 'vaids' (*A.O.*, p. 51), 'Beldars' (*A.O.*, p. 112), 'Vadari' (*A.O.*, p. 115), 'Ghadasi' (*A.O.*, p. 157), 'mali', 'korvis' (*A.O.*, p. 158), etc. Other Marathi words that occur in *An Outsider* are 'dhoti' (*A.O.*, p. 21), 'Peepal' (*A.O.*, p. 30), 'bajra' (*A.O.*, 31), 'paisa' (*A.O.*, 39), 'murlyea', 'Kalawantin' (*A.O.*, p. 40), 'dombari' (*A.O.*, p. 41), 'aarati' (*A.O.*, p. 54), 'anna' (*A.O.*, p. 56), 'Puja' (*A.O.*, p. 75), 'bidis' (*A.O.*, 80), 'surpatya' (*A.O.*, p. 92), 'Basing' (*A.O.*, p. 96), 'Nayak' (*A.O.*, 112), 'Chowk' (*A.O.*, 115), 'paan' (*A.O.*, 116), 'paanwallah' (*A.O.*,137), 'namaste'

(*A.O.*, 164), 'Deeksha' (*A.O.*, 165), 'Kabbadi' (*A.O.*, p. 169), 'morcha' (*A.O.*, p. 168), 'Rickshaw' (*A.O.*, p. 178), 'mangalsutra' (*A.O.*, p. 179), and 'chawls', 'Sanyasi' (*A.O.*, p. 196), etc. These words impart a distinct flavour to the narrative. This is an example of code-mixing and switching. It is a stylistic literary device. A single speaker in code-switching uses different varieties at different times. In *An Outsider* as well as *Upara,* the local dialect and the standard language are mixed up. There are many examples of conversational code-switching. Both the versions of the autobiography in English and Marathi rely on the process of borrowing.

In *Upara*, there is frequent mention of things required for worship such as 'Nividachi pitali', 'Udabattya', 'kapur', 'a small piece of gud' i.e. jaggery, 'gulal', 'bukka', 'kunku halad' etc. Names of various trees, fruits and crops like 'Limba', 'Pipal', 'Piparini', 'Vad', 'Keli', 'usa', 'papaya', 'bajra' occur repeatedly in the autobiography. Places of pilgrimage like Malvadi, Jejuri, Kurvali, etc. are mentioned. There is a long and exhaustive list of many towns and villages that are traversed by the writer's clan in search of bread and butter. Majority of these lexical elements in *An Outsider* enlisted above possess multidimensional religious and cultural connotations. Equivalence in English or mere translation of such terms into English by retaining the original word in Marathi fails to unfold the cultural ethnicity of the word. The word 'Diwali' (*A.O.*, p. 79) has been described as 'festival of lights celebrated in October, November.' For millions of Indian readers, 'Diwali' is so special because of its religious and cultural link ups. These have not been hinted at. 'Bhakri' (*A.O.*, p. 19) has been described as 'a meal'. Arjun Dangle's *Poisoned Bread* describes 'bhakri' as 'coarse, unleavened bread' in its glossary.[15] Limbale's glossary in *The Outcaste* gives its meaning as 'unleavened bread made of millet' (*A.O.*, p. 114). Marathi 'Kavul Lava' (*Upara*, p. 28), has been translated as 'applying flower' (*A.O.*, p. 51). Such translations fall short to convey various cultural and/or religious nuances associated with a certain word. It is rather surprising that in *An Outsider* the footnotes include only thirteen words. The rest of the words (mostly Marathi) are without any explanation.

The translator has tried his best to translate some popular sayings/phrases/idioms/proverbs into English. Laxman Mane has made use of 'Kal aala vhata, par yel aali navhati' in *Upara* (p. 43). In *An Outsider* it reads as "the messenger of death had arrived but the moment had not." Laxman Mane has used a combination of colloquial language, Kaikadi, and Dalit words in his *Upara*. He has drawn heavily on English words in the second half of the autobiography. In addition, there are instances of code-switching and borrowing. Hence, the translation of *Upara*, an autobiography written in regional and local language, was a tedious task. Translation of the text becomes more tedious when emotions run high. In the life of any human being, there is an ebb and tide in affairs arousing a wide gamut of emotions. There are many emotional scenes of fear, anger, happiness, protest, etc. described in *Upara*. It is interseting to observe how the translator has handled various scenes depicting emotions. The change in the language of the narrator in scenes depicting different emotions is remarkable in *Upara* but in English translation many of these nuances are lost. Both Laxman's parents, in moments of anger, switched over to Kaikadi. The father's language was very abusive. As an example the incident of rape of Parumami can be quoted. The limitations of translation in a foreign language immediately come to fore. The change in Laxman Mane's language and style of speaking is crystal clear after his education and shifting to a city. His language and expression had undergone a sea change. This change in his mannerism and language is mirrored in *Upara*. The language in the first half of the narrative and that of the second half are different. Only few English words are used in the narrative initially. The pronunciation of these words is hackneyed in the first part. 'Band' becomes 'bend' or 'byand', 'rehearsal' is 'resal', 'Kenal' is actually a 'canal', 'photu' is 'photo' and 'rid' is 'raid', etc. As Laxman went in for higher education and shifted to a hostel, more English words became a part of his vocabulary. His Marathi language also became pure and polished. His initial language which was a mixture of 'rural, Dalit and Kaikadi' language gradually paved the way for more refined Marathi. This very important aspect of the development of the personality of the writer is reflected in Marathi *Upara*. The English language, perforce, retains the same tone right from the beginning to the end in *An Outsider*. Thus, a very crucial component is wanting in the English translation.

Laxman Mane's style of narration, very dramatic to begin with, acquires polish and refinement later on due to education and due to the elite company in which he leads his later life. (The effort to recreate the language used in that period/phase of life shows honesty of the writer and invokes appropriate response or emotion in the reader.) Yet in moments of emotional anxiety and uncertainity, Laxman instinctively switches over to 'gramin' and Dalit language. The language acts as an integral part of the writer's life and hence words which otherwise would have rubbed the reader on the wrong side acquaint him with the rural set up and ethos. It is true hat the abuses, expletives and vituperative language used in the text is sometimes redundant. Here it would be very interesting to point out an observation of Mane about his language. He says,

> As for us, we Kaikadis are protected by our own dialect. We could say whatever we liked and the outsiders would not know anything. It's not the same with the Pinglas. Our man was talking like a Maratha, so the people just watched the fun and laughed. His wife's face was burning with shame (*A.O.*, p. 86).

Common people were not able to understand Kaikadi language. Naturally, in times of quarrels when this language was used, it had a two-fold advantage. The problems remained confidential and personal. Secondly, no one could understand what kinds of abuses were used. This aspect can be understood well through *Upara*.

A remarkable feature of *Upara* is its change in language of people belonging to different castes. When one *Savarna* talks to another *Savarna*, the language used is cultured and polished. As an example, the marriage incident of Barge's daughter can be mentioned (*A.O.*, p. 99-100). When a *Savarna* person talks to an Untouchable, his language undergoes a subtle change. The conversation among Raosaheb Khalata, Dattu Kaikadi and Laxman's father illustrates this. The same conversation throws light on how a person from a lower caste addresses a *Savarna*. There is plenty of internal discrimination prevalent amongst the lower classes. This is witnessed in Laxman's father's conversation with Dagadya Ramushi. The language used for communication between a dombari and Lakshya's father shows how two different lower caste persons talk to each other. How the mannerisms of the grown people are blindly imitated by their progeny is substantiated by the scene of children's play. Many varieties of language usage are reflected in *Upara*. Some of the noteworthy usages are: Master's conversation with Lakshya's father (p. 16), Ba's replies to the questions of other people (p. 12), father's conversation with a Wadari (p. 77-78), Lakshya and his friend's meeting with a prostitute and her language (p. 49-50), language of women in the Holar community (p. 147) and the language of civilized, cultured, well educated persons like Dr. Narendra Dabholkar (p. 140) and Mr. V.S. Khandekar (p. 122), etc. are worth commenting upon. In *An Outsider*, all this variety disappears as everything is narrated in plain, simple English. The variety of dialects and styles used in Marathi can not be shown and translated or transliterated into English. This lacuna in *An Outsider* is due to the fact that *Upara* is 'polyphonic' (Multi-voiced). The language that is used in the caste Panchayat (*Upara,* p. 32-33) is an apt pointer in this direction. It brings to attention different voices and the clash of social perspectives and points of view. Jonathan Culler has said, "Narrative voices may have their own distinctive language, in which they recount everything in the story, or they may adopt and report the language of others. A narrative that sees things through the consciousness of a child may either use adult language to report the child's perceptions or slip into a child's language."[16]

In *An Outsider*, Parumami's rape has been reported in an adult's language with a child's perception. The grafting of his parents' in a theft case has been described in an adult's language with an adult perspective. Laxman confesses, "I was burning with an inner anger. Even at my age, I could understand the situation" (*A.O.*, p. 61). The dispute in the Panchayat related to Dharmea and Punnappa (*A.O.*, p. 56) is again narrated in an adult's language within an adult perspective. In another Panchayat dispute ,a punished man was made "to carry (on his head) an earthen pot filled with shit." The members of the Panchayat made holes into the pot with stones as he went around the god. The shit and piss fell on his body. This incident has been described in the language of an adult. Yet here both perspectives (that of an adult and child) are merged. Laxman writes, "In my mind's eye I saw myself in the place of the pot carrier. It is long past the day of that event, but I have not been able to wipe out the incident from my mind" (*A.O.*, p. 109). The description of Sami's engagement and wedding and that of his fight with village children is given from a child's point of view. This combination of an adult and child's language with both or single perspective makes the narrative more authentic and interesting. The treatment of both these perspectives in *Upara* and *An outsider* is different and worth studying. In English, the same language is employed whereas in Marathi, due to dialect variations, it is much more appealing and effective. As has been pointed out by Rich Atman, all texts carry a multiplicity of meaning or polysemy.[17] Thus the narrator has used 'Heteroglossia'—literally different languages. For Bakhtin, language is not to be considered a unitary phenomenon; rather, it is 'heteroglot'. It is divided up into languages which represent interest within dialogical relations such as the specific language uses which facilitate exchanges between humans within particular social groups, within professional groups and within particular genre.[18] All these subtle and finer aspects of language usage are lost in this translation.

Laxman Gaikwad's *The Branded* is the autobiography of a person belonging to '*Uchalya*' or '*Pathrut*' community. As has already been mentioned, it was known as a criminal tribe in Maharahstra. The original Marathi autobiography is *Uchalya*.

It heralds the debut of Laxman Gaikawad in the world of creative literature. Prior to this, he had written a ballad depicting the miseries of the exploited lot in 1977. *Uchalya* has received several awards including Sahitya Akademi award in 1988. Gaikwad confesses,

> I had little opportunity to acquire education and sophisticated culture. These are the reflections of a non- Matric social worker.... It is an attempt of a sensitive mind to pen what it has felt and experienced. This writing has been inspired by the stimulating encouragement of Laxman Mane of Upara fame and Sri Balkrishna Renke, the Secretary of the Nomadic and Vimukta Tribes' association (*T.B.*, p. ix).[19]

The Marathi *Uchalya*[20] has been dedicated to all his friends helping him in the fight for transformation. The dedication page is omitted in the English translation. A 'Translator's Note' has been added to the English edition. The Marathi word *Uchalya* literally and figuratively means a thief or a pilferer. It is the name of one of the communities notified as criminal tribes in the All India Criminal Tribes Act. Thus, it is a socially and legally branded community. The word *Uchalya* has been translated as *The Branded* in English. As Laxman Gaikwad reveals later in the text, whether the tribe and its members, commit a theft or not, they are always *Branded* and hence ill-treated and marginalized in the society. This aspect is very well connoted with both the English and Marathi titles and hence they are appropriate. *Uchalya* has been translated into English by Prof. P.A. Kolhatkar. Prof. Kolhatkar initially worked in the Indian Air Force and later taught English at the Bombay University. He being a keen lover of literature has translated several works from Marathi into English.

Uchalya has been published into Marathi by Srividya Prakashan, Pune. Its English translation has been published by Sahitya Akademi. The front side of the blurb describes it as 'Sahitya Akademi Award Winning Autobiographical Novel in Marathi'. It has the name *The Branded* written on it in all capital letters in bold font and underlined form. The Marathi title *Uchalya* is written below it in all capitals but a small font size is used. It is exactly the opposite of what has been practiced for *An Outsider*. In this strategy, the reader first focuses his attention on the English title *The Branded*. Of course, the purpose served is the same as that of *An Outsider*. The identity and response to Marathi *Uchalya* has been effectively used. The attractive cover page shows the bare back of a hand-cuffed man. Thus, the cover page conveys symbolically the significance of the title and contents of the autobiography. The translator of the autobiography, Kolhatkar has talked about the tone of the text. He writes,

> Gaikwad's book is an eloquent attempt to expose this prejudice and bring people round to the view that the people of these tribes are human beings and are in need of a helping hand from all to bring them into the mainstream of social life (*T.B.*, pp. v-vi).

P.A. Kolhatkar admits that it was "the compelling—tone of the work-militant as well as frank that prompted me to undertake this translation" (*T.B.*, p. vi). *Uchalya* contains 188 pages. The autobiography commences with the childhood of Gaikwad and ends with his activism. These 188 pages come one after another without any break. The English translation consists of 253 pages. No chapter scheme has been introduced here too. Yet space has been utilized to indicate change and discontinuity. Bhalchandra Phadke feels that the Dalit writer expresses his rejection, protest and agony in his own language.[21] *Uchalya* is the autobiography of a young activist born in the criminally branded '*Uchalya*' community. As he has said,

> NO NATIVE PLACE. NO birth - date. No house or farm. No caste, either. That is how I was born. In an Uchalya community, at Dhanegaon in Taluka Latur (*T.B.*, p. 1).

Gaikwad has put the words 'NO NATIVE PLACE' in all capital letters driving home his sense of alienation. Due to the peculiar circumstances of his community, he could not acquire much education. He has also articulated the need for sociological evaluation of his work of art rather than a literary one. Yet any work of art cannot come into being without language. Language plays a crucial role in any work. The writer unknowingly reveals his language habits, culture and *samskaras* in his text. If a writer is very particular about language, he makes an attempt to bring out its linguistic features through his text. A writer who does not possess theoretical linguistic knowledge also unknowingly enhances the linguistic richness of his literary creation. This imparts a unique nature to the work of art. Thus, in Dalit literature language has retained its social and cultural novelty.

Laxman Gaikwad spent most of his life in areas surrounding Latur. This area is rural and hence rural language is used in the autobiography. This area is in the vicinity of Andhra and Karnataka. Gaikwad has said, "We speak Telugu" (*T.B.*, p. 94). The Marathi spoken by the family is also influenced by it. Some words especially used by the '*Pathrut*' community also figure in the narrative. The language component of *Uchalya* can be classified as follows:

- Words in the colloquial language
- Words used in the rural set up
- Telugu words
- Words used by the 'Uchalya' community
- English words
- Other words from Hindi, Urdu, etc.

Many colloquial words are used in *Uchalya*. The change in language is noticed after the writer shifts to a hostel in Bhabalgaon. Then his language often becomes an admixture of colloquial Marathi and rural language. This tendency is noticed till the end of the autobiography. Many words used in the rural set up also blend with the narrative to impart to it a rural flavour and ethos. Telugu was the mother tongue of Laxman's family. Hence many Telugu words are strewn in the narrative. The meaning of these Telugu words is given in brackets in *Uchalya* to facilitate understanding. Gaikwad belongs to the Pathrut community. Naturally there are many words specially used in the vocabulary of the Pathruts. These words have enriched the Dalit vocabulary due to their novelty and uniqueness. In addition to these, there are many sentences in the native tongue of the Pathrut community occuring in the text. These sentences make the narrative more authentic and realistic. Laxman Gaikwad has made use of many idioms, phrases, and proverbs in the autobiography. Majority of them are found in the second part of the autobiography when Laxman starts living in a hostel. His social circle had widened reflecting a change in his vocabulary. His language had become more idiomatic. Laxman Gaikwad has imparted a deeper meaning to his experiences by the use of idioms. Another interesting feature of the language in *Uchalya* is that the language is heavily influenced by proximity to Andhra and Karnataka. The grammatical correctness in the use of gender, number and verb is not seen in the Marathi used here.

In *Uchalya,* many Hindi and Urdu words have crept into the fabric of the narrative changing its tenor. In *Uchalya*, many English words too are used. Their usage increases when Gaikwad starts working in a mill. As such, all technical words are in English and workers pick them up instinctively as a matter of routine. It is observed that most of the English words used in the text relate to work area and problems. These words do not occur here as English words. These words recur with varied distorted pronunciations. The word 'duty' comes with six different pronunciations. The same tendency is noticed about the use of the word 'hybrid' and 'chairman'.

The character refinement of the protagonist is evident through these examples. Many English words are uttered with hackneyed pronunciation. The speakers are not even conscious of pronouncing them wrongly. There are many terms indicating relationships. In *Uchalya,* Laxman has addressed his parents as 'Maay'and 'Baba'. In English, 'mother' and 'father' are used as equivalents. For his siblings, in both editions, Dada, Anna and Bhau are used. 'Tata' is his maternal grandfather. He is called by the same term in both languages. 'Bhabhi' and 'Vahini' have been translated as sister-in-law. Grandfather and grandmother in English are 'Aajya' and 'Aaji' in Marathi. His wife's grandmother is addressed as 'Mami' both in English and Marathi. For father, sometimes the translator has used the term 'Baba'. Santaram bhauji is addressed by the same term in both the languages. Yet surprisingly mother is never addressed as 'Maay'. The tendency to shorten first names of children noticed in *Upara* is also seen in *Uchalya*. 'Narya' (p. 12), 'Tukya' (p. 12) and 'Dagadya' (p. 15) are some examples. The tendency to call by clipped names is also seen in names of animals—'Pilya', 'Champi', 'Gulbya' (p. 13), etc. Laxman Gaikwad is addressed differently by people belonging to six different classes of the society. Another very interesting conclusion emerges out of the study of *Uchalya*. Gaikwad has used the same word twice (in succession) in sentences. *Uchalya* abounds in such sentences containing the linguistic device of reduplication.

The social hierarchy also resulted in different mannerisms in varied speech communities. The mode of addressing a person changed according to his social status. The police personnel always abused the Pathruts and the Pathruts addressed them as 'Sayab' (p. 2) and 'Saheb' (p. 158) respectfully. The washerman and Pathruts addressed each other as 'tumachyat' (p. 11) with due respect. The members of the Pathrut community addressed each other informally with 'Aara' (p. 13). Kulkarni master and the Brahmin lady are also given respect. In the mill, Laxman called all his higher-ups as 'Saheb'. The mill supervisors and other officials addressed them contemptuously and abused, humiliated them. Laxman's language underwent significant change as he progressed in life. His work as an activist made him mingle with nomadic tribes and hence almost till the end of *Uchalya,* a mixture of colloquial Marathi and rural language has been used.

Evaluation of any work of art is a subjective process. Gaikwad would like *Uchalya* to be evaluated sociologically rather than literarily. *Uchalya* being a socio-cultural document, the responsibility of the translator was manifold. He had to translate the source text into the receptor language, here a foreign language and in the process translate and convey the culture, habits, customs and civilizations of the tribe to non-Marathi readers. The problem of the translator here was herculean as the source text was replete with social and regional dialect forms. Moreover, the source text is about a marginalized community. As the translator P.A. Kolhatkar himself confides,

> They have been in a way outcastes lower than the lowest scheduled caste, on the bottom-most rung of the social hierarchical ladder. The politics, education, religion, economics of the mainstream society never touched them and they have been living in their own world of superstition, of primitive norms of justice and of ignorance (*T.B.*, p. v).

A delineation of all these social aspects and cultural nuances was indeed a tall order. The tone of the autobiography was also different. The translator says, "Gaikwad's book is an eloquent attempt to expose this prejudice and bring people round to the view that the people of these tribes are human beings and are in need of a helping hand from all to bring to them into the mainstream of social life" (*T.B.*, p. v-vi). As Kolhatkar confesses,

> It is this compelling tone of the work—militant as well as frank—that prompted me to undertake this translation. I have tried to be as near as possible to the authentic spirit of the book. Sri Laxman Gaikwad has not had much formal education. He has not the polish and advantages of a man of letters. The book suffers from many shortcomings which would be regarded as unpardonable in a well-educated writer. I have tried to stick to the way of narration adopted by Laxman Gaikwad so that the reader of this translation may savour the same experience which I, as the reader of the original savoured. (*T.B.*, p. vi).

In order to retain the flavour of the original *Uchalya*, the translator has used all proper nouns with their clippings. Laxman is addressed in various ways as 'Lachimen' (p. 16), 'Laxman' (p. 18), 'Lakshya' (p. 27), 'Lachhmantata' (p. 34), etc. Other proper nouns are also clipped—'Narya', 'Tukya' (p. 44), 'Hanma' (p. 44), 'Dagdya' (p. 14), 'Kerya' (p. 46), 'Babusha', 'Makya' (p. 47), 'Shankarya' (p. 53), 'Padme' (p. 65), 'Sayabu' (p. 67), etc. are used. The elders are addressed by full names such as 'Dagadusaheb Deshmukh' (p. 73),

'Ankush Mekle' (p. 76), 'Lingaram Chamle', 'Gyanoba Kuthwade' (p. 77), 'Govind Patil' (p. 83), 'Kisan Patil' (p. 66), 'Keshavrao Sonovane' (p. 96), 'Chandrabhagabai' (93), 'Santaram', 'Tukaram' (p. 06) and 'Tulashiram' (pp. 10-12). Suffixes indicative of relationships are used. Some examples are 'Manikdada' (p. 03), 'Shambhubhau' (06), 'Bhagwan Anna' (09), and 'Kesar Vahini' (p. 40), etc. are used. Words such as 'Bhavaji' (p. 49), 'Kaka' (p. 53), 'Bhauji' (p. 56) and 'Uncle' (p. 59) are also used. The suffixes of respect are also added to certain proper nouns such as 'Dagadusaheb' (p. 73), 'Chandrabhagabai' (p. 93), 'Keshavrao' (p. 96), 'Rizmal Sheth' (p. 112) and 'Guruji' (p. 18). 'Saab', 'Saheb' (p. 96), 'Ma'am' (p. 21), 'Madam' (p. 24) are employed to convey respect. There are umpteen numbers of references to gods and goddesses in the text. These are—'Yama' (p. 3), 'Laxmi' (p. 3), 'Yellamma' (p. 17), 'Bhawani' (p. 26), 'Ambabai' (p. 27), 'Rokdoba' (p. 77), 'Siddheswar' (p. 27), 'TuljaMai' (p. 49), 'Pandurang' (p. 56), 'Hanuman' (83), 'Balaji' (p. 107), etc. References to scriptures like 'Ramayana', 'Shivaleealmrit' (p. 83), 'Bhagvadgita', 'Pothi' and 'Puran' (84), are also found. There is a reference to 'Gautama Buddha' and 'Mahavir Vardhaman' (p. 79), too. Many other words associated with religion occur. Words like 'jogva' (p. 79), 'bhajans', 'abhangas', 'kirtans' (p. 82), 'gandha', 'Kirtankar', 'Veena' (p. 56), 'Halad-Kunku' (p. 26), help evoke typical religious ethos. Another characteristic tendency of the translator comes to fore. He has made plurals in the English style by adding 's' to the common noun in Marathi—'abhangas', 'bhajans', 'Kirtans', etc. When there are so many references to gods, it is but natural that there should be references too Hindu months of the calendar (like 'Aashadha-Shrawana', p. 39), and Hindu festivals (like 'Dusserah' (p. 12), 'Kar' (p. 12). Many food-items recorded in the oeuvre include 'bhakri' (p. 6), 'jeelebi' (p. 08), 'Wal' (p. 13), 'dhapatya' (p. 14), 'mand' (p. 20), 'bhajis' (p. 27), 'Mutke Kadbole' (p. 39), 'Chapati', 'Bundi' (p. 44), 'Dal' (p. 71), 'Roti' (p. 46), 'Puran' (p. 84), 'Pedhas' (p. 99), and 'Papad', 'Pakora' (p. 101), 'Pithale' (227), etc. Various containers, pots and pans are mentioned. These are 'Mutkula' (p. 9), 'Paratis', 'ghangal' (p. 29), 'Salada' (p. 27), and 'ghagar'

(p. 34). Names of various leaves consumed in absolute starvation are Marathi names. These are—'gadhav kata', 'Tarvata', 'kurdu', 'dagdi' and 'shepu' etc. (p. 40). 'Jakham Jodicha pala' (p. 43) is also mentioned. All these terms have been retained in Marathi for want of equivalence.

There are number of castes and sub-castes mentioned in *The Branded.* The exhaustive list includes 'Vanis' and 'bammans' (p. 6), 'Marathas' (p. 8), 'Kunbi' (23), 'Mang' (p. 27), 'Mahar' (p. 36), 'Ramohsi' (p. 61), 'dombari' (p. 65), 'Gurav' (p. 101), 'Vaidus', 'garudis', 'masanjogi' (p. 104) and 'Yalama caste' (p. 103). The plural of 'bamman' (p. 17) is 'bammans' (p. 6). The feminine gender is 'bamnin' (p. 2) and it is also called 'brahmins' (p. 17). The Indian readers are acquainted with the hierarchy of castes in India and so are able to understand caste discrimination practiced amongst the lowermost strata of the society. Bur for non-Indian readers, the exhaustive list, without any explanation, means nothing. The various names by which the '*Uchalya*' community is known such as 'Santmuchchar' (p. 4), 'Pathrut', 'Takari', 'Uchale', 'Girnewadar', 'Kamati', 'Ghantichor', 'Wadar' (p. 5) etc. are also enlisted. Various items of clothing are indicated as 'dhoti' (p. 1), 'Uparana' (p. 50), 'Saris' (p. 47), 'Petticoat' (p. 65), 'Jumper' (p. 65), 'Chemise' (p. 65), 'Blouse' (p. 47) and 'Salwar' (p. 113). Foodgrains like 'milo' (p. 37), 'Jowar' (p. 38), 'bajri' and 'white jowar' (112) are mentioned. The narrator Laxman Gaikwad wanted to create rural atmosphere in *Uchalya.* To evoke that kind of rural set up, he has used many typical Marathi words in the narrative. The translator too has retained those words with the same purpose. Words like 'Taluka' (p. 1), 'Patil', 'Polite Patil' (p. 3), 'yamadoot' (p. 3), 'Panchayat', 'Panchas' (p. 5), 'Chappals', 'dongals' (p. 6), 'panchakola' (p. 9), 'Mangalsutra' (p. 15), 'Guruji' (p. 18), 'Wawar' (p. 19), 'bidi of Kulwa' (p. 23), 'Allah' (26), 'Uda Uda', 'Karbhari' (p. 27), 'chhatak' (p. 29), 'Karta' (p. 31), 'Kargota' (p. 33), 'Khata' (p. 34), 'Sarpanch' (p. 36), 'Pan' (p. 38), 'Patravali' (p. 46), 'Chadar' (p. 47), 'bhasma', 'bhanumati' (p. 51), 'Musalman' (p. 59), 'Raosab' (p. 65), 'Ashram shala' (p. 70), 'Khanduls' (p. 74), 'Rui' (p. 85), 'Paats'

(p. 101), 'Mahamaya' (p. 103), 'ganja' (p. 104) and 'ulthana' (p. 106), etc. create unique Maharahstra village atmosphere.

This codemixing, switching and borrowing was absolutely essential to create the complex culture of the '*Uchalya*' community. As compared to *An Outsider*, in *The Branded* the translator has made use of more footnotes. In *An Outsider*, there are only 13 footnotes as opposed to hundred in *The Branded.* Yet there is no explanation given for many Marathi words used in the text. To any reader, especially a Maharahstrian reader, not much explanation is necessary as the autobiography deals with hegemonic Hindu culture. For a foreigner or for a layman, the task of understanding all cultural aspects of the autobiography would be formidable.

Idiomatic expressions impart a unique rustic look and flavour to the narration. Yet it makes the task of translating them into a foreign language difficult. It is interesting to analyze the translation of all these vocabulary items in *The Branded*. '*Bamanyala dili vasari halu halu paay pasari*' (p. 67) has been translated as "Then I too like the proverbial brahmin, who given permission to occupy the front porch, occupies the whole house gradually, began to spread the tentacles of my activities" (*T.B.*, p. 83). A lot of meaning is condensed into the Marathi proverb. Being aphoristic in nature, its exact translation is difficult. The economy of words in the Marathi saying has vanished into its translation. '*Tambya thevun gadav yet nahi*' (p. 70) has been translated as "even an earthen jar will not be loaned, on the pledge of a metal bowl" (T.B., p. 87). The saying '*Muki ne keli takrar par haak na bomb*' (p. 160) is an all time favourite of Dalit autobiographers. Laxman Mane has used it in *Upara* and Bhagwan Ingle has mentioned it in *Dhor*. Here its interpretation is "A dumb woman complains, but there's neither a whimper nor a howl" (*T.B.*, p. 198). '*Dagadapeksha veet mau*' (p. 186) is "A brick is softer than a hard stone" (*T.B.*, p. 230). '*Tee balantinbai datacha pani peevun jagat hoti*' (p. 161)' is "The woman lived only on water" (*T.B.*, p. 198), '*Mug gilun gappa rahilo*' (p. 164), has been translated as "...I was forced to keep quiet" (*T.B.*, p. 202).

The change in the personality of Gaikwad can be guessed from the change in his language. This is reflected in *Uchalya*. His language became pure and refined. Gaikwad has instinctively, like Mane, swung back to rural dialect in anxiety, despair and sorrow. The death of Anna and its description in *Uchalya* validates this point. The use of 'Heteroglossia' forms another interesting feature of language usage in *Uchalya*. At home, Laxman's family used a combination of rural, Dalit and Pathrut community's language.

Many varieties of language usage are observed in *Uchalya*-Hirabai's conversation with police, Gaikwad's discussion with the Police Inspector (*T.B.*, p. 161), Jadhav's abusing Laxman in the mill (*T.B.*, p. 122), Laxman's speech in the mill (*T.B.*, p. 122-23), Laxman's request to his boss for salary (*T.B.*, p. 80), the conversation of Gaikwad with Sikh Fouzdar (*T.B.*, p. 129), etc. This variety comes into play due to the dialects used by Pathruts. In English translation, everything has been narrated in the same prosaic style due to the limitations of the target language. There are not many scenes of humour in the text. Humour in *Uchalya* is the product of pidgin.

Gaikwad has made use of some other stylistic devices. The autobiography begins with the use of graphology. The intense beginning sets the tone and at once, acquaints the readers with the existentialist predicament of the narrator. The first sentence is given in all capital letters. The first paragraph, very short in length, reads as,

> NO NATIVE PLACE. No birth-date. No house or farm. No caste, either. That is how I was born. In an Uchalya community, at Dhanegaon in Taluka Latur (*T.B.*, p. 2).

Graphology has been employed to emphasize his rootlessness and alienation. Thus, the writer has made use of a tone unit to present information. It is an example of semantic focus—importance is given to semantic status.[23] This mode of direct thought presentation is in direct speech and its main purport is to speed up the narrative. This kind of typographical variation is not possible in Marathi.

An analysis of Dalit autobiographies translated into English thus reveals a new vocabulary (words, phrases, idioms and proverbs) and different imagery used in the text. It introduces readers to a new universe and culture. They acquaint the readers with new imagery. The figurative language used in both these Dalit autobiographies has also imparted these texts polysemy. They acquaint readers with Dalit ethos and deal with various cultural and aesthetic aspects of Dalit life and bestow upon Dalit texts linguistic and stylistic grace. Dalit autobiographies have retained in English translations many culture specific terms such as names of gods, goddesses, festivals and items of food, etc. along with peculiarities of vernacular grammar, gender, and number, etc. These Dalit writers, per force, had to work under linguistic and cultural constraints. The use of local dialect in these autobiographies also appears with distinct variations and 'is indicative of the social distance between them.' The use of social deixis in Dalit autobiographies encodes the social identities of participants or the social relationships between them or between one of them and persons and entities referred to. Many aspects of language usage depend on these relations and find manifestation in 'polite' pronouns and titles of address such as honorifics.[24] This aspect is lost completely in translation.

No translation can be a Photostat of the original. Dalit autobiographies being socio-literal-historical-cultural documents, in their translation, some cultural loss has taken place due to want of equivalence. Yet these translations have succeeded in depicting Dalit '*Vedana*' (agony) and '*Vidroha*' (protest) along with a host of other emotions. The problem of equivalence and cultural loss has been taken care of to a certain extent by providing footnotes or glossary. Some footnotes have been inserted in *An Outsider* and *The Branded.*

"Dalits had started asserting their identity through cultural endeavours", says Bhongle.[25] He adds, "...Dalit literature was considered as a convincing way of asserting the cultural identity of the community which was exploited culturally, socially, and economically for centuries together."[26] Dalit autobiographies are an assertion of this identity. In the English translations of these Marathi autobiographies, some tiles have been retained. This holds true of *Upara* and *Uchalya*.

In almost all Dalit autobiographies in Marathi, there is a combination of colloquial language, vernacular language, Hindi and English words and words from other regional languages. 'Boli' language has been employed in these autobiographies for the uneducated, illiterate, and rustic characters. The use of social deixis and honorifics is also noteworthy. The change in the language proficiency of a character depending on his education, background, interaction with other people in villages and cities is noticed in Marathi editions. This aspect is wanting in the English editions. Code mixing, code switching, and borrowing which form an integral part of the narrative strategy of writers is less prominent in English translations.

Marathi and its dialects follow a unique construction pattern and word order. In one language itself, many times, it is difficult to come across synonyms. In translation from one Indian regional language to another, this problem is acute and yet can be tackled due to the affinity in culture and dialects. Naturally in another language such synonymy is difficult to obtain. The real task of the translator and his choices begin from here. In a particular language, words and groups of words possess broader and deeper meaning than their ordinary usage. This deeper meaning is imparted due to emotional, representative, symbolic, social, cultural and aesthetic connotations. Words also acquire a different meaning due to rhythm, alliteration, etc. Then the meaning of the words is context relevant. All these complexities lead to the basic surmise that no translation can ever be perfect. The reader of a translation with an ability to read the original should not expect to be wholly satisfied with it. Sujit Mukherjee has pointed out,

> The translator is tested twice over. First he is tested in terms of reception—What he makes of the original text.... The second testing is of the translator's command of the two languages involved—that of the original and that of the translation....[27]

The translators have made available texts for the readers which they otherwise, would not have been able to know about and read. That is why, L.W. Tancock is in accord with Sujit Mukherjee when he says,

> The aim of any translator is to communicate a work of literature intact to a reader of a different language. The ideal translation, like the ideal stage play should have the power to suspend the reader's disbelief, to make him think he is reading an original piece of work written in his own tongue.[28]

English language is alien to Indian culture and ethos and hence fails to provide exact equivalents for vernacular words and idioms. To capture any culture in its true essence, target language, if a foreign language, falls insufficient and inadequate. The disrespectful and informal addresses in Marathi cannot be conveyed in English. The use of English words in conversation, their hackneyed pronunciation, its effect on the listener, etc. can not be conveyed in English. Code mixing or borrowing from other languages into Marathi is very difficult to depict in English equivalence. Use of Dalit and Mahar words, Kolhati and Kaikadi words, Urdu, Kannad and Telugu words etc. is very difficult to depict. Different dialects of Marathi are very difficult to be captured in English. In almost all Marathi Dalit autobiographies, dialectical peculiarity plays a significant role. In both these autobiographies, language acts as an index of the narrator's development. Standard Marathi and dialects of Marathi are used effectively to shed light on such development. Such a development of character reflected through the medium of a language can not be shown in English.

The translation of both these Dalit testimonies into English is at times very superficial. It fails to capture the feelings and emotions of characters. At such times, it is like a 'statue' that resembles the original but is devoid of its 'life-blood' i.e. emotions, feelings, and essence. Sometimes, the translator acts in a haste and becomes slipshod. The translator feels that he can improve upon the original by emendations and insertions of his own (the reference to the 'Cross' in *An Outsider*) and in the process becomes a transcreator. The translator here takes too much of liberty. Interpretation of long drawn symbols and images, figurative and idiomatic language is difficult as it can be interpreted and translated in many ways. Conflict whether psychological or social or political is also very difficult to translate as its true spirit could prove to be too elusive to capture. Examples of all these things have been incorporated in the analysis of translation strategies. Each language has got its own grammar—word order, rules of gender and number. This makes the task of the translator more tedious. Some observations can be made regarding the translations of these two Marathi Dalit autobiographies into English:

- Standard English has been used in the translations.
- The dialects of the source language, code mixing and switching, borrowing, etc. have been ignored in the translation to a certain extent.
- The equivalence provided for words in the source language does not cover its features in the target language in a comprehensive manner.

All said and done, the translated documents have served their purpose. They have created awareness in the readers about the plight of these marginalized communities living at the lowest rung of the social ladder and have strongly put forth their demand of an egalitarian society in which human and humane values would rule supreme.

Notes

1. Kotapalle, Nagnath, *Gramin Sahitya: Swarup ani Shodh*, (Pune: Mehta Publishing House, 1985), p. 59.
2. Lanjewar, Jyoti, *Samkalin Sahitya: Pravrutti ani Pravah*, (Nagpur: Vijay Prakashan, 1985), p. 287.
3. Phadke, Bhalchandra, *Asmitadarsh*, Diwali, 1983, p. 89.
4. Mane, Laxman, *Upara*, (Mumbai: Granthali, 1980). All subsequent references in the parentheses are taken from this edition of the text.
5. Mane, Laxman, *An Outsider*, (New Delhi: Sahitya Akademi, 1997). All subsequent references in the parentheses are taken from this edition of the text.

6. Corbett, Edward and Robert J. Connors, *Style and Statement,* (Oxford University Press, 1999), p. 25.
7. Pathak, Vandana, "The Dialectics of Praxis and Gnosis: Translation of Laxman Mane's *Upara*", *L.A.D. College Research Journal,* Vol. I, 2004-05, p. 10.
8. Bama, "Dalit Literature", *Indian Literature,* Sahitya Akademy's Bimonthly Journal, 193, Sept-Oct-99, p. 98.
9. Manohar, Yashwant, *Nave Sahityashastra,* (Nagpur: Vijaya Prakashan, 2001), p. 182-183.
10. Kulkarni, Arati, *Dalit Swakathane: Sahityarup*, (Nagpur: Vijay Prakashan, 1991), p. 139.
11. Valmiki, Omprakash, *Joothan: A Dalit Life,* trans. Arunprabha Mukherjee (Kolkata: Samaya, 2003), p. vii.
12. Valimiki, *Joothan*, p. xxx.
13. Wankhede, M.N., "Friends, the Day of Irresponsible Writers Is Over", *Poisoned Bread,* Ed. Arjun Dangle, (Orient Longman, 1994), p. 316.
14. Prestan, D.R., *Sociolinguistics and Social Language Acquisition,* (Oxford House Publishers Inc, 1989).
15. Dangle, Arujun, ed. *Poisoned Bread*, (Orient Longman, 1994), p. 325.
16. Culler Jonathan, *Literary Theory A Very Short Introduction,* (Oxford, 2000), p. 87.
17. Cobley, Paul, *Narrative,* (London: Routledge, 2001), p. 214.
18. Cobley, Paul, *Narrative,* p. 233.
19. Gaikwad, Laxman, *The Branded*, (New Delhi: Sahitya Akademi, 1998). All subsequent references in the parantheses are taken from this edition of the text.
20. Gaikwad, Laxman, *Uchalya,* (Pune: Srividya, 1987). All subsequent references in the parentheses are taken from this edition of the text.
21. Phadke Bhalchandra, *Dr. Ambedkar ani Dalit Sahitya,* p. 224.
22. Mulate Vasudeo, *Dalitanchi Atmakathane, Sankalpana va Swarup,* (Aurangabad: Swarup Prakashan, 1999), p. 278-79.
23. Leech and Short, *Style in Fiction,* (Longman, 1980), p. 338.
24. Levinson, Stephen, *Pragmatics,* (Cambridge University Press, 1983), p. 89-90.

25. Bhongle, Rangrao, "A Semiotic Study of Dalit Poetry in Mararthi", *Indian Literature*, Sahitya Academi's bi-monthly journal, ed. Nirmal Kanti Bhattacharjee, Sahitya Akademi, New Delhi, 233, May-June 2006, p. 172.
26. Bhongle, Rangrao, "A Semiotic Study of Dalit Poetry in Mararthi", *Indian Literature*, Sahitya Academi's bi-monthly journal, p. 172.
27. Mukherjee, Sujit, Translations as Discovery and other Essays on Indian Literature in English Translations, (New Delhi: Allied Publishers Pvt. Ltd.), p. 141.
28. Tancock, L.W., "Some Problems in Style from Translations in French", *Aspects of Translations*, (London: Secker and Warburg Ltd.; 1958), p. 45.

14

Godaan: The Complex Architectonics of Cultural Translation

Neeta Modi

Translation is not an easy art because the translator is consciously or unconsciously always within the confines of the original.

Translation means 'to carry across', 'to transfer'. John Dryden represented translation as a judicious blending of 'paraphrase' and 'metaphrase'. But he cautioned against 'imitation' i.e. adapted translation. "When a painter copies from the life...he has no privilege to alter features and lineaments."[1] However there is a common misconception that translation is a straight forward verbatim replacement between any two languages. In fact translation involves a lot of "spilling over" not only of languages but also of cultures.

Culture is the sum total of signs, beliefs, artifacts, social arrangements and customs created by human beings. Today people of different nations, races, genders, religions, languages and cultures have merged together into a global village. So now when languages and cultures are constantly coming in close contact, the role of the translator has become not only very crucial but also very arduous. Translation involves transposition of not only words, expressions, ideas and thoughts from one language (source language) into another (target language) but also of cultures. The cultural aspect of the text also has to be borne in the mind. The process of translation i.e. recoding across cultures should correspond to the target culture to make it credible and comprehensible to the target readers. A good translator is one who is not only bi-lingual or multi-lingual but also bi-cultural or multi-cultural. He is the bridge between cultures and civilizations. He shapes the target language and also enriches his own (source) language with ideas, thoughts, loan words, calques, grammatical structures, idioms and vocabulary from the former.

It is almost impossible to translate words and phrases that are heavily and exclusively grounded in a culture. When to paraphrase, when to use the nearest local equivalent, when to coin a new word, when to transcribe, when to add an explanatory note or glossary, has created a lot of controversy and confusion. The culture-bound words or phrases which defy translation have always fascinated the translators.

When the writer and the reader share a common cultural background they comprehend the text easily. But when their cultural background is different or unfamiliar there is difficulty in proper interpretation. During translation if some culture specific elements in the source language are not dealt with properly the target language reader finds them insensible, incomprehensible and may face "cultural shock". "Cultural shock" is a common experience for a person from another culture. To avoid it translators should have a thorough knowledge of the culturally derived values, attitudes and outlooks in the two languages concerned. A translation should be faithful, expressive and close to the original work. Thus it is the job of the translator to bring together two different persons, his author and reader and to help his target reader understand and enjoy the author of the source text as correctly and completely as possible.

India has an ancient tradition of translation but it was never thought of as something different from creative writing. In ancient times much translation was done between allied languages like Sanskrit and Praakrit. Such translations were 'shadows' of the original texts.

Creative translations of ancient Sanskrit spiritual texts like *the Ramayana*, *the Mahabharata*, and *the Geeta* are generally termed as "Transcreation". Transcreation if understood as 'rebirth' of the original text is the best solution for the problems faced in translating culturally oriented texts. According to G. Gopinathan it can be defined as "an authentic re-interpretation of the original work suited to the readers or audience of the target language in the particular time and space".[2] This re-interpretation has a social purpose and includes explanations, summarization and aesthetic innovation in style and techniques. Poets like Tagore, Aurbindo, Ramanujan, Agyeya and Dharamvir Bharati also used this technique. Through it the problems of 'untranslatability' can be solved to an extent.

Every society has its own unique mythology, history, and way of life, culture and language which differentiate it from others. While translating, a translator must have essential knowledge of all these elements of the source language text so as to do justice to them in the target language.

Literature, especially translation brings societies and people nearer. Tagore, Sharat Chandra, Premchand, Tolstoy, Gorky, Shakespeare, Milton, Wordsworth are all familiar and dear to us in spite of cultural and linguistic barriers. However, it is very difficult to find proper parallels for words, phrases and expressions to re-code them in the target language. It is difficult to capture and communicate the cultural gestures and elements of a work in the receptor culture.

A translator has to face many problems and challenges while rendering Hindi or any Indian language text into English. Translation is beset with not only linguistic snags but also cultural ones. It means transmission of culture as well. It involves two different languages and two different cultures, so it is translation of language as well as of culture. The cultural factors are difficult to handle, and the problem of untranslatability increases all the more if the differences between the source and the target languages and their respective cultures is too much.

Godaan, the novel written in Hindi by Munshi Premchand poses many challenges during translation into English as it is deeply embedded in Indian culture. The culture incorporates language, dialect, native food, garments, folk music, musical instruments, native kitchenware, customs, traditions, social structure, relations and their terminology. It also includes natural world, flora-fauna, seasons, festivals, mythology, beliefs, omens, superstitions, native medicines and even the games and sports played in that region. Therefore culture is 'all inclusive' and encompasses anything and everything that is specific to the region and related to the life and living of its natives. It is thus imperative that the translator has, preferably first hand knowledge of the source culture to do justice with the job at hand. But the problem still remains at the other end, i.e. with the target language and the target readers. Generally there are no exact parallels of many culturally related terms in the target language and this causes untranslatability.

The novel is in Hindi but has been liberally sprinkled with many dialectical words and phrases. Premchand has even used Sanskrit-influenced words and phrases in Godaan but very dexterously and tactfully so that they nowhere hinder the free flow of the narrative.

Chirasthayi jeernavastha (p. 5), kolaahal pratikshan prachand, krishak-prakrati (p. 43), samashtivaad, apmaan aur aaghaat ko dhairya aur udaarta se sahne ka abhyaas (p. 53), manodgaaron par kathor nigrah (p. 56), Eershyamishrit vinod, shraddhapoorn swar (p. 65), laalsaapradipta netra, shishta prem ki durbalata aur nirjeevata (p. 73), saadhvee, papishtha, trast hriday (p. 123), Bhishagaacharya (p. 192), dharmabhiru man trast, aartswar (p. 221), aardrkanth (p. 229), duraasha (p. 244), kushkanya (p. 256), vilasini ramani (p. 289), ahamanyataa ka dhwansa (p. 342), etc. are some of the examples.

Godaan is full of Sanskrit neeti and maxims. Hori – Gobar dialogue on page 10 "Vrikshon mein fal lagate hain, unhain janata khaati hai, kheton mein anaaj hota hai, wah sansaar ke kaam aata hai, gaay ke than mein doodh hota hai, wah khud peene nahin jaati, doosre hee peete hein; meghon se varsha hoti hai, usase prithvi tript hoti hai" reminds us of

> "pibanti nadyaha swaymeva nodakam swayamna khaadanti falaanivrikshah

> Dharadharo varshati natmhetve paropkaraay sataam vibhutayah."

And "kheti mein jo marjjad hai wah naukari mein to nahin hai" echoes in the famous sentence from Upnishads

> "Krishimitkrishasva, vitte ramasvah bahu mattyamaanah."

The sentence "aurat ko bhagwaan sabkuchh de, roop na de, nahin to wah kaaboo mein nahin rahati" (p. 260) is a reflection of Sanskrit maxim

> *Bhaaryaa roopwati shatruh* and seems culturally untranslatable. It has no significance or meaning for a western reader.

Premchand has written *Godaan* in the backdrop of villages like Belari and Semari near Lucknow but his graphic description represents the culture not only of this region but of the whole nation. Most of the characters are illiterate and hence use words in dialect like "*parsan* for *prasann, niyav* for *nyaya, ser* instead of *sher, bamhanai* for *brahmanitva, partach* for *pratyaxa, vises* for *vishesh, paraschit* for *praayashchit, saraarat* for *sharaarat, kaasi* for *kaashi, kulachchani* for *kulaxani, istaam* for stamp, *kagad* for *kaagaz.*" Regional words are used thus in plenty and are difficult to translate. Major characters of the novel Hori, Dhaniya, Sona, Jhuniya, also make use of regional dialect. Some examples are noteworthy:

Hori - natan kheti bahurian ghar (p. 23)
londe kaheen fad par jame honge (p. 23)
jal mein rahakar magar se bair budbakpan hai (p. 26)
shaaid bhinsaar ho raha hai (p. 27)

Dhaniya - andhe kookar ki tarah hava ko bhoonka kare (p. 42)
Dekho apne sapoot kee leela, usey apni sel se chhutee nahin (p. 111)
Vah muaa bahattar ghaat ka paani piye hue (p. 111)

Jhunia - baithane ko maachi doongi (p. 26)

Sona - jaa tu gobar path (p. 36)

Dr. Mehta's dialogues in the guise of Afghan

Amse poochhata hai kaisa loot, kaisa daaka?....
Am yaan se kissi ko nahin jaane dega (p. 73)

Such lines loose their beauty as well as cultural connotations when translated.

The childish prattle of Selia's son Ramu is quite humorous, relaxing and defy translation. He calls *roti—oti, doodh—tut, saag—chhag, koudi—toli.* When asked his name, pat comes the reply '*Lamu.*'

Rural life and culture is highlighted by Premchand through the effective tool of language. Influence of city on the language is also evident. The rural characters speak Hindi sprinkled liberally with regional words and thus make their language more natural, realistic and effective. Cultural meanings are woven intricately into the texture of the language.

Aber, bhurkas, gapadchoth, darsan, asnaan, parsaad, muskiraana, durdasaa, tirasanaa, rapot, kamisnar and many more are all used naturally and spontaneously by the characters. Translation may hinder the spontaneous natural flow of the narrative.

The abundant but specific kinship terminology of India shows the value and importance attached to it in our society, whereas in the West it is quite general and vague. The feelings, the association, the affection, the reverence and the awe attached to these terms resist translation. *Naana—naani, dada —daadi*, become merely grandfather-grandmother. Same is the case with *maama-maami, kaaka-kaaki, foofa-bua, taau-taai, mausa-mausi*, they are uncle-aunt. They simply loose their rich associative connotations and evocative value when translated. We in India still have joint families and extended relationships. We cannot do without our specific terms. Western culture does not give much importance to family or blood relations and hence have no specific and a very limited kinship terminology which is insufficient to convey the wide range of Indian relationships.

Several terms of kinship in the novel like *Dada, Amma, Kaka, Kaki, Beta, Bahu, Bhai, Bhabhi, Jeeja, deedi, Saala, Saali, Saas, Sasur, Devar, Devarani, Sasuraal* are extremely culture specific and are loaded with emotional effervescence. They convey feelings of respect, dignity and intimacy. Affection, motherliness, concern, innocent cajolery, security, awe and a lot more are the associations connected with these terms. Translation can hardly do justice to the rich and varied sentiments evoked by them.

In *Godaan*, the protagonist Hori on meeting Bhola greets him thus *raam raam Bhola bhai* (p. 8). In India certain conventional societal or community addresses are also prevalent. They may sound weird to the Western reader who is unfamiliar with the social hierarchy of India.

The Zamindaar is addressed as "Rai Saaheb" by the villagers out of respect. Hori is "Bhaiya" for his younger brothers. Bhola, Damdi Bansor and others call Hori "Mehto". Datadin is a brahmin, highest in the social ladder so villagers address him as "maharaj" as a mark of honour.

Educated characters like Mehta and Khanna are addressed as *Mehtaji, Khannaji, Bhai Saheb*. The women are "*Deviji*" and Malti is "*Baaiji*" for the illiterate young black woman. The police inspector is addressed as "sir" by Hori and others.

As a part of our culture, we in India address our elders as *Aap* to show respect. The difference between honorific *Aap* and familiar and intimate *tu/ tum* cannot be rendered in English. If we try to translate such things, the idea and the sense behind this plural honorific address would be lost.

Proper names also reflect the culture of an area or country. Godaan has many proper names with rural touch like *Hori, Dhaniya, Gobar, Jhuniya, Bhola, Sona, Roopa, Dulaari* and many more.

Food is a very important part of culture and varies from region to region. Some food items are related with a season or festival and remind us of some story behind them. This again is culture specific and cannot be experienced by one who is not familiar with that culture.

Godaan also has some specific food items especially rural like 'jowar – roti', 'arhar – dal' with raw mangoes, 'laddus', 'halwa', 'puri', 'gulaab jamun', 'sherbet', 'chapatti', 'gur', 'sattu', 'chaat', 'ras', etc.

Not only food items but native kitchenware, things of daily use, dress, medicines, musical instruments, religious rituals are all culture bound and defy translation.

The novel refers to dress materials and clothings like khaddar, achakan, pyjama, saari, chunari, dhoti, pagadi, dupatta, mirjai, kachhani, kurta and salwar.

'Dhol-Majeera', the native musical instruments, *bailgaadi, ikka, tonga*, etc. are the rustic means of transport while *gulli-dandaa* and *kabaddi* are native sports. *Beedi, chillum, paan, gilori*, all these are untranslatable and can only be transliterated.

Caste, customs, traditions, social-structure also challenge a translator. Caste system and social hierarchy is quite strong in India even today. The Brahmin father and son Pandit Datadin and Matadin would not accept food or even water from Selia as she was a cobbler by birth and hence impure, untouchable.

Hori is ostracized for giving shelter to pregnant Jhuniya. Datadin, the Brahmin Pandit asks him to distribute rice to the community and feast the Brahmins to save his Dharma. Datadin's son Matadin has an illicit affair with a cobbler girl Selia. To atone his sin he reads the Geeta, observes all religious rituals, has a dip in Holy Ganga, performs a big Yajna and feasts many brahmins and is taken back in the fold of his caste. Dhaniya and Gobar are outraged by this hypocrisy. Dhaniya realizes that the society judges the rich and poor by two different moral codes. Gobar remarks "the world sides with those who have money". So community and ostracism becomes silly. Hori is forced to pay a fine of ₹ 100 and 30 mounds of grain by the Panchayat, whereas Matadin goes scot-free. Still Hori believes that "It is the voice of God that speaks through the Panchs." This shows his implicit faith in the age old customs and traditions.

It is very problematic to portray culturally bound aspects. Though Hori's life is full of sufferings and miseries, he has a unique self-complacency and fatalism. Complacency is an integral part of Indian philosophy. His fatalism also becomes his plus point as it helps him in facing his sorrows and despair. He attributes his miseries to his fate or destiny and faces them calmly. The socio-economic system of India makes the role of fate all the more important as it has the capacity to make the life of thousands and lakhs of people tolerable. Hori has faith in life. He does not know what will happen tomorrow and is perhaps not even worried about it as he has no such foresight. He is an optimist and has great faith in God and this keeps him alive and going. Hori symbolizes the farmers of the older generation and Gobar represents the labourer of the new generation. We are all aware how Gobar is replacing Hori in Indian culture. Hori is an individual as well as representative of a class. He has many qualities of a typical Hindu. Indian culture is reflected in his complacency and fatalism. Like other Hindus he has his own beliefs, faiths and superstitions. He has Hindu culture too in his blood. He cannot keep a penny of a Brahmin even if the Brahmin is dishonest. Pandit Matadin charges exorbitant interest on the loan but Hori pays without any doubt or question. He tells Gobar that he cannot forget '*Neeti*'. *Neeti haath se na chhodana chhahiye beta! Humne jis byaaj par rupaye liye hain, voh toh dene hee padenge. Phir Brahman thahare! Inkaa paisa hume pachegaa? Aisaa maal toh inhin logon ko pachata hai.* In this way he is a staunch Hindu and believes in "*Varnaashram* system" and therefore considers a Brahmin important in the social hierarchy.

But when the issue of sheltering Jhuniya comes up, Hori is not afraid of the '*varnaashram* system' or of being ostracized by the society. He listens to his heart, gives shelter to Jhuniya and also repents and pays for it a lot. He does thus everything to save Hindu culture and even becomes a mere labourer from a farmer. All these are very tricky and sensitive issues for a translator. He has to be very cautious while trying to translate culture.

Every society or nation has its own customs and traditions which give it an identity. In India people greet one another with *Namaste, Jai Shri Krishna, Har Har Mahadev* or *Ram Ram. Ram Ram Bhola Bhaiya*; says Hori on meeting Bhola in the opening of the novel. Gobar touches the feet of his parents before leaving for the city and so does Jhuniya. The elders in turn bless them. This is a mark of respect unheard of in the West. It may look ridiculous to them but it is part of our culture. Similarly women cover their heads and even their faces with 'sari' as a decorous tradition. Nohari, Jhuniya, Sona, Dhaniya, cover their heads in keeping with the custom. The lady of the house is referred to as *Lakshmi.* Bhola tells Hori that "A good wife is a *Lakshmi,* bhai," and when Hori thrashes Dhaniya, Datadin asks him not to beat 'the *Lakshmi* of the house'.

Indian woman has a weakness for ornaments. Sona mentions *Nathunia* and *Kanthaa.* After marriage she wore *Hansali* and *Hemul* in the neck, *Karnaphuli* in the earlobes, silver bangles, *kaajal* in her eyes and vermilion in the parting of her hair; a true picture of a 'happily married woman'. Some ornaments can be worn only by a woman whose husband is alive. There are several restrictions for a widow; not only in ornaments but also in dress, colours, and even her appearance in social functions and religious ceremonies. The pain, the agony and the sufferings of a widow cannot be understood by the readers unfamiliar with this culture.

All these things are deeply embedded in culture. One who is well-versed with Indian culture can only understand their significance. So a translator has to be careful while translating them in the target language and culture.

'To bring fire from the *chulhaa*'; 'to draw water from the well'; 'to carry the water-filled pitchers on one's head' and treating the guests like a God *(Atithi Devo Bhav);* are all illustrations of typical Indian culture. Dhaniya tells Hori, "either do no invite a guest, or if you do, feed him well", when Bhola comes to their house.

The villagers were orthodox, superstitious and believed in *Nazar, Tona-Totaka* (black-magic), *vaidyas, hakims* and faith-healing. When Gobar-Jhuniya's son falls ill they show more faith in black magic and faith-healing than in medicines.

Translation of popular beliefs, superstitions, omens, etc. is difficult. It is a good omen to see a cow, and a married woman early in the morning. Sight of a widow, a cat walking across the way, wailing of dogs, all these are supposed to bring disaster or ill-luck.

It is auspicious to have a Tulsi plant in the front courtyard of a Hindu house. Selia spots one in Sona's courtyard in the novel. It is highly revered, associated with purity and is worshipped. The Goddess ruling Tulsi is known as the personification of bhakti to the Supreme Being. Such cultural patterns which do not belong to the target language culture are difficult to translate.

There is description of the spring season, the romance, the joy and fragrances lavishly falling on the world. The Koel perched on the mango branches cooed softly, sweetly touching the heart with its harmonious melodies, awakening several desires and hopes; Mahuwa branches were cluttered with a flock of Myenas; Neem, Sirus, Karounda and mango trees were laden with sweet intoxicating flowers; Hori's troubled heart, drowned in so much colour, broke into a song.

Even when translated, such culturally loaded portrayal fails to evoke and convey the associative emotions, the wealth of connotations and cultural details in a person unfamiliar with our culture.

Indian mythology is one of the richest elements of Indian culture that enriches it further and makes it a unique one in the world. Bhola tells Hori that there was no one to look after his house and family after his wife's death: *Ghar mein Mahabharat machaa rehataa hai.* Later Datadin cites instances from Mahabharat and Puranas enumerating the Brahmins who had married girls of lower castes and their children were accepted as Brahmins.

A scene from *the Ramayana* is enacted at the function organized by Rai Saheb. References to mythology too create difficulty for a translator. Transmitting culture through translation is quite complicated as well as significant.

Customs and traditions are part of culture and we the Indians are steeped into them right from birth to death. There is hardly any occasion that does not have elaborate ceremony, be it birth, *naamkaran*, thread ceremony, engagement, marriage or any other festival. Even after death certain rituals are performed. The significance or the value or the latent symbolism behind them becomes a stumbling block for a translator. They can be transliterated and then explained in the glossary if they have no equivalents in the target language and culture.

Proverbs and idioms are storehouses of wisdom accumulated over centuries. These often have "proper nouns with history or cultural significance which can't be mapped on another linguistic and cultural space."[3] Premchand has effectively used several proverbs and idioms in *Godaan*. Viz. –

Talve sahalaanaa (p. 1)
Pet – tan Kaatnaa (p. 1)
Ek- ek koudi daant se pakadanaa (p. 1)
Bin gharani ghar bhoot kaa deraa (p. 10)
Baal ki khaal nikaalanaa (p.12)
Paanv mein shanichar honaa (p. 16)
Choti ka paseenaa aedi tuk aanaa (p. 18)
Man bhay mundia hilay (p. 19)
Laad de, ladaa de, laadne wala saath kar de. (p. 21)
Naak kaaatanaa (p. 28)
Pagadi neechi hona (p. 28)
Gardan par savaar hona (p. 29)
Gale par chhuri chalaanaa (p. 30)
Dwesh ka mayajaal badi-badi machhalion ko hee fansaataa hai. (p. 36)
Kafan ko koudi nahin. (p. 37)
Khoon khoulanaa (p. 39)
Munh sikodanaa (p. 53)
Dwaar par naak ragadanaa (p. 215)
Munh dhonaa (p. 217)
Kaha-sunee honaa (p. 218)

Munh dekh kar beeda denaa (p. 219)
Rupayaa haath ka mail hai (p. 219)
Naak sikodanaa (p. 219)
Bhoot sawaar honaa (p. 219)
Haath paon foolanaa (p. 221)
Jaisaa baap waisaa betaa (p. 222)
Anguli par nachaanaa (p. 224)

Cultural implications are subtly woven thus in the very texture of the language and it depends on the translator to project them or reflect them in the translated work. It is his duty to initiate the target language readers into the sensibilities and deeper nuances of the source language and culture.

A brief but captivating and graphic description of festivals of *Holi, Phag*, singing of *Aalha* in the month of *Aashaadh, Kajli* in the months of *Saavan – Bhadon* and then recitation of the Ramayan during Navratri are cultural identities and hence untranslatable. In villages native musical instruments like *Dhol* and *Majira* can be heard for six months out of twelve in a year. There is one occasion or the other to celebrate, to sing and to enjoy forgetting all sorrows and tensions.

Religious culture relates to the religious beliefs and faiths of a society which are quite specific. *Ganga* is the holiest river for Indians. It is believed to take the soul to the doors of Heaven. Similarly *Gangajal* is an essential ingredient of every religious offering. The villagers follow dharma strictly. Pandit Datadin wants Heera to swear by the holy water of the *Ganga* if he has not poisoned the cow. When Heera is found missing, his brother Sobha suggests that he might have gone to take a dip in *Ganga* to atone his sin.

Hori has great faith in God and religion (dharma). He is ready to pay the fine imposed on him by the panchayat as he believes that 'it's the voice of God that speaks through the *Panchs*'. Again when Bhola comes to take away his bullocks Hori says that he will be ruined if the bullocks go but if Bhola's dharma sanctions it then he may take them. So implicit is Hori's faith in dharma and God.

Reading the Geeta, swearing by the holy water of *Ganga*, and the holy thread is also religion (and therefore culture) bound.

Thakur Dhyansingh performs a *pooja* and sends sweets to each house. Hori feels it would be insulting to attend the *pooja* without offering any thing for *Aarti*. He was worried more about his social prestige than the religious sanctity involved.

Pandit Datadin refers to the present age as 'dark age-*Kaliyug*'. He goes to Benaras with his son for expiation of his sin. But Dulaari feels sin cannot be atoned by money. Once the dharma is gone it is gone. One can't buy it with money. After spending a huge amount on the pandits of Benaras, Matadin is again declared a Brahmin and taken back into the fold. A big 'Yajna' is performed, many Brahmins feasted and mantras are chanted. As a part of purification ceremony Matadin has to taste cow dung and urine. This is supposed to purify him by killing the bacteria of defilement in his soul. But Matadin revolted against this penance, dharma and discarded his sacred thread as he knew his patrons would neither accept water from him nor allow him to touch their utensils or food. And therefore he returns to cobbler Selia and eats food cooked by her.

Nokheraam, a Brahmin fasted on every *ekadashi* and feasted five Brahmins. Pateshwari, a Kayasth held the recitation of *Satyanarain* every full moon and invited ten Brahmins. Both vied thus for superiority. These cultural elements do not have equivalents in the target language culture and hence are almost untranslatable.

Religious beliefs, customs, rituals, ceremonies present hurdles in translating a text. Such sensitive and cultural issues demand full attention of a translator. Weddings are a grand affair in India as they follow different customs and traditions. *Kanyaadaan* has great importance attached to it. It is not merely a marriage of two persons as in the West. It is again a very culture specific term full of associations and rich symbolism. It can be fully comprehended and appreciated only by one acquainted with our culture.

Hori also has great faith in the Indian tradition of *Kanyaadaan* and wants to marry off his daughters as lavishly as he can with good dowry. The idea of Sona's *kushkanya* wedding saddens him and Dhaniya. But Nohari helps them with money. Defeat comes in the form of Hori's helplessness when he is forced to sell his second daughter Roopa.

This is Indian culture, this is their religious belief. All these ceremonies, beliefs, faiths and rituals are so deeply rooted in the culture that the efforts to translate them render them culturally incomprehensible and the readers may get "cultural shock".

Gobar, Gobar paathanaa, Kande, Uple lose their resonance when translated as 'cow-dung cakes'. So holy is the cow and its dung and urine that they are used as purifiers during religious ceremonies and rituals. When Heera poisons the cow out of jealousy it is regarded s a heinous crime, because great religious importance is attached to a cow in India. It is considered as a mother, very holy, very sacred. Premchand's novel *Godaan* amply exemplifies this. The protagonist cherishes only one desire in life – to own a cow and serve it. He considers it a great honour and prestigious to have a cow and also very auspicious to see the cow very first thing in the morning. For him and others cow is a Goddess from Heaven.

But even that remains unfulfilled and he dies an untimely tragic death. Out of four basic components of Indian culture- *Geeta, Ganga, Gau and Gayatri*, Hori chooses only one and is defeated even in that.

Like *Kanyadaan*, *Godaan* also has cultural implications. *Daan* is neither charity nor donation; it is not even gift or endowment. Mere lexical equivalents of cultural patterns or contexts or references are not adequate enough for the target language readers to interpret culturally loaded words, lines or text.

The very title of the novel *Godaan* defies translation. It is so culture-bound that it has no English equivalent. In Indian (Hindu) culture *Godaan* is very significant after *Yajna* or any other auspicious function. *Godaan* by a dying person helps him to cross the dangerous *Vaitarini* river while going to Heaven. He only has to hold the tail of the cow and she takes him safely across the perilous river, as per *Garud Puraan.*

The title *Godaan* reflects satire, pity, hollowness, hypocrisy, social evils, rural life and agrarian culture. A person who fails to fulfill his only dream wish to buy a cow has to give a cow in charity before breathing his last just to improve his next life. It is a sharp satire on religious rituals which touches our heart and moves us to tears. The irony is that when Hori is about to die Dhania has to part with the only *20 annaas* she possesses; the *purohit* takes it in the name of *Godaan!*

A translator has to perform a dual function of translating the local colour as well as the meaning. He should himself be thorough with both the languages and cultures involved in order to be credible and comprehensible to his target language readers. It is his job to bring home the culture by interpreting the text linguistically and culturally. A translated work, as stated earlier cannot be an exact copy of the original. But a good translation can serve as a bridge between two languages and cultures and help the target language reader comprehend and enjoy the text as much as the source language reader might have. Translation of cultural elements is complicated but vital task to attain this goal.

Untranslatability can be dealt with by using innovative devices and procedures like:

Transliteration
Adaptation
Borrowing
Substitution
Omission
Addition
Compensation
Reduction
Deletion.

Or by the use of:

Calques

Paraphrase
Cultural equivalents
Descriptive equivalents
Translator's note
Glossary

The enigmatic question - should one translate culturally loaded or culture specific words, phrases, elements and aspects or leave them as such? does not have universal answers. It depends upon the translator and the text. The best solution is to leave it at the discretion of the translator.

Notes

1. Christopher Kasparek, *The Translator's Endless Toil*, p. 84
2. G. Gopinathan, *Translation, Transcreation and Culture: The Evolving Theories of Transltion in Hindi and Other Modern Indian Languages.*
3. H. Desai, *Muse India*, (2007)
4. *Godaan* (Hindi), Saraswati Press, Allahabad.

15

Translation of Tennessee Williams' *A Streetcar Named Desire*

Sarita Mane

The present paper is an attempt to make use of the comparative model of Translation Studies research in which certain features of the source language or text are compared with their translation into a target language or text (Chesterman, 2000). It examines parallel corpora, the extracts drawn from both Tennessee Williams' *A Streetcar Named Desire* (1947), the source text and Vijay Tendulakar's *Vasanachakra* (1966), the target text and studies it in relation to the sociocultural context.

Kate Sturge (1997), makes a distinction between 'normalising' and 'estranging' strategies. Normalising strategies produce translations that imbue the source culture with values, concepts, emotions, etc. that are rooted in the target culture, whereas estranging strategies emphasize the strangeness of source texts. The present paper is an attempt to examine Tendulkar's translation of *A Streetcar Named Desire* in terms of the translator's use of both normalising and estranging strategies.

The colonial encounter led to the emergence of a new literary polysystem in Maharashtra. Christian Missionaries such as Dr. William Carey, Rev. J. Murry Mitchell, and others produced a number of translations of the Bible and other sacred texts in order to disseminate the word of God among the natives. Some British administrators such as George Jervis,

Thomas Candy, with the help of the Marathi Pundits, produced many translations of non-literary texts in order to disseminate secular and moral knowledge among the natives. When the natives themselves began to translate imaginative literature from Sanskrit and English, a number of new forms of literature such as the lyric, the novel, biography, etc. emerged in Marathi. As the British were the masters, almost all translations were made from the British tradition. Writers like Hall Caine, Charles Garvis, Mrs. Henry Wood, G.W.M. Reynolds, and others were chosen for translation. It is worth noting that no American novelist or dramatist figures in this initial list (Sawant, 2001).

American novels started to be translated only at the beginning of the 20th Century. American novels such as Harriet Beecher Stowe's *Uncle Tom's Cabin*, Mark Twain's *The Prince and the Pauper*, Upton Sinclair's *The Damaged Goods* and *No Pasaran*, John Steinbeck's *Moon is Down*, Pearl Buck's *Mother* and *The Good Earth* cast their impact on the Marathi literary sensibility through translations. After post-independence, however, along with American novels, several short stories, poems, plays, essays, articles, etc. from American literature have been translated into Marathi.

Translations have always played a very important role in the formation of the modern Marathi drama. Especially Shakespeare's plays offered, and still continue to offer, an opportunity and a challenge to different Marathi translators. It was only after Indian Independence that there took place a shift from the British influence to the American influence. As soon as the British left India after the serious setback to their Empire during World War II, America emerged as a superpower. During the Cold War era, in order to prevent the spread of communism outside Russia and China, America opened such centres as The United States Information Service in four Indian cities of Delhi, Mumbai, Kolkatta and Chennai. It also established American Studies Research Centre at Hyderabad. These initiatives led to the increased perception of America as a distinctive nation and culture on the world map.

There is no paucity of translation from other regional languages into Marathi. Experimental plays like Adya Rangacharya's *Suno Janmejaya;* Girish Karnad's *Hayavadana, Tughlaq* and *Yayati;* Badal Sarkar's *Evam Indrajit, Pagala Ghoda, Baki Itihaas, Julus;* Mohan Rakesh's *Adhe Adhure, Laheron Ka Rajhans* and *Ashad Ka Ek Din;* Mohit Chattopadhya's *Guinea Pig;* Surendra Verma's *Draupadi* and Utpal Datta's *Shaturmrug* have been translated into Marathi from other Indian languages. It is very significant that Marathi writers have translated American novelists such as Mark Twain, John Steinbeck, Upton Sinclair, Ernest Hemingway. They have also translated the plays of Western dramatists such as Maeter Linck, Gogol, Luigi Pirandello, Eugene Ionesco, Fredrico Lorca, Jean Anouilh, Carol Moore, Samuel Beckett, Bertolt Brecht, J.P. Sartre, Albert Camue, Arthur Miller, Eugene O' Neill and Tennessee Williams.

Vijay Tendulkar, a major Marathi playwright, was very much influenced by Tennessee Williams in choice of themes and their treatment. Both of them deal with themes like man-woman relationship, love and sex, violence, alcoholism, man's existential loneliness, class-conflict, gender relations, sexual norms, homosexuality and problems evolved from contemporary events. Both these playwrights are known for presenting contemporary reality: Tennessee Williams, from his Southern American milieu and Tendulkar, from the middle class and lower middle class background of Maharashtra. Tendulkar has been criticised for "showing hideous, horrific and repulsive melodramatic actions on the stage as does Tennessee Williams" (Dani in Madge, 2007: 115). Tendulkar takes keen interest in experimenting with both form and content. He makes use of language and style in such a way in his works that they become effective as in the plays of Tennessee Williams.

As a translator, Vijay Tendulkar has made a significant contribution to translation. He has translated Tennessee Williams' *A Streetcar Named Desire* (1947) as *Vasanachakra.* What's more, he has to his credit, besides some translations of novels, two other translations of American plays such as John

Mark Patrick's *The Hasty Heart* as *Lobh Nasava Hi Vinanti* and Van Doren Mark's *The Last Days of Lincoln* as *Lincoln Yanche Akherche Divas*.

The fact that Tendulkar gave his valuable time for translating American plays into Marathi has literary significance. About translating *A Streetcar Named Desire*, Tendulkar writes, 'The work of translating *Streetcar* showed me how difficult it is to produce a good translation as compared to the production of original work of art. I was not happy with the quality of translation for which I had to spend the entire year. We lose everything in faithful translation and the attempt to capture it leads to loss of words'. Tendulkar's comment draws our attention to the problems of interlingual and intercultural translation. He has faced a number of different problems while transferring different coordinates of American culture to the target Marathi culture. The present paper is a modest attempt to explore *Vasanachakra* as Tendulkar's exercise in cross-cultural transfer. It makes use of representative extracts dealing with cultural components such as religious belief, mythologies, superstitions, customs, art, literature, various beliefs, traditions, and world-views of people.

Tendulkar makes use of a variety of strategies in his translation. The model used by Tendulkar for translation can be called an eclectic model as it is practical.

(1)

A corresponding air is evoked by the music of Negro entertainers at a bar-room around the corner. In this part of New Orleans you are practically always just around the corner, or a few doors down the street, from a tinny piano being played with the infatuated fluency of brown fingers. This 'blue piano' expresses the spirit of the life which goes on here.

(*A Streetcar Named Desire*: 115)

koparayavarach ek madhyagruha. Tithun negro vadakanche sangeet kani yet ahe. New orleanschya ya bhagat,vakabdar asha kalya botani dhundpane vajawala janara chotasa piano, jave tithe, ha 'palikadech' vajat asto. He 'nilepan', ha 'piano' yani ithun vahanarya jeevanacha janu pran wyakta hoto ahe.

(*Vasanachakra*: 1)

The translator gives the glimpses of the people of the low culture living in a big city like New Orleans where in a slum, people have their own ways of enjoyment in a bar-room. The passage appears to be faithful in terms of the sense and feel of the original. The translation is from the point of view of target language. A long complex sentence from the original source text is broken into short and simple sentences in the translated text. For example, 'A corresponding air is evoked by the music of Negro entertainers at a bar-room around the corner. In this part of New Orleans you are practically always just around the corner' is translated as 'koparayavarach ek madhyagruha. Tithun negro vadakanche sangeet kani yet ahe'. Instead of literal translation, at the vocabulary level, the translator has used appropriate words to suit the context. For instance, 'fluency of brown fingers' is translated as 'vakabdar asha kalya botani', 'spirit' is aptly transalted as 'Pran'. This 'blue piano' is split into 'he'nilepan', and 'ha piano'. The translated extract appears more transparent because of the strategies used by the translator.

(2)

Two women, one white and one coloured, are taking the air on the steps of the building. The white woman is EUNICE, who occupies the upstairs flat; the coloured woman a neighbour, for New Orleans is a cosmopolitan city where there is a relatively warm and easy intermingling of races in the old part of town.

(*A Streetcar Named Desire*: 115)

Imaratichya payarayanvar don baya hawa khat baslya ahet. Yatali ek gaurkai ani dusari kali aha. Gori ahe 'Eunice'. Hi varachaya majalyavar rahanari. Kali bai tichi shejarin. Karan New orleans he 'cosmopolitan' shaher a he. Gawachaya junya bhagat rang-vanshatale bhed tase rahilele nahit.

(*Vasanachakra*: 1)

This extract of translation deals with the theme of racialism or the question of colour-bar. It is a cultural fact though this problem has lost its earlier intensity in big cities. The translator wants to bring this problem to the notice of the readers of the target language. As far as the language part of the translated text is concerned, the translator has made use of informal language. This can be seen through the use of words like 'don baya', and an idiomatic phrase like 'hawa khat baslya ahet'. The translator has translated white woman as "gori bai"/ "gaurkai" and the coloured woman as "kali bai". The words used in Marathi don't appear to be equivalent to the English words. The English words have the connotation of racialsim and it cannot be suggested through the Marathi words which appear to denote only the colour of the skin. To add to the readibility of the translated text at the level of vocabulary, the translator has used different words for the same English words. For example, the word 'white' is translated as 'gori' and 'gaurkai'. As far as the translation of these words is concerned it appears literal. It carries no force of the original version. Thus the translator has used vocabulary that connotes the low social and cultural background of the characters. For example, the word 'women' is translated as 'baya' (instead of 'striya'). "Two women, one white and one coloured, are taking the air on the steps of the building". This complex sentence is translated into two simple sentences. The main clause and the subordinate clause which is rankshifted in the English version are put in different sentences. As a result, the translated version sounds simple. Other sentences in English are also complex. But in Marathi version they are split into simple sentences. The translator has retained the word 'cosmopolitan' as it is in the source text. It may be because this English word is commonly used in Marathi more than its Marathi equivalent "vishwabandhuatwacha"/ "vishwabandhuatwa" (sarvatrik)

(3)

She continues to laugh. BLANCHE comes around the corner, carrying a valise. She looks at a slip of paper, then at the building, then again at the slip and again at the building.

Her expression is one of shocked disbelief. Her appearance is incongruous to this setting. She is daintily dressed in a white suit with a fluffy bodice, necklace and ear-rings of pearl, white gloves and hat, looking as if she were arriving at a summer tea or cocktail party in the garden district. She is about five years older than STELLA. Her delicate beauty must avoid a strong light. There is something about her uncertain manner, as well as her white clothes, that suggests a moth.

(*A Streetcar Named Desire*: 117)

Ti hasatach rahate. Hatat ek bag ghetaleli' Blanche' koparayavarun ata pudhe yate. Hatatalya kagdachya chitoryakade ekda baghte,nantar samorchya imartikde pahte, punha chitore nyahalate ani punha imartikade pahte. Mudrevar manasvi avishvas. Ya sagalya drushashi visangat ase tiche vyaktimatva. Pandhra shubhra poshakh, pisapisanche tyavar ghatalele polke, tyach pramane galyatali mal, kanatale motyache ear-rings,hatatale pandhre hatmoje ani hat yamule ti mothi subak disate ahe.Ya bhagatalya ekhadhya unhali chahapartila kiwa madyapanachya karyakramala yavi tashi ti vatate. Stellahun hi sumare pach varshani mothi.Hichya najuk saunderyala prakhar prakashache ketakshane wavde. Vagnyatala asthirpana ani shubhra vesh yani ti kahishi divyavar zepavnarya patangasarkhi vatate.

(*Vasanachakra*: 3)

This passage is an example of representation of typical American woman wearing typical American clothes and ornaments. This brings out the contrast between an Indian woman and a western woman in terms of garments and items of beautification. It is a part of distinction between source culture and target culture. The translator has retained the similes as they are there in the SL text. It appears that he manages to portray a typical western woman through this translation. The reader can visualize the same on the strength of this word picture. The translator has made the mistake of tautology for e.g. kanatale motyache ear-rings, hatatale pandhre hatmoje. At the same time he has translated some words quite appropriately. For example, the word 'a slip of paper' as 'chitore', 'must avoid' as 'ketakshane wavde', 'a fluffy bodice' as 'pisapisanche polke ', 'valise' as 'hatatali bag' and 'white suit' as 'pandhara shubra poshakh'. Here also long and complex sentences are divided into short and simple sentences. Here pandhara and shubra are collocated words. The writer is able to evoke the typical picture of sophisticated western woman.

(4)

BLANCHE: I was so exhausted by all I'd been through my-nerves broke. [*Nervously tamping cigarette.*] I was on the verge of- lunacy, almost ! So Mr. Graves - Mr. Graves is the high school superintendent - he suggested I take a leave of absence. I couldn't put all of those details into the wire... [*she drinks quickly*] Oh, this buzzes right through me and feels so good !

(*A Streetcar Named Desire*: 122)

Blanche:Aja je kahi ghadala hota tya saryana itki maragalun gele bagh mi ki - manachi ubharich khachali mazya! (Nervously hatatalya cigaretashi chala kerit)mhanaje agdi vedach lagnyachi avastha ali hoti javalpass! Ani Br. Graves - shaleche superintendent amachya-tyancha mhanana padla ki,binpagari tar binpagari pan raja ghyavich mi.Taret he saglach kahi lihana jamala nahi mala - (zatkyane madhya ghete) kasa jaljalat jata ghashakhala! khoop bara vatataya ata mala.

(*Vasanachakra*: 9)

The translator has used the device of code-mixing. For example, he has kept the words from English as they are. These words are 'cigarette', and 'superintendent'. He has tried to make the translated extract more effective by using the device of repetition which is not in the original, 'he suggested I take a leave of absence' which is translated as "tyancha mhanana padla ki, binpagari tar binpagari pan raja ghyavich mi. 'This buzzes right through me and feels so good' is beautifully translated as "kasa jaljalat jata ghashakhala! khoop bara vatataya ata mala.' The translation of the word 'buzz right through me' as "jaljalat jata ghashakhala' appears typical. In this extract the translator has retained many English words as they are. At the level of syntax, the translator has tried to make the target text as natural as possible.

(5)

BLANCHE : Yes, it is, it is or I wouldn't say it! You just have to watch around the hips a little, stand up.

(*A Streetcar Named Desire*: 122)

Translated as:

> Blanche: nahi nahi - agati kharach ahe te! yeravi kashala mhanale aste mi ? Kamareshi barik jara jyasta pasaralyayas tu. Ubhi raha pahu!

(*Vasanachakra*: 9)

If we compare the original and the translated sentences, it is noticed that the translator has not translated them literally. He has made use of altogether different expressions but they sound natural. The original sentence is 'Yes, it is, it is' but he uses negative sentences to convey this sense. Taking Indian culture into consideration, the translator has avoided the literal translation of the word 'hip' to make it sound less vulgar, less erotic and sexy. He has made use of metonymy here. e.g. "waist" instead of "hip". The Translator's culture consciousness can be noticed here.

(6)

BLANCHE : The other one? [*she laughs sharply. There is an embarrassed silence.*] How quiet you are, you're so peaceful. Look how you sit & there with your little hands folded like a cherub in choir!

(*A Streetcar Named Desire*: 123)

Blanche: ani ti dusari ? (khachun baste. Doghinmadhaye kinchitkal avaghadli stabdhata) kiti shant vatates tu ! He tuze chotese haat chativar bandhun kashi charchmadhlya chotya devdutachya chitrasarkhi baslyes bhag!

(*Vasanachakra*: 10)

This extract is an example of faithful translation. Through this example we get an idea of the Christian church and the singers singing the choir or religious songs. The use of simile adds to the vividness of the picture. The device of elaboration is used to explain the culture-specific phenomenon. For example, 'a cherub in choir' is elaborately translated as 'charchmadhlya chotya devdutachya chitrasarkhi'.

(7)

BLANCHE: Well, I never had your beautiful self-control. I am going to take just one little tiny nip more, sort of to put the stopper on, so to speak.... Then put the bottle away, so I won't be tempted. [*She rises.*]

(*A Streetcar Named Desire*: 123)

Blanche: ho, ani tuzyasarkha chandar sayam mazyakadehi navata.Aankhi thodasa madhya gheyin mhanate ! mhanaje kay mhanatat tasa - 'Agadi Akhercha Ekach Pyala'—ani he bagh, mag matra hi batli tikade thevun de tu. Ugach mala moha nako vhayala. (ti uthte)

(*Vasanachakra*: 10)

This extract is an example of making a deliberate use of some cultural details from the target culture. In Marathi literature Ram Ganesh Gadkari's 'Ekach Pyala' is a very famous play about a man addicted to alcoholic drinks. There is no reference to this in the original text but Tendulkar in his translation uses an expression that refers to Ram Ganesh Gadkari's play: 'Agadi Akhercha Ekach Pyala.'

(8)

BLANCHE: I, I, *I* took the blows in my face and my body! All of those deaths! The long parade to the graveyard! Father, mother! Margaret, that dreadful way! So big with it, it couldn't be put in a coffin! But had to be burned like rubbish! You just came home in time for the funerals, Stella. And funerals are pretty compared to deaths. Funerals are quiet, but deaths - not always. Sometimes their breathing is hoarse, and sometimes it rattles, and sometimes they even cry out to you, 'Don't let me go!' Even the old, sometimes, say, 'Don't let me go.' As if you were able to stop them! But funerals are quiet, with pretty flowers. And oh, what gorgeous boxes they pack them away in! Unless you were there at the bed when they cried out, 'Hold me!' You'd never suspect there was the struggle for breath and bleeding. You didn't dream, but I saw! Saw! Saw! And now you sit there telling me with your eyes that I let the place go! How in hell do you think all that sickness and dying was paid for? Death is expensive, Miss Stella! And old Cousin Jessie's right after Margaret's, hers! Why, the Grim Reaper had put up his tent on our doorstep! ...... Stella. Belle Reve was his headquarters! Honey-- that's how it slipped through my fingers! Which of them left us a fortune? Which of them left a cent of insurance even? Only poor Jessie - one hundred to pay for her coffin. That was all, Stella! And I with my pitiful salary at the school. Yes, accuse me! Sit there and stare at me, thinking I let the place go! *I* let the place go? Where were *you*. In bed with your - Polak!

(*A Streetcar Named Desire*: 126-127)

Blanche:mi,mi,mi ghetale sagale ghav tondavar,mazya angavar!Ti sari sari marana mi mele!Tya sarya masanvatichya ferya!Baba gele,Aai geli! Ti tasha bhayankarpane Margarat geli- itaki phugli hoti ti tyana ki peteet mawat navhti ! Kacharyachya dhigasarkhi petwun dyawi lagali ani tu, Stella, smashanat hajar rahata yawa ya betana dar veli yewun pochalis ani maranachya manana nantarchya smashanyatra chhan. Smashanyatra mothya shantatet par padatat; pan marana-nehamich nahi tashi ghadat - kahi vela - kahi vela shwas jadavato ni kahi vela gharghar lagate, ni kahi vela tar-mithya ghalun te kinchaltat ki 'mala nahi jayacha ! mala sodu nakos ga !' Agdi jakha mhataryancha sudhha toch akrosh, "mala nahi jayacha! Mala ghatta dhara !" Janu tyanna kuni thambau shakata ! Pan smashanyatra, tya tya agdi mukya mukya astat, chhan chhan phulanni sushobhit kelelya. Ani melelyanchi rawangi karatat ti tar kiti chandar unchi petyanmadhun-mhanaje tumhi titha tevha.

nasalatach- "mala dhar,mala sodu nako,mala nahi jayacha,"asa ti panchpran ekvatun ordat astat.tevha tumhi naselatach-tar tumhala kalayacha sudhha nahi ki sadhya eka shwasasathi kevdha jiwacha aakant zala hota itha, kevdha rakta vahila hota. Tula swapanat sudhha kala nasel te; pan mi baghitala ! baghitala ! baghitala ! Ani ata tu titha tashi beghun,tashi basun asa arop kar mazyavar ki me ghar ghalvalal !Te-te sagale ajar ani ti marana-tyancha sagala kharcha kasa sosla asen mi, kasa bhagvala asen ? Stellabai, maran kharchacha asata. Maran far mahag asata ani Margarat jate na jate toch pathopath Jesina number lavala. Janu-janu kahi yamrajani amchya umbarthyavar tal thokla hota! Bel Rev mhanje janu tyacha ekmev karyalayach houn basala hota ! Bai ga. Ghar he asa mazya hatun nighun gela. Yatlya kuni aplya mage kahi dabola thevala ? Te raho mhante mi, yatla ek tari vimyacha chadam maga theun gela ? Nahi mhatala tar fakta Jessie - tina tewadhe aplya shavapetisathi shambhar theuan dilele hote. Bassa - itakach. Ni mala kaya milanar shalet ? Milata char didkya ! Barobarya, tu kar arop mazyawar ! Vichar jaab mala ! Titha tashi bais ani bagh mazyakade dole phadun, mich ghar ghalawala asa dhok manashi ! mi ghalavla ghar ? ani mag tu kutha hotis - tya tuzya Polyak barobar bichanyat ?

(*Vasanachakra*: 14)

The basic theme of this passage is death which is a part of an existential angst. It is vividly and realistically described from the point of view of a very sensitive character named Blanche who is a witness to the death scene. She describes a dying person's struggle to live. This situation moves the people of all cultures. So the translator has translated it creatively. Of course, he makes some changes to appeal to the people from the target culture. For example, the words like 'coffin' as 'shavpeti', Georgeous boxes as 'bhari shavpetya' and 'Grim Reaper' as 'yamraj'. These are culture-specific Christian details. In the west, the dying persons are expected to make provision for the expenses of their burial rites. So Blanche complains that her relatives have not made sufficient provision for their sickness and deaths. The translator has retained metaphoric expressions and an ironic tone of the speaker. He has used the device of elaboration.

(9)

BLANCHE: Honey, it wasn't the kiss I objected to. I liked the kiss very much. It was the other little- familiarity - that I -

felt obliged to-discourage—I didn't resent it! Not a bit in the world! In fact, I was somewhat flattered that you - desired me! But, honey, you know as well as I do that a single girl, a girl alone in the world, has got to keep a firm hold on her emotions or she'll be lost!

MITCH [*Solemnly*]: Lost?

(*A Streetcar Named Desire*: 176)

Blanche: Ladkya, a-re chumbanala harakat nahvati kahi mazi. Mala far far avadala te. Mala nako vatata na-te nirala. Tyatala to dusara saraitpana - tyala uttejan dyayach nahvata mala-kon mhanata mala avadala nahi te mhanun? Agdi nahve ! Khara sangu ka, tula mi itki havishi vatale-yanach khoop moharun gele bagh mi. Pan ki-nai, ladakya, mala mahitaya tas tulahi ahe mahit, ki lagna na zalelya mulila, jagat agdi ektya ektya asalelya mulila, apalya manavar na, phar phar motha taba thevava lagato. Nahitar - kahitari bhalatach houn basel ticha !

Mitch : (bharavalela) Bhalatch?

(*Vasanachakra*: 69)

This passage also relates to patriarchal inhibitions with regard to a woman or a girl. She is supposed to keep a firm hold on her emotions. Suppressions of emotions and feelings on the part of a woman is supposed to be a cultural value.

The translation here is not word-for-word but is creative and free. A single girl has some moral binding on her. She has to protect herself. Otherwise she is held responsible for her downfall or moral degradation. The translated piece appears natural and equivalent to the original.

(10)

BLANCHE: A cultivated woman, a woman of intelligence and breeding, can enrich a man's life - immeasurably! I have those things to offer, and this doesn't take them away. Physical beauty is passing. A transitory possession. But beauty of the mind and richness of the spirit and tenderness of the heart - and I have all of those things - aren't taken away, but grow! Increase with the years! How strange that I should be called a destitute woman! When I have all of these treasures locked in my heart. [A choked sob comes from her.] I think of myself as a very, very rich woman! But I have been foolish- casting my pearls before swine!

(*A Streetcar Named Desire*: 211-212)

Blanche: asha veli ekhadi susanskrut stri, buddhiman ni kuleen stri, ekhadya manasacha jeevan khoop samarudha karu shakate - kalpana suddha yenar nahi itka ! Mazyakade he sarea bharpur ahe ni devun kahi te sampanara nahi. Shariracha sauandarya kshanbhangur asta. Ahe mhanata mhanata osarun janara ek dhan. Pan manacha sauandarya, atmyachi shreemanti ni kaljatala givhala - he sara sara ahe mazyakade - he sare kunich nahi nehu shakat. Ulat dyava tevada vadhtach. Varshavarshana vadhatach jata ani mala kuni abhagini mhanava ? He sara apar vaibhav itha - kalajat kondalela astana ! kevadaha ashcharya ! (ek dabla hundaka tichya othanwate umatato) mhanu det kuni kahi, mala swatala matra mi phar phar bhagyawan watate shrimant watate. Pan mich murkha - nalayakanchyawar sagala ugach udhalit ale! Casting my pearls before swine !

(*Vasanachakra*: 105-106)

The theme of this passage is the idea of a cultured man who possesses the beauty of the mind, richness of the spirit and tenderness of the heart. It is a common core of culture found as a universal trait. The translation of this passage is simple, beautiful and effective. The translator has retained the original saying, "casting my pearls before swine!" from the source text as he has elite audience before him. The translation appears impromptu. The balance between the two languages appears to be retained. The translator has the common core of the culture before him while translating the passage from one language to another.

To conclude, it can be argued that Vijay Tendulkar has translated Tennessee Williams' *A Streetcar Named Desire* as *Vasanachakra* word for word. In Peter Newmark's words, Tendulkar's is a semantic translation rather than a communicative translation. Tendulkar was mainly concerned with introducing the dramatic art of Tennessee Williams, the playwright he held in high regard, to the Marathi audience. Instead of producing an adaptation and thereby nativising the source text to cater to the requirements of native literary culture, he adopted the SL-oriented approach and made an attempt to produce a faithful translation. In *Vasanachakra*, he has used a variety of strategies of translation such as elaboration, explicitation, simplification, deletion, addition, code-mixing, repetition, paraphrasing, alternatives, allusions, and experimentation at the level of vocabulary and syntax, and a strategy of alteration especially at the level of imagery. Tendulkar's translation makes a combined use of both normalising and estranging strategies. He normalises many marked or unusual source text features in order to accommodate the target text for the language audience. However, he largely dramatises difference in order to introduce American elements directly in his translation. By using the above-mentioned strategies of translation, Tendulkar has overcome successfully the difficulties of translating cultural content from *A Streetcar Named Desire* into *Vasanachakra*.

References

Chesterman, A. 2000. "A causal model of translation studies", in *Intercultural Faultlines. Research models in translation studies I: Textual and cognitive aspects* edited by M. Olohan. Machester: St. Jerome, pp. 15-27.

Dani, A.P. 2007. "Vijay Tendulkar's *Gidhade* (The Vultures) and John Webster's *Duchess of Malfi*" in *Vijay Tendulkar's Plays: an Anthology of Recent Criticism* edited by V.M. Madge. New Delhi: Pencraft International.

Sawant, Sunil. 2001. *The American Novel in Marathi: A Study in Translation Culture*. Unpublished thesis submitted to Shivaji University, Kolhapur.

Sturge, Kate. 1997. "Translation Strategies in Ethnography". *The Translator*, 3: pp. 21-38.

Tendulkar, Vijay. 1966. *Vasanachakra*. Mumbai: Popular Prakashan.

Williams, Tennessee. 1947. *A Streetcar Named Desire* in *Tennessee Williams* by Martin E. Browne. London: Penguin Books.

16

"The Marching Song of Columbus": A Transcreation

A.K. Farakate

The central issue in the theory and practice of translation, as discussed by the scholars and translation practioners, is Translation Equivalence (TE). Still further the equivalence in poetic translation is a more serious issue. Translating poetry is an ordeal before the translators. The task becomes challenging for the mysteriously creative nature of poetry and communication of emotive meaning rather than referential meaning. Roman Jakobson declares that all poetic art is technically untranslatable; and only a creative transposition is possible (1959:232). Even though it is often called an impossibility, poetic translations have been attempted by the translators with more or less success. These translations have played a vital role in cross-cultural bridging across different languages and language communities. Marathi is one of the major Indian languages. It has evolved its own translation culture. There had been a number of attempts at translating Marathi poetry into English. One such effort is the translation of Kusumagraj's poetry into English by a veteran scholar Vilas Salunke. The collection of Kusumagraj's selected poetry entitled *Blooms of the Earth* (1999) translated by Salunke is published by Writers Workshop, Kolkata. In this paper an attempt is made to examine the linguistic and stylistic equivalences established by the translator, by means of ST-TT (Source Text-Target Text) pair oriented analysis in order to appreciate the worth of the TT as a transcreation. The poem selected for the study here is "The Marching Song of Columbus" from the collection *Blooms of the Earth* (1999), which is the translation of *Kolambasache Garvageet* from Kusumagraj's *Vishakha* (1942).

Vishnu Vaman Shirwadkar alias Kusumagraj (1912-1999) was born in Pune. He belonged to a village named Shirawade in Nashik district of Maharashtra. He spent almost all his life in Nashik city which is situated on the banks of the river Godavari.

An eminent Marathi litterateur V.S. Khandekar appreciated Kusumagraj's poems and introduced his trend setting volume of poems entitled *Vishakha* (1942). The volume is still applauded by the critics as well as the common readers for the poems promoting patriotism and humanitarianism as well as for the poems of passionate love and romantic spirit. Kusumagraj is a contemporary of Mardhekar, Rege and Karandikar but his idiom is simple and full of musical quality. He continued the traditional poetic forms marked by rhyme and metre. He combined the romantic spirit and the national spirit. As a modern poet he enjoys a unique position in the evolution of Marathi literature. Kusumavati Deshpande and M.V. Rajadhyaksha take note of his poems as:

> These (Kusumagraj's) are poems of young love and of nostalgia: romantic poems in short. The romantic note was perfectly in tune with the nationalist upsurge: a happy concord between an aspect of the poet and the theme—and the hour. The nationalist poems have genuine passion, but their expression is not merely passionate. They do not splutter with anger, or mouth battle-cries; and they do not trade on the clichés of patriotism. They are good poetry first–good modern poetry. (1988: 141)

Kusumagraj successfully handled many literary forms in his long literary career of 65 years which includes 16 verse volumes, 18 plays, 3 novels, 8 short story collections, 6 short plays, a dozen one-act plays and 7 books of essays and prose writing. Besides a number of Maharashtra State awards to his credit, his play *Natsamrat* won him the Sahitya Akademi

Award in 1974. He was chosen President of Akhil Bharatiya Marathi Sahitya Sammelan in 1970. He was honoured with Jnanpeeth Award, the highest literary honour in India, in 1987 for his significant and inspiring services to literature.

Before we proceed to examine the equivalences in *The Marching Song.*, let us be clear, of course in brief, on certain concepts concerning translation analysis. Here the ST and the TT are considered to be two different linguistic, cultural constructs and are studied for how far the meaning is transferred from the source language (SL) into the target language (TL) and the cultural gap is bridged by the translator while trying to retain the poetic form. As far as the translation of poetry is concerned, the retention of potential meaning holds the key in the act of translation. Such retention may result out of an attempt to keep up 'literary' meaning and not literal meaning. In order to understand and appreciate this aspect of poetic translation, one has to be aware of the new orientation to the translation theory which takes translation as a cross-cultural event (Snell-Hornby, 1990: 82-84). During the analysis in this paper, the aptness of linguistic equivalence or the management of lexical items connected with formal correspondence (Catford, 1965: 32-34) is paid attention to. But while commenting upon formal features, the cultural context has to be taken care of. Eugene Nida makes it clear that it is quite impossible to deal with any language as a linguistic signal without recognizing its relationship to the cultural context as a whole. This also makes it clear why Nida uses the phrase "the closest natural equivalence" (1975: 33) in this connection. In the analysis the closest natural equivalence is duly appreciated. Next to this, due attention is paid to stylistic equivalence. According to Anton Popovic stylistic equivalence concerns the elements aiming at the expressive identity. (Cited in Bassnett, 1980: 25)—in short the way of expression that makes a piece of writing 'poetry'.

: TT:

The Marching Song of Columbus

Roar with your thousand tongues, O sea
Unsettling stars in the universe,

Stir up your way to watery mountains
Shaking even the earth's corners!

With the sun hiding in the underworld,
Sky-demons dance in drunken mirth,
And their queen, the lightening, blazes
Its torches to split the earth!

Or is this watery surge a wild dance
Of the Archangel fallen from heaven?
He has come out to take revenge, dancing
With his bands of devils on the ocean.

Dethroned Angel, go on with your dancing,
Burst clouds upon us ceaseless,
Shoot meteors showering a rain of fire-
Born sailors, we are fearless!

Comrades! Life at sea is a battlefield
Forever, we've no regret as we roam
Free over the blue like the stars above-
The boundless globe is our home.

Did we set sail to turn back in fear
And run away from strife?
We'd sooner meet out watery grave
Than guard a vanquished life.

Millions of lives are born, but they wither
Like leaves of grass in this world,
We go sailing under seven skies with
New horizons before us unfurled.

Nothing can stop us, no love of wealth
Nor the narrow prison of home,
Blazing mankind's flag we will conquer
The land and ocean as we roam!

Unfurl those proud white sails and tell
The silly ocean what is in store:
'While boundless are our hopes and dreams
You are bound by your shore!'

(Kusumagraj, Trans.
Vilas Salunke, 1999: 29-30)

(1)

Kolambasache Garvageet is a poem inspiring to struggle fearlessly to achieve the goal and not to give up due to hardships. The poet has taken the example of the determined voyager Christopher Columbus (1454-1506). Columbus was an Italian explorer who persuaded King Ferdinand and Queen Isabella of Spain to pay for an expedition to find new route to Asia by crossing the Atlantic. It is believed that Columbus discovered America in 1492. Kusumagraj here presents Columbus as a symbol of determination who inspires with his own example to face the adversities fearlessly and continue the march. The poem was written in 1936. This is the period when Indian nation was struggling hard for freedom. Kusumagraj's this and some other poems aimed at raising morale of the people of India. They promoted the fighting spirit. This is an important contextual significance associated with this poem.

The poem is a dramatic monologue in which Columbus talks first with the vast sea and then with the devil in the form of violent storm and then to his crew encouraging them to fight the storm and continue the march ahead. Columbus dares the turbulent sea to continue his destructive activity and warns the sea of his readiness to fight any challenge. He challenges the devils of the sky to come down and perform their frightening dance. Even the dancing band of devils on the sea cannot make us recede, he says. Let this dance cause the fiery meteors fall, but the sailors are fearless.

Columbus encourages his colleagues by asserting that the life of the sailors is meant to fight without pause. The ship is not set into the sea to go back and to save the defeated lives but to march ahead despite the calamities. Sailors are not like other millions of creatures who live and die without purpose. A sailor's march can never be stopped even by wealth or woman or the narrow prison of home. His march is to hoist the flag of humanity in the ocean. Finally, Columbus despises the ignorant sea saying 'our hope to win is infinite but you have the limits of your own coast.'

(2)

2.1 The title of the TT "The Marching Song of Columbus" has a touch of determined journey. The literal translation of the title would have been 'The Proud Song of Columbus' but the translator has preferred 'literary' to literal. The address *Samudra* (ST: Line 2) in Marathi is translated as '*O sea*' (TT: 2) where the extra vocative O is used as a mark of address. The mark of address in Marathi is inflectional and 'inbuilt'. Also a comma after *samudra* offers a pause to emphatically pronounce the next appealing words. In order to adjust the line length perhaps, the translation of the word *pratidhvanine* (ST: 1) which means 'by means of echoes', is avoided by the translator. This is an important word as it is the cause to 'unsettle' the stars. The stars are there in the universe which needs no mention. But the translator has used the phrase *stars in the universe*. The post-modifying phrase *in the universe*, so, is redundant. This redundancy, of course, is an unnecessary gain which is a kind of loss for the gain of predetermined line length. In the same manner while translating *dishakon* (ST: 4), the part of the compound *disha*—is left untranslated and only—*kon* is translated as *corners* (ST: 3), further made redundant by the addition of the pre-modifying phrase *the earth's*. Also, *virat vadal* (ST: 3) which means 'the tempest', is only *waves* (TT: 3) for the translator and *parvat panyache* (ST: 3) is *watery mountains* (TT: 3) which can never be equivalent to *the mountains of water* (the waves as huge as mountains).

In the second stanza of the TT we notice a serious flaw of misinterpretation of the function of finite verbs. The ST has finite verbs *matu de* (ST: 5), *dadu dya* (ST: 6) and *pajalu de* (ST: 8). The verbs in Marathi give open challenge to the adversities. This is not retained in the TT. The verbs *dance* (TT: 6), *blazes* (TT: 7) show actual actions in simple present. In this stanza the force of challenge is lost. One which is challenged in the ST is simply happening in the TT. Note for example *dadu dya patali savita* (ST: 6) which means 'Let the sun hide in the underworld', is proposed as *With the sun hiding in the underground.* (TT: 5)

2.2 The same continued redundancy is noticed in the third stanza e.g. *watery surge* is not only unnecessary but it unnecessarily makes explanation of *swargatun kosalalela* (fallen from the heaven); so in a way disambiguates the potentiality of meaning. Shockingly, *saitan* (ST: 10) i.e. devil is to the translator *Archangel* (TT: 10) and *Angel* (TT: 13) in the next stanza. This is a serious misinterpretation of the word. Actually in the poem 'devil' is dethroned and to the translator 'angel' is dethroned. This dethroned 'angel' as a part of his revenge forms a band of devils to perform their destructive dance. This is a serious negative shift in translation. In the phrase *Born sailors* (TT: 16), *Born* unnecessarily adds emphasis to *sailors*. The translator has not translated the adverb *akhand* (ST: 15) which means 'ceaselessly' but he has translated the adverb *asech* (ST: 13) which means 'as this' as *ceaseless* (TT: 14) which is unfit in the stanza. Compromisingly, he has preferred the adjective *ceaseless* to rhyme with the adjective fearless (TT: 16). But still further in line 16, instead of translating as *Born sailors are fearless*, he translates as *Born sailors we are fearless*. The equivalent for *sahakaryano* (ST: 17) as *Comrades!* is a perfect dynamic equivalence (Nida, 1975: 33) which in English is an effective vocative rather more effective than *sahakaryano* of Marathi. The line *dishanche amhala dham* (ST: 20) is well interpreted (disha→directions→the boundless globe) and so translated as *The boundless globe is our home*. (TT: 20) But still the line preceding this one i.e. *free over the blue like the stars above* (TT: 19), there are two prepositions *over* and *above*. While over is apt, above is stranded which has no semantic connectivity with any constituent in the next line which is a complete clause in itself equivalent to *dishanche amhala dham*. In the same stanza *aseem* (ST: 19) of *aseem neelamadhye* (in the vast infinite blue) is left untranslated which dilutes the intensely felt vastness of the blue sky in the ST.

2.3 The first two lines of the sixth stanza (ST: 21, 22) could not have been translated with economy in two English lines as the translator has planned to. So only one line (ST: 20) is translated in the space of two lines of TT as

(ST: 20): Kay sagari taru lotale parataya mage
(TT: 21, 22): Did we set sail to turn back in fear
And run away from strife?

This makes the translator to leave *ase ka ha apula bana* (ST: 22) i.e. 'Is this our promising spirit?' without translation. This actually is the loss in the process of translation. Also, *tyahun gheu jali samadhi* (ST: 23) proposed as *we'd sooner meet our watery grave* (TT: 23) should have been 'We'd rather meet...' as the word *tyahun* suggests 'rather' and not 'sooner'. The translator has coined new phrase *watery grave* here to mean *jali samadhi* (death by water) which lacks the forcefulness of 'promise' or 'pledge' implying 'we'd rather die' or 'meet death by water'. The equivalent for *jivanu* (ST: 25) is proposed as *lives* (TT: 25). Actually, the term 'jivanu' is a disdainful expression as it implies 'trifle creatures' and not human beings in a true sense. Also, *nirmito nav kshitije pudhati*! (ST: 28) means '(we) create new horizons ahead' but in the TT we notice new horizons already existing, and these are unfurled before the sailors. *Nothing can stop us* (TT: 29) is an apt dynamic equivalence proposed by the translator for *marg amucha rodhu na shakati* (ST: 29) but in the same line *na dhan, na dara* (nor wealth, nor wife or woman) is only *no love of wealth*. This too is a serious loss. The word *manavateche* (ST: 31) is ambiguous having potential meanings 'of mankind' and 'of humanity'. The translator's choice is 'mankind' and no doubt his choice is based on quantity of sounds in 'mankind' in order to be in harmony with the music of the line. In the ST Columbus wishes to conquer the continents first and subsequently unfurl the flag of humanity. But we are sorry to notice that in TT (31, 32) the flag is first unfurled and then the continents to be conquered.

In the last verse of the poem the translator has shown commendable command of language while translating the last quotation. Of course he has added *what is in store* (TT: 34) to rhyme with *shore* of the last line and avoided the translation of *pamarala* (TT: 36). But this meaningful freedom makes fantastic end of the poem retaining the inspiring spirit of the sense as follows:

'While boundless are our hopes and dreams
You are bound by your shore.'

2.4 As far as stylistic equivalence is concerned the elements aiming at expressive identity (Popovic, cited in Bassnett, 1980: 25) are well taken care of.

First of all we notice conspicuously the graphological appearance of TT. The translator has tried to retain appearance of the stanzas on the paper parallel to the ST though line lengths could not have been retained. A number of stanzas and a number of lines in each stanza are equal to that of the ST. The second important feature of stylistic equivalence is that the translator has created end rhymes those are parallel to that of ST. In the ST we have rhymes such as *tare-sare*, *sangram-dham*, *bana-prana*, *kara-sara* and assonances such as *savita-palita*, *saitan-thaiman*, *mathyavarati-bhiti,* etc. In the same way we have in the TT the rhymes such as *mirth-earth*, *roam-home*, *strife-life*, *store-shore* and assonances such as *universe-corners*, *heaven-ocean*, *ceaseless-fearless*, *world-unfurled*. Such efforts on the part of the translator are of course commendable but he had to compromise by losing certain content and adding certain details or explanations.

(3)

The translator Vilas Salunke has more or less taken freedom of interpretation but the translation could not be termed as free translation. Mostly at the lexical level the translator has attempted literal translation in order to maintain its emotive value. He has not attached fixity to the meaning. But sometimes he explains or disambiguates as we noticed the case of *watery surge* (TT: 9) in 2.2 above. The main strategy of translation predetermined by the translator is 'rhyming translation' (Lefevere, 1975: 19-70). In order to be faithful to this strategy he had to lose certain important poetic contents or else had to be redundant every now and then as discussed above in 2.1 and 2.2. His additions are actually not gains but losses. Once you fix the strategy you must be ready to pay the price i.e. loss or gain, both unwelcoming.

In the last stanza the word *garvane* (ST: 31) which means proudly, is in fact adverb but the translator has used it as adjective 'proud' to save one syllable. In the concerned TT line (TT: 31) *proud* is the attribute of sail and not adverb of unfurl. This sort of 'maladjustment' has been done to achieve the rhyme or the stylistic features.

Though the graphological features are taken care of, due to the different constitutions of languages there is inevitable constitutive shift (Popovic, 1970: 78) which is easily noted in the short rhyming lines of ST and long redundant lines of TT. The second person plural pronoun 'we' is many times 'implied' in Marathi, but in English it has to be actually employed in the TT. There is also noted a negative shift in translation due to misinterpretation as in *Archangel* (TT: 10) above.

In this way, the compromise in translating is inevitable. The compromises are, in fact, due to the different formal features of the languages—source language (SL) and target language (TL), and the culture specific linguistic items. The translators manage these features by compromising with certain expressions in the ST. Still some compromises are due to the predetermined translation strategies as noticed in the present TT *The Marching Song of Columbus*. We can sum up the compromises in respect of this TT as follows:

1. The economy of expression that Kusumagraj has achieved in his poem has not been achieved by the translator. He had no option but to compromise. Though he has been successful in retaining the number of stanzas and the number of lines, he has not been able to retain the line length.
2. The system of sounds in the ST is such that their pronunciation is hard or harsh to listen to be apt to the forcefulness of challenge to the adversities and not smooth to make a sweet song. e.g.

   tamrasurva prashuni matu de daitya nabhamadhale
   dadu dya patali savita

   or the words such as *thaiman*, *saitan*, *khand khand* create a kind of roughness and forcefulness. This effect has not been retained. So the forcefulness of the system of sounds achieved by the poet may not be felt by the TL readership.

3. Certain nuances of linguistic expressions are actually culture specific e.g. *jivanu* is the expression despising comfort going people by calling them trifle creatures. Also, the words such as *palita*, *pamar* have their own Marathi cultural implications. As regards such expressions the translator has to introduce cultural filter that is a strategy in order to balance the greater or smaller pragmatic differences where as Katharina Reiss writes, "For a given pragmatic aspect we have to look for a common denominator in the experience of readers of both in the original and in the target language." (1987: 50). Still that is a kind of compromise. Here the translator has not introduced any. Rather he has preferred to avoid translating some words e.g. *pamar*. In brief, the translator had to inevitably compromise with the nuances of linguistic expressions.

In spite of these compromises, the target text "The Marching Song of Columbus" offers independently certain poetic experience as a metapoem (Holmes, 1970: 94-98) or a poem based on poem. The poetic experience being offered by the TT to the TL readers may not be as intense as that is offered by the ST to the SL readers as it is not just linguistic but cultural transfer. It is a kind of diluted experience. But this does not diminish the value and importance of the TT as a poem. Its creative worth cannot be ignored. In fact it is a transcreation offering an aesthetic pleasure of creative literature and maintaining the emotive value of the expression. The present English version has its own appeal and its own expressive identity. This impression of the TT as a metapoem can be summed as follows:

1. Rhyming translation is the major achievement of the translator. The translator has explored the possibility of such a parallel form of poetry and so it is in fact a parallel creative activity. The outcome of the

translator's exploration supports the argument that poetic translation is a transcreation.

2. The TT retains the mood incorporating the confidence of the speaker in tune with the ST. This in fact is a poetic experience underlining the high morale of man or man's confidence to overcome the adversities.
3. The translated version is in fact a poem based on a poem, and the freedom and risk taken by the translator is in favour of a good independent verse; and without doubt, the present TT entitled "The Marching Song of Columbus" can be enjoyed and appreciated as an independent verse.

References

Bassnett, Susan McGuire. (1980) *Translation Studies*. London: Methuen.

Bassnett, Susan, and Andre Lefevere, eds. (1990) *Translation, History and Culture*. London: Pinter Publishers.

Catford, J.C. (1965) *A Linguistic Theory of Translation*. London: Oxford UP.

Deshpande, Kusumavati, and M.V. Rajadhyaksha. *A History of Marathi Literature*. New Delhi: Sahitya Akademi.

Holmes, James, ed. (1970) *The Nature of Translation: Essays on the Theory and Practice of Literary Translation*. The Hague: Mouton Press.

Jakobson, Roman. (1959) "On Linguistic Aspects of Translation." *On Translation*. Ed. Reuben Brower. Cambridge Mass: Harvard UP. pp. 232-39.

Kusumagraj. (1973) *Vishakha*. Pune: Continental Prakashan.

———. (1999) *Blooms of the Earth*. Trans. Vilas Salunke. Kolkata: Writers Workshop.

Lefevere, Andre. (1975) *Translating Poetry: Seven Strategies and a Blueprint*. Amsterdam: Van Gorcum.

Nida, Eugene. (1975) *Language Structure and Translation*. Introd. Anwar S. Dil Stanford: Stanford UP.

Popovic, Anton. (1970) "The Concept of Shift of Expression in Translation Analysis." *The Nature of Translation: Essays on the Theory and Practice of Literary Translation*. Ed. James Holmes. The Hague: Mouton Press. pp. 78-85.

Reiss, Katharina. (1987) "Pragmatic Aspects of Translation." *Translation Across Cultures*. Ed. Gideon Toury. New Delhi: Basil Publications Pvt. Ltd. pp. 47-50.

Snell-Hornby, Mary. (1990) "Linguistic Transcoding or Cultural Transfer? A Critic of Translation Theory in Germany." *Translation, History and Culture*. Ed. Susan Bassnett and Andre Lefevere. London: Pinter Publishers. pp. 79-86.

17

Translation in Tamil Poetics

J. Samuel Kirubahar and *M. Muktha Manoj*

Translation has almost become a universal force with an aim to bring out a complete interaction between languages of various ethnic families at global level. Such an idea has promoted comparative approach not only between languages at different intervals but also between literatures written in different languages at different intervals. As Indian languages stamp Indian culture, translation is used as transferring agent to seek national integration covering a broader spectrum of various disciplines such as Linguistics, Computational Linguistics, Literature, History, Psychology, and Social Science.

Metaphrase / Literal Translation

In Indian context, translation can well be defined on two grounds based on the earliest known Poetics in India, namely:

1. Transcreation / Interpretation
2. Metaphrase / Literal Translation

Transcreation has always been the practice of the bards right from the Vedic age as comprehension of the real meaning behind the Source Language Text (SLT) and description of the same in the Target Language Text (TLT). This kind of translation could be termed as Intralingual translation where the verbal signs of one language are transferred by means of other signs in the same system. The great sagas like *Ramayana* and *Mahabarata* have been transcreated in different languages without affecting the original thought content of the Source Language Text (SLT) effecting new grandeur and flavour in the poetic technicalities of the Target Language Texts (TLT).

History has proved that the different renderings by Kamban and Tulsi are mere adaptations of Valmiki's *Ramayana*. Metaphrase or literal translation could also be termed as Interlingual translation in which the unit of one language is transferred by means of other equivalent unit in the target language. This sort of translation has not gained momentum as the practitioners are seldom encouraged on such grounds. To a considerable extent, the translator's awareness of different functional patterns of other languages in different translation situations has decided the success of translations. It is almost felt that every translation is created in time and space and can never be an innocent tool to set against a context in which the translated text is transposed. There are different strategies and methods, which could war with one another but adequacy has always been an important criterion for quality in translation.

Throughout its history, Tamil language has been influenced by other languages in spite of the despondent cry that the purity of the language should be preserved in all forms. Tamil Poetics is embedded on an idea that the borrowing or rendering would be a disgrace to the language which has preserved its heritage right from the inception of its heritage. Close political, cultural, and linguistic contacts between Tamil and other languages have increased the number of loans and transfers from other languages. Besides these factors, fads, ideas, technologies, and needs which came from overseas brought with them their unique terminology. The first Tamil book printed in India *Tambiran Vanakkam* has contributed Tamil words to express Christian doctrines and used spoken form to compose books. The inevitability of translation has been felt by the great poet Bharati as he demands western arts and science should be translated into Tamil. Bharati proclaims

> Puttam Putia Kalaikal – Panca
> Putac ceyalkalin Nutpankal Kurum,
> Metta Valarutu Merke – Anta
> Menmaik Kalaikal Tamilinil Illai
> Pira Nattu Nallarinkar cattirankal
> Tamil Moliyir Peyarttal Ventum.

In Tamil poetics, translation as a discipline has been felt right from the time of the earliest known grammatical 'urtext' *Tolkappiyam*. Translation has been considered an art form rather than science. The language itself is inescapably blended with the poetics. Tolkappiyar in "Ceyyuliyal" (Ars Poetica Art of Poetry) declares:

> Tokuttal, Virittal, Tokaiviri Molipeyarttu
> Atarppata Yattalotu Anai Marapinave (*Tolkappiyam*)

Tolkappiyar's insistence on poetics and its grammatical disciplines is analogues to Saussure's structuralist poetics. His classification is remarkably parallel to Saussure's insistence that "language is not a nomenclature, a way of naming things which already exist, but a system of differences with no positive terms" (*Critical Practice: 38*). Tolkappiyar, categorically lists that 'Tokuttal' (composition), 'Virittal' (expansion), 'Tokaiviri' (art of composition and expansion wherever necessary), 'Molipeyarppu' (translation or transcreation) and, 'Atarppatayattal' (art or science of approximation in a circumlocutary process) are the basic traditional concepts in translating a text. His argument borders on the suggestion that far from providing a set of labels language differentiates concepts which require amplification and justification. Tolkappiyar's 'Tokuttal' signifies the art of composition where the different ideas and perceptions scattered in and around the Source Language Text could be composed to be a single unit in the Target Language Text so as to convey the meaning in its own literal way as a free rendering of the text exemplified by *Purapporul Venpamalai* which is composed of *Panniru Patalam*. Similarly the label 'Virittal' refers to the art of literal expansion or amplification of both the poetic content and generic element as *Periya Puranam* and *Tiruttontar Tokai* are the amplified materials of *Tiruttontar Tiruvantati*. The other classification 'Tokai Viri' means both an art of composition and expansion with which a text could be made in the target language as the grammatical commentary Nannul has been translated by composing the grammatical concept 'Kurriyalukarap Punariyal' in 'Uyirirup Punariyal'. The nomenclature 'Molipeyarppu' raises an ambiguous question whether the term means translation or transcreation. Tolkappiyar's brevity means both translation and transcreation as *Nannul* considers *Ramayana* an illustrative example of this sort, *(Nannul Kandikaiyurai: 39)*. Tolkappiyar goes along with Saussure in keeping up the traditionalities of the language accepting that language is a matter of convention or 'Marapu' (*Critical Practice: 41*).

Nannul treats translation as a separate entity to exist along with the composed and expanded texts. Tolkappiyar's ideas on translation have been based on a single word which involves the problems of the semantic range and the distribution of that term in the language, the syntagmatic and paradigmatic relationships the word has with other terms in the language, the social context of its use, and the function it has at the level of discourse. M. Ganapathi Pillai in *Molipeyarppum Collakkamum*, supports Tolkappiyar affirming that the translation should preserve the original ideas of the Source Language Text with all semantic, syntagmatic, and paradigmatic relationships. Tolkappiyar's Tokuttal (composition) and Virittal (expansion) may be termed as abridgment and adaptation but if the translation does either of these things, as Ian Finlay argues, it is no longer a translation but a mere summary, precise, or version in a different language (2). At the same time, it is to be accepted as Joseph T. Shipley argues:

> Translation will destroy the author's precise balance of thought, feeling, written word, sound: the loss is undeniable; but it has been greatly exaggerated. The Italian proverb *Traduttore, traditore* (translator, traitor) is a victim's hyperbole. The merit of books lies in the beauty, richness and adequacy of their symbols, rather than in the sound of their language. The greater the work, the less will it suffer from transplanting. (342)

Tolkappiyar's '*Tokuttal*', '*Virittal*' and '*Tokaiviri*' are based on the condition that if words stood for pre-existing concepts, they would all have exact equivalents in meaning from one language to the next; but this is not true as the truth is that different languages divide or articulate the world in different ways. Tolkappiyar's stand in translation is comparable to the stand of structuralist philosophers on the reason that his theory of translation is analogous to that of Ferdinand Saussure's that language is a 'system of signs where in a 'sign' is consisted of 'signifier' (the sound image or the written shape) and a 'signified' (a concept).

Tamil poetics has always been influenced by the notion of translation. Not only *Tolkappiyam* but also the great classical poems written during the period of Cankam reflect the practice, art, and craft of translation. The earlier Cankam classics reflect two different distinctions in translation, namely:

1. Col peyar (word – for word translation)
2. Moli peyar (literal translation)

as Cankam classics proclaim:

Kalpiranku Aritai vilankiya
Colpeyar Teetta curanirantore
Panipatu colai Venkatattumbar
Molipeyar Teetta Ayinum Malkuvar.

In Cankam age, translation had never been considered a disciplined study with classified rules and reservations of its marginality. However, many books were translated, transcreated, and transferred from languages like Sanskrit, Pali, and Prakrit. Mostly translation was in stream line with the grammatical texts and they became commentaries on the grammatical aspects of literatures.

Akam poetry ememplifies itself with context bound and context free translations and as a result commentaries on Akam classics have to amend their interpretations to illuminate the real sense conveyed in the context of the commentators and translators that could well be exemplified by the word "Adip pavai" The lack of knowledge of the real meaning of the word and its nature and function has led to such a kind of a misconception of the meaning of the literal word. Researchers feel that "Adipavai" could not be a mere 'mirror image' but should be a 'puppet' as it signifies a lady as puppet on the hands of a man.

Tolkappiyar suggests that the need for translation should have been stimulated by the extreme blend/mix of Sanskrit words in Tamil. This has been the first stage in language combination in Tamil Poetics as Tolkappiyar suggests:

Vatacol Kilavi Vatavelut Toriyi
Eluttotu Punarnta collakumme

Nannul has also accepted the use of Sanskrit word in making literature as it accounts:

Iyarcol, Tiri col, Ticaic col, Vatacol
Anaitte ceyyul Ittac colle.

Nannul claims that words like 'Iyarcol' (Common words), 'Tiri col' (learned words such as simile, metaphor, symbol and so on that are used in literature and literary discourses), Ticai col (Provincial words, or words peculiar to or derived from any of the Tamil provinces or from any of the Indian cognate languages), and 'Vata col' (words of Sanskrit origin) could be used in poetic process. Eugene Nida's classification of words into centripetal, centrifugal and lineal concepts is very close to Nannul's 'Iyarcol', 'Tiri col', and 'Ticaic col' as 'Iyarcol' like 'centripedal' is a common denominator of meaning which defines the meaning of a word, 'Tiri col' like 'centrifugal' is a meaning of a word which rides off in all directions, and 'Ticaic col' like 'lineal concepts' refers to what a word should mean depending on the province or cognate. (Eugene Nida: 32) Both Nannul and Nida approach the meaning of a word and its use in a traditional way so as to impart the right understanding of the 'detexte'. This progressive idea that includes 'Ticaic col' and 'Vatacol' in the poetic process has given an impetus to use a vast amount of borrowing or loan from Sanskrit, Pali, and Prakrit origins and as a result the great classics like *Pattup Pattu, Ettut Tokai, Pura Nanuru*, and *Pattinap Palai* are abound with loan words and literal borrowings from other languages both in content and form. In short, translation as a discipline can be classified under three different heads as existed along with the early Tamil poetics, namely:

1. Word-for-word translation—Tolkappiyar's period

2. transcreation of structure and texture with the literal expansion and amplification—Cankam Literature
3. transfer of thought content from SL text into TL text —Period after Cankam Literature.

As a result, trans-proper (proper translation) and interpretation (comprehending the SL text and describing the same in the TL text) have become the fashion of the practitioners. The art of interpretation has increased the use of polylingual usage that is 'Manip Piravala Natai' in Tamil, in fifth century B.C. in Tamil spoken and written forms. Translations of this age tend to be mere adaptations with the bilingual and Polylingual usage which has been effected with the reason that there has been no positive associations in Tamil language with other languages. As a result, the narrow parochial attitude to save the purity of the language has curtailed the efforts to enrich the vocabulary and diction with added loan words to form a comparable equivalent diction in Tamil. However, the need to enrich the language has been felt and Tamil Poetics has liberally borrowed words from other language origins, particularly from Sanskrit origin. The need to establish the equivalence on the linguistic and pragmatic levels is minimized by Tamilicisation of Sanskrit words based on functional, phonemic, and morphological modifications so as to remain as Tamil diction. To amplify the point Kamban's *Ramayana* could be cited. In it one can find modifications such as:

Sanskrit	Tamil
Raman	Iraman
Hanuman	Anuman
Lankai	Ilankai
Hirtayam	Irutayam (heart)

The change is effected on the reason that the borrowing of foreign words always entails phonetic modification because the accentual peculiarities may not fit with the native phonetic habits. It has been generally felt that the nouns in Tamil should begin with the vowel sound rather than consonant and mostly the case marker 'i' is used before the consonant beginnings. Tolkappiyar also states.

Vatacor Kilavi Vatarelut toriyi
Eluttotu Punarnta collakumme

Tolkappiyar indirectly suggests that transformations have been based on metonymic and metaphoric shifts in Tamil poetics. Such a theory is not only limited to Sanskrit but also to other languages such as Arab, Persian, English, French, Dutch, Urudu, and so on. Buddhists and Saivites have extensively used borrowings from Sanskrit in Tamil Poetics and have modified the diction. This Practice has been accepted as a tradition as the St. Pavananthi says:

Epporul Eccolin Evva ruantor
Ceppinar appatie cepputal marape

And as Tolkappiyar suggests:

Valakkenap paturatu uyarntor merre
Nikalcci avarkat takalan

This has led to two different views on types of theory such as:

1. the general view which basically recommends any word combinations, making, and coinage.
2. the particular view, which has described conformity between two languages.

However, the need to identify equivalents, similarities, adequate substitutions, and translational peculiarities of texts with various functional styles in genres like Kurumba, Limmerick, Haiku are all entirely new. Tamil literature provides a variety of ways and means for the study of the science of literary genetics. However, it also provides difficulties in translation as, the 'urtext' Tolkappiyam's theme or 'Turai' situations are very difficult to translate. Even the translation of a word is based on the mechanism of probable prediction of the interpreter's delivery in a significative context as 'Chilly' is 'Milakai'—named after the reason that the vegetable ('Kai' in Tamil) is hot as pepper ('Milaku' in Tamil). In translating words, the communicative intention has always been balanced so as to keep the functional parameters of the

TL text. Derivative names or genres have found the place and not the specific term or primitive nouns which are not common to all in translating as Tolkappiyar suggests: "Molip porut Karanam vilippat tonra". Tolkappiyar suggests the importance of significance behind each and every word translated rather than the denotative value, socially invested meanings, and the symbolic determinism of a word as is the case with words such as 'university', 'Vice-chancellor' and 'train' which had been rendered as 'Carvakalacalai', 'upa—Attiatcar', and 'Pukaivandi' are now changed into 'palkalai kalakam', 'Tunai Ventar', and 'Totar Vandi' respectively due to their significance. Similar cases of difficulty in translating Tamil to English arises out of certain phrases, conventional usages, riddles, puns, nouns, pronouns, grammatical labels such as 'Irattaik Kilavi' and so on as the word 'Kavi' (poet) is a pun in Tamil as it signifies both the poet and the monkey. The word 'Kavi' is derived from the Sanskrit word 'Kabi', meaning monkey, with the syllabic change into 'Kavi', the poet. Kalamekap Pulavar uses the word 'Kavi' in the original sense of the term to create an atmosphere of pun to satirise versifiers. Cankam literature offers a variety of untranslatable words such as 'Akaval Makalir', 'Panan', 'Patini', 'Netunici', 'Veriyattu', and so on due to non availability of equivalent epithets.

Translation is also a covert behaviour of the mental process by which two types of equivalence could be achieved as listed below:

1. a translated words can be recognised as loan words from the SL text with an imposed modification on the phonemic and phonetic structures to suit the SL text.
2. a Tamil cognate can undergo semantic expansion under foreign influence.

Nannul used the term 'Payiram' which has undergone semantic changes and expansion. It was used to express the strength of an army and served a warning given before the battle. The contextual significance is lost and now the word is related to 'Foreword' 'Preface', 'Introduction', and 'Editor's Opinion' in synonymic condition. Nannul says:

Ukavurai Patika Maninturai Nunmukam
Puravurai Tanturai Punainturai Payiram

Equally it is not very easy to find equivalents in Tamil as the language lacks a comparable diction with its narrow boundaries in semantic, syntactic, and lexical structures. The words like 'Time Budget', 'Water Budget' have no equivalents and there is no prefix and suffix in Tamil to create new words. Shanmuga Velayutham in *Molipeyarppiyal (The Art of Translation)* pointed out that the English Prefix 'Photo' could be translated into Tamil as 'Oli' (synonymous to the world 'light'.) in words like photograph, photography, photosynthesis, and Photometry and would get words like 'Olivarai', 'Olivaraiyam', 'Olic cerkkai', and 'Oli alavaiyam' respectively in Tamil translation. Similarly, Manavai Mustafa in *Kalam Tetum Tamil* translated 'Photography' as 'Nilar Patam'., but when photography is 'Olip patam' as Shanmuga Velayutham has translated, it poses a problem whether the prefix 'Photo' is 'Oli' (light) or Nilal (image). However, the Tamil tradition has accepted 'Photography' as 'Pukaip Patam' and not as 'Nilal Patam' or 'Olip Patam' and even the word 'Photo' is retained in spoken form in Tamil in its transliteration form as the words like Enzyme, Isotope, Radar, Laser and other scientific terms have been retained in its foreign form in transliteration. In the field of transliteration too problems arise out of certain vowels and consonants like the cases listed below:

1. 'Ka' represented by both K, G, of English Phonemes
2. 'Ta' represented by both T, D of English Phonemes
3. 'Pa' represented by P, B, and F, of English Phonemes

To avoid variations, complications, and uncertainities in making characters, it is felt that Tamil alphabet is to be simplified. Tamilologists feel that the alphabet must be made to have a unisign instead of two or more signs. However, no theory is comprehensive and acceptable one as language is constantly in a flux and cannot be reduced to a static concept. This inherent ability has made it an art of approximation. Even modern theories are not prescriptive and suggestive as that of

Tolkappiyam and Nannul but descriptive and transliteral subjecting themselves to suit the demand of the vocabulary to fill up the vacuum in communication as translation is perceptible to the extent that it has been embedded in words and phrases that are of subtle shade of thought, implied meanings, and indirect literary echoes besides aesthetic embellishment at the verbal level.

References

Belsey, Catherine. *Critical Practice.* London and New York: Methuen, 1985.

Mustafa, Manavai. *Kalam Thetum Tamil.* Chennai: Mira Publication, 1967.

Nida, A. *Towards A Science of Translating.* Leiden. E.J. Brill, 1964.

Pillai, Ganapathi. *Molipeyarppum Collakkamum.* Chennai: Vanathi Pathippakam, 1980.

Shanmugavelayutham. "Molipeyarppu Ilakkiyam". *Tamil Ilakkiya Kolkai-9.* Chennai: Ulaga Tamilaraychi Niruvanam, 1984.

Shipley, Joseph. T. *Dictionary of World Literary Terms.* 1943. London: George Allen and Unwin, 1930.

18

Barriers in Cross-Cultural Communication with Special Reference to *Ponniyin Selvan* by Kalki

Sangeetha Jayakumar

Translation is a central core of linguistic activity. It involves the transfer of 'meaning'. Language is the medium of expression for the society, so when translation happens the meaning is expected to be retained.

Language also has a close link with culture. Sapir and Whorf declare that "no language can exist unless it is steeped in the context of cultures...."[1]

Language is the heart within the body of culture. For example, when the surgeon operates on the heart, he cannot neglect the body that surrounds it. So the translator should not treat the text in isolation from culture.

Translation from the SL to the TL has five steps.

SL TEXT → ANALYSIS → TRANSFER → RESTRUCTURING → TL TEXT[2]

i.e.; the text from the SL is analyzed and then there is a transfer that leads to restructuring and finally translation in TL is accomplished by the translator.

Roman Jakobson in his work "On Linguistic aspects of Translation" classifies the types of translation as follows:

- Intralingual translation: an interpretation of verbal signs by means of other signs in the same language.
- Interlingual translation: an interpretation of verbal signs by means of some other language.
- Intersemiotic translation: an interpretation of verbal signs by means of signs of nonverbal sign systems.[3]

The translator has barriers in doing justice to the 'original work'. This article would discuss those barriers in translating a work, pertaining to Indian culture to the Western culture and language. *Ponniyin Selvan* by Kalki which is translated by C.V. Karthik Narayanan as *The Pinnacle of Sacrifice* is taken for special reference.

Edward Sapir claims that 'language is a guide to social reality'. He says: "no two languages are sufficiently similar to be considered as representing the same social reality."[4]

In tune with the social reality, the translator must also consider the religious and political differences. The Western readers of *Ponniyin Selvan* must be familiar with the political background of Tamil Nadu, India. It was not a democratic country then. Rather it was reined by the Kings of Chera, Chozla, and Pandiyas.

Christianity is the religion of commonality to many English countries. But in India, people follow various religions and worship different deities. Even among Hinduism there are further subdivisions like 'Saivism' (p. 25) and 'Vaishnavism' (p. 26);

> Saivism—worship of the deity Lord Shiva.
> Vaishnavism—worship of Lord Vishnu.

The readers must be familiar with the religious scenario in India in order to understand these concepts.

Even to comprehend the word 'Sanyasi' (p. 2) the Westerners must be aware of 'Nirvana' (p. 25) and the concept of attaining Sanyasam. Sanyasis are those who leave all their materialistic possession and seek sanctuary at the feet of the Lord. Nirvana has a literal meaning or a colloquial meaning which says nakedness but in this context it means attaining Sanyasam or attaining 'Moksha' which means attaining divinity. Sages or Saints who give up all their worldly possession and seek abode in God's feet have presumably attained this stage of Nirvana.

The Universal readers will be aware of the medicinal value that a 'neem' tree has. But it also has religious significance, here in Tamil culture.

"There was a huge neem tree opposite the temple that had somehow withstood the gale" (p. 50).

For the reader the inner meaning, that is, the neem tree having religious value and that it is worshiped by the people as a symbol of the deity 'Amman' (p. 76) will not be understood. So the reader fails to understand the co notated religious significance.

The religious practices in India differ from those in the Western countries. Indians have 'Pujaris' (p. 48), who do 'pooja' (p. 47) for the deity and they chant 'mantras' (p. 117).

Pujari can be translated as priest but even then a reader cannot understand the original concept of a pujari who differs from the priest with a white robe who preaches the message of God. Rather a pujari does puja that is, he worships God by chanting mantras which is considered to be a language spoken between God and the pujari. Then he distributes the 'Prasadham' (p. 48) to the devotees which is considered to be the sacred communion which is offered to God. Such words fail to apply to the English social, religious and cultural patterns.

There is ordinarily no full equivalence through 'translation' since each unit contains within itself a set of non-transferable associations and connotations.

The translator of *Ponniyin Selvan* retains the word 'kannae' (p. 86). If one tries to find the English equivalent for this word it means the "eyes" but the co notated meaning here is "oh! Dear".

Even when one considers the word 'Dharma' (p. 101) it can be translated to "righteousness". But the author will fail to emphasize the concept of Dharma if he translates it to the

English equivalent, so he retains the same Tamil word in the text.

So, such words are non-transferable and it should be only associated with the co notated meaning.

The terms like 'rakshasas' (p. 52), 'yamma' (p. 53) are new to the English readers. They will be aware of Satans and the fallen Angel "Lucifer" but rakshasas are like demons which have scary appearance and they perform demonic dances.

The concept of 'yamma' or 'yamadharmaraja' (p. 54) that is the "God of destruction" will be unfamiliar to the readers.

When the author mentions 'Samudraraja's fury' (p. 19) the reader might interpret it as a name of some person maybe a King's fury but according to the context it means that the fury of the "Sea God". Due to his fury the floods have hit the country and there is destruction everywhere.

Certain meanings can be only determined by the context, which will not be intelligible to the other readers out of context.

While translating, the function or the purpose of the word should be taken into consideration and not the words themselves.

The translator translates the word 'josier' (p. 72) as "astrologer" but according to the purpose the translator has retained the word as josier in many places.

The Western reader should know the various words used to represent relationships.

'Amma' (p. 24) refers to mother.
'appanae' (p. 15) refers to father.
'Anna' (p. 67) refers to elder brother.

But in this context the words does not represent only the blood relationships. These words are used to represent respect. A speaker in his conversation addresses the other as Anna or Amma to show his due respect.

So in certain cases the function of the word must be taken into consideration and not the words themselves. Certain utterances will be situation-bound. We must consider the phrase in its particular context, i.e.; as a moment of high tension in the dramatic text.

The sudden cries like 'Aiyo!' (p. 34) is a sudden outburst of fear, or pain or sorrow. It is situation-bound. A phrase like 'Adada!' (p. 70) refers to exclamation which gives different meaning according to the voice-inflexion of the speaker. Adada can mean that you "admire" something or also it can mean that you feel "sorry" for something, the meaning differs according to the inflexion in the tone of the speaker.

Phrases like 'chi chi' (p. 47) expresses "disgust". You don't like something or the speaker tries to remove certain unwanted thoughts from her mind so she uses the word 'chi chi'.

'Aha!' (p. 36) is a cry of pain or sorrow. In translating such words the translator must accept the untranslatability of the SL phrase in the TL on the linguistic level.

The 'Demonic dance' (p. 18) as represented by the writer will not be understood by the English reader. 'Ravanan' (p. 89) with his ten heads makes the reader to visualize a person with ten heads and also probe into the difficulties of having ten heads while sleeping, walking, brushing and also the imbalance in the physic. For a Westerner it proves to be an illogical concept, but the writer uses it as a hyperbolic statement to represent that 'Ravanan' has the strength of ten people.

'Appa' (p. 67), 'Anna' (p. 67), 'Ayya' (p. 30), 'kuravai' (p. 37), 'Ammani' (p. 83), 'Thayae' (p. 85), 'Athan' (p. 66), all these phrases are representation of class, status, age, sex, etc. So the attempt to impose the value system of the SL culture onto the TL culture is useless.

Allbrecht Neubert said that Shakespeare's sonnet "Shall I compare thee to a summer's day?" cannot be semantically translated into a language where summers are unpleasant. The concept of God the father cannot be translated into a language where the deity is female. Similarly words like 'Durga' (p. 17), 'Amman' (p. 76), 'parameshwari' (p. 17), 'Ranabhadrakali' (p. 26), cannot be translated into a language where the female deity is not worshiped in its various forms.

Idioms, phrases, puns, proverbs pertaining to one particular language and culture cannot find equivalence in TL.

"Before my very eyes" (p. 23) actually shows the mother tongue influence. The speaker says the incident happens "in front" of his eyes but the translator just translates those words accordingly due to his MTI.

"Storm ragged in Pazhuvettarayar's heart as well" (p. 41). The writer means that the person was in confusion or was in some dilemma.

So Idiom or Phrase while translated will have a substitution, not an equivalent one. It only tries to serve the same purpose. What is unique can have no counterpart.

> "Bhagavan Buddha! Buddham Gachami! Dharmam Gachami! Sangam Gachami!" (p. 17).

Equivalence cannot be found but have to be created. There is a lack of vocabulary to describe words like 'Nirvana', (p. 25) 'Anthapuram', (p. 68) 'Gopuram' (p. 28) 'Naligai' (p. 62) 'Yugam' (p. 70) 'Mandapam' (p. 47).

'Anthapuram' refers to a place where the King and Queen take rest where the commoner's entry is restricted. It cannot be translated as "Guest house" or "farm house".

'Gopuram' means the entrance of a temple or the entrance of a city. It cannot be translated as "Toll gate" or "entrance"

'Naligai' means "seconds", to retain the poetic essence the writer uses the word as such. 'Yugam' is understood only by readers within this social ethnicity. Many decades put together forms a Yugam which does not have an English equivalent.

The English phrases 'I'm going home', or 'He's at home' can readily be provided with translation equivalents in most languages, but the terms 'democracy', 'untouchability', 'caste system' are language-specific and culture-specific.

The reader will have a concept of the term based on his or her own cultural context. It differs according to the country.

e.g.: The American Democratic Party
The German Democratic Republic
The Democratic Wing of the British Conservative Party

So, although the term is international, its usage in different contexts shows that there is no longer any common ground.

Hence, the true essence of the literary work and the nuances in that language will be lost due to such barriers in translation. But, in spite of these discrepancies, certain great works in Literature have to be translated so that great ideas of the writers can be relished by universal readers. Also, due to globalization, people are much interested in knowing the ethnicity of other cultures, so only a translated work can provide with such an insight. Because a literary work is like a mirror which reflects the cultural, political, religious, social background of a society. So only the literary work can provide a wide scope of information. Therefore despite many barriers translation helps to meet such needs.

Notes

1. Edward Sapir, *Culture, Language and Personality*. Berkeley, Las Angeles: University of California Press, 1956. p. 69.
2. Nida E.A. and C. Taber. *The Theory and Practice of Translation*. Leyden, Brill. 1974.
3. R Jakobson, "On Linguistic Aspects of Translation", in R.A. Brower (ed.), *On Translation*. Cambridge, Mass,: Harvard University Press, 1959. p. 234.
4. Edward Sapir, *opt. cit.*

19

The Context of Indian English: A Case of Manju Kapur's *Difficult Daughters*

A.M. Sarwade

I

Language of literature is the object of study in Stylistics. As per the theories of Stylistics (particularly the theories of Russian Formalism and those who study Foregrounding) the language used in literature is the deliberate use by the writer with some specific aims and objectives. As such, the literary language cannot be taken on its face value as the ordinary, spontaneous use of language is taken. For that matter, the linguist can no doubt study the language of literature but s/he has to be careful in not missing the stylistic and deliberate point of view of the writer. As a result, constant and more specific attention needs to be paid to the peculiar use of language in the text. Such use, again, needs to be investigated from different perspectives—individual, social, cultural and stylistic.

English language has been and is being used by the Indians for the last two hundred years or so, not only for day-to-day communication but also for what can be called the 'creative use of language' i.e. in literature. Indian English literature is the one in which English language, the foreign language in the Indian context, is used deliberately by the Indian writer who has acquired it as a second language. According to the theorists of the Second and Foreign Language Acquisition, the goal of language learning is what they call the acquisition of the 'near-native competence' (Selinker) or what Hymes calls the "Communicative Competence". Such competence includes the ability of the learner to use language not only grammatically, but also appropriately depending on the nature of participants and the context of situation. However, the Indian writer in English cannot use and cannot be expected to use English language as it is used by the native speakers of that language. In this context, what Nils Enkvist has articulated may be recollected. According to him, one of the most important problems of foreign language learning is the acquisition of the sense of style. By 'sense of style', he means the varieties of language which are changeably used as the participants and the contexts differ. The literary work of art, more particularly novel, consists of such different contexts and participants requiring the novelist to change the language with respect to these contexts and participants. Most of the time, in Indian novels written in English, the contexts and participants are Indian. It means that the novelist requires to show the awareness not only of the varieties of English used across different contexts and by different participants but also s/he should be aware of the Indian ways of life which can provide Indian sensibility to the use of English language. This is what Verghese calls the 'main problem of Indian creative writers in English' i.e. 'evolving an Indian mode of writing in English'.

Verghese says that English is not a spoken language in India. (No doubt, time has changed since and English is now used for day-to-day communication, particularly in metropolitan cities and mostly for Information Technology and Business matters.) The rhythms of speech and idioms of any language are created by the people who use it. Since English is used to serve very limited functions for its users in India, the Indian novelist cannot depend on the common people (whom s/he presents in his/her works) for the enrichment and development of the language s/he uses in his/her works. As a result, the novelist has to depend on him/herself for the effective use of English to communicate the cultural and emotional life of the people in the novel. That is, the novelist has to use the language in such a way as possibly and probably be used by the characters in the daily communication. Still, the novelist can use English language successfully and render his characters appropriately in his/her works depending upon the novelist's ability to imagine how the character will probably use the language in the situations elaborated in the novel. However, in such imaginative uses of language, the novelist should be conscious enough in that the language articulated by the characters must render a realistic portrayal of the character. (Verghese, 181) That is to say, the language used by the different characters in the novel and the narrator of the novel should not only be different from character to character and context to context, but, what Verghese calls, should also be 'realistic' to the Indian scenario.

Another important difficulty in the use of English for creative purposes is that while depicting the Indian experience through English the novelist has to translate the idioms from regional languages into English. The novelist cannot do so without violating the basic rules of the English language. In this context, Verghese says:

> In translating native idioms into English for the sake of reflecting cultural undertones and overtones, violation of English language can be permitted only if the violation is significant and meaningful. The Indian novelist in English should be tactful when he violates the language. The criterion whether the violation is necessary should be internal and not external: that is, it should be a violation permissible within the context of the novel. (183)

Raja Rao, in his Forward to *Kantapura*, also voiced similar arguments. He is of the opinion that English is our intellectual language and not emotional one. By that he points to the same difficulty of the Indian novelist of using suitable language to the Indian background of his characters. In the absence of the actual input from the real people, it is difficult for the writer to use language in his/her text in the day-to-day context.

In the light of the above discussion of the difficulties of the Indian novelist writing in English, let us now examine how Manju Kapur has used language in her *Difficult Daughters*.

II

Manju Kapur was born in 1948 in Amritsar. She teaches English literature at Miranda House College, New Delhi. Her first novel *Difficult Daughters* (1998) earned her substantial success in both financial and literary matters. She is awarded the Commonwealth Writers Prize for Best First Book. As with her contemporary Indian women novelists, a feminist tradition is strongly apparent in her novels. The search for control over one's (particularly a female protagonist's) destiny is the recurring theme in her novels. Her other novels include *A Married Woman, Home, and The Immigrant.*

Difficult Daughters is set around the time of India's Independence struggle and is said to be partially based on the life of Kapur's mother, Virmati. The novel depicts the story of a woman torn between the family duty, the keen desire for education (and naturally for freedom) and the illicit love. Virmati, a young woman born in Amritsar in a joint, austere and high-minded household, falls in love with the already married neighbour—a Professor. She enters into a scandalous relationship with the Professor. The relationship between Virmati and the Professor Parallels India's battle for freedom, and eventually Virmati becomes the Professor's second wife. Mostly, Amritsar and Lahore provide the setting to the novel.

As could be seen from the above outline of the novel, most of the characters and events are Indian in their socio-cultural contexts. Again the setting is pre-Independence India, which demands a meticulous attention on the part of the writer to use language to create the historical sense. With these points in mind let us now try to find out some of the peculiar ways in which Kapur has used English language in her novel.

The novel is written in third person omniscient narrative with dialogues of the specific characters intruding occasionally. One chapter, Chapter IXV is written using Epistolary technique consisting of the communication between the

Professor and Virmati through love-letters. It is expected that the language of the narrator i.e. Ida, the daughter of Virmati and the Professor, should be different from that of the other characters. Since the narrator narrates the story happened in the past, her language should be pretty sophisticated as compared to the language of the other characters that belong essentially to the earlier period. In the same vein, such characters of the bygone period should also reflect the socio-cultural and historical ethos of India at that time. The opinion held by the sister of Lala Diwan Chand, the grandfather of Virmati, and the language through which she expresses them is true to her period:

> Marriages are in the hands of God. (21)

This particular stance towards the institution of marriage was very common in India in the early decades of 20th century. Kapur has done nothing but simply translated it literally into English so that it would convey the historical and the cultural ethos of India. Moreover, the phrase 'in the hands of' strikes the readers as unusual because unless the reader has some knowledge of Indian socio-cultural context, it is not possible to understand the meaning of it.

The views of the other characters regarding marriage, the role of women and the education of women also reflect the socio-cultural and historical tradition of India and Kapur provides us with the translation of these colloquial and everyday utterances:

> Kasturi: Still, it is the duty of every girl to get married. (13)

Here marriage is thought in terms of the sacred duty of the women. Again:

> A woman's *shann* is in her home. (13)

Such utterances aptly illustrate how the role of woman was encapsulated in the Indian society. This other-worldly nature of thinking is also evident in Lajwanti's defence of the unmarried status of her daughter Shakuntala:

> It is the will of God. (13)

Referring to the importance of education and its significance, Kasturi voices the assumptions of the earlier generation:

> Study means developing the mind for the benefit of the family. I studied too, but my mother would have killed me if I had dared even to dress in anything other than was brought for me. (14)

These lines of Kasturi clearly manifest how education in general and women's education in particular was looked upon. The quote also epitomizes the way women were expected to behave even though they were educated. The use of the expression "would have killed me" is again very common and should not be taken literally, because the connotations of the word in the present and, for that matter, the Indian context are quite different. Such usages are what Leech calls 'semantic deviations'. Literally, the clause means that such behaviour on the part of the children would not have been accepted by the people and also the society.

The novel also abounds in the translations of Indian idioms from regional languages and also metaphorical thought process of the characters. For example, Kasturi says:

> Now it is you who are eating my head. (19)

The literal meaning of the utterance cannot be accounted for the intention of both the character and also the novelist. The phrase 'eating my head' would be quite inappropriate and ungrammatical in English language. But the Indian readers may not find it unintelligible, for it is the part of their thought process and the way they use language. This is conventionally indirect Speech Act of Complaint where the mother is indicating her annoyance to the behaviour of her daughter. What Lajwanti says about Shakuntala is another evidence of the metaphoric cognition of the characters:

> She is very delicate, Baoji, how can she stand it when I can't? Poor Shaku has to *walk up and down my back and across my head* to relieve the pain. (23)

Lakoff and Johnson in their book *Metaphors We Live By* have given their cognitive-linguistic theory of metaphor.

According to them, the way we use language and the way we perceive reality is shaped by the cognitive make-up of the individual which is, in turn, shaped by the socio-cultural realities in which the individual finds him/herself. In the present context, what Kapur has done is simply translated such Indian expressions into English literally, which also help to provide what Verghese calls 'Indian sensibility' to the literary work. The use of the phrase 'poor Shakhu' in the present case doesn't consider the literal meaning of the word 'poor'. On the other hand, it is a recurrently used term to indicate the innocence of the person with which it is associated. This is called the extension of the original meaning of the word. Indian English abounds in such extensions. Not only does Kapur use Indian idioms with literal translation in the novel, but she also has shown her competence in the use of English idioms:

> Breeding like cats and dogs. (7)

And

> Harvest time and again. (7)

The novel also gives a feast of implicatures. According to various pragmaticians (Levinson, 1983; Yule, 1996), Conversation Implicatures are highly dependent on the socio-cultural background in which the conversation takes place. For example, the following dialogue between Ida (daughter of the Professor and Virmati) and her maternal uncle, Kailashnath Mama:

> Ida: You know the college where my father taught?
> Kailashnath: Who doesn't? (44)

The answer in the form of a question and the expression like 'who doesn't?' is the Indian way of asking rhetorical question and can also be seen as Conversational Implicature as the outcome of the cognitive make-up. It has been argued that Conversational Implicatures result when one or more of the Cooperative Principles are not observed in the conversation. Griece has elaborated the four Cooperative Principles with reference to which the participants in the conversation interact: Maxim of Quality, Maxim of Quantity, Maxim of Relation, and Maxim of Manner. It is expected that people should follow Cooperative Principles by engaging with each other for meaningful communication in which they act as agents. The implicature in the above example results because Kailashnath flouts the Maxim of Quality. That is to say, on the face of it, the response doesn't answer explicitly the question posed by Ida. However, as per Indian norms of conversation, this response is acceptable which means roughly that 'there is not a single person who doesn't know the college where your father worked'.

The statement present in the form of a question is yet another typical way in which Indians use English. Again Kailashnath's answer "What is too far in Amritsar?" (44) as a response to the question "Is it too far?" will not be acceptable in Standard English, but it is - in the Indian context.

There is the essential difference between the way the narrator uses the language and the characters use language in the novel:

> Shakuntala Pehnji who have done her M.Sc. in Chemistry, had gone about testing the wine of freedom. Wine, whereas all Virmati had ever drunk had been creamy milk in winters, designed to deaden the senses with its richness, and frothy cool *lassi* with its lacy bubbles in summer. (17)

Not only the language of the quote is sophisticated, but also the images of wine and milk are used changing upside down the Indian conventional opinions. Wine is associated with freedom, whereas milk is seen as having the effect of deadening the senses. Such alterations can be accounted by the fact that the narrator is essentially a modern personality; she knows the total of the narrative of the novel; and, also she has imbibed the Western ways of thought associated with the Indian education.

It will be appropriate here to juxtapose and investigate some of the pieces of dialogues in the novel from the perspectives of Politeness and Cooperative Principles. These principles are elaborated by different pragmaticians. Politeness is understood in terms of conflict avoidance strategies. In conversation, Politeness facilitates interaction by minimizing the potential for conflict in all human interaction. Linguistic strategies are employed by the participants to realize politeness which manifests one's respect and recognition of another's public image. The choice of such strategies depends on the 'power and solidarity' between the speaker and the hearer. The following is the dialogue between Virmati and Lajwanti when the latter comes to Dalhousie:

> 'Beti, I am here now, you rest,' said Lajwanti frequently to her niece.
>
> 'No, no, Taiji. You are here for a holiday,' said Virmati.
>
> 'What holiday is it for you, beti, with your mother so sick and needing constant care'. (12)

This piece of dialogue sheds light on the relationship between Virmati and her aunt Lajwanti and also on how the language 'communicates more than what is said'. The use of the honorific—Beti by Lajwanti and Taiji, by Virmati—show their relationship and how both of them try to be polite and cooperative to each other. However, to understand the significance of the Politeness used in the example above, it is necessary to understand the background of the speech event: both Kasturi and Virmati had gone to Dalhousie for climate change for the former and Lajwanti joins them afterwards. The predicament of Lajwanti is that, as per the Politeness maxim of the Indian situation, she has to offer herself at work even though she has come to Dalhousie to take rest for herself. It explains Lajwanti's first utterance. Though Virmati has to look after her mother, the baby and now her aunt, as per the same maxim and power and solidarity between her and Lajwanti, Virmati cannot, as soon as was told, go and take rest. The excuse given in the form of an implicature explains the things. However, as the narrator points out, the second utterance of Lajwanti has the implications that Virmati herself is a pleasure loving girl. But she does so in such a way that Virmati may feel how much her aunt cares for her. The complaining tone of the utterance makes it possible for Lajwanti to bring her point home.

This conversation between Lajwanti and Virmati can be compared with the dialogue between Shakuntala (Lajwanti's daughter) and Kasturi:

> 'I hope I am not disturbing your convalescence, Chachi,' she said teasingly to her aunt.
>
> 'Beti', said Kasturi in a mock scolding voice, 'how can family disturb? You are getting very modern in your thinking. We hardly get to see you as it is.'
>
> 'What to do, Chachi? These colleges really make you work.'
>
> Hai re, beti! What is the need to do a job? A woman's shaan is in her home. Now you have studied and worked enough Shaadi.' Here Kasturi's eyes glistened with emotion. 'After you get married, Viru can follow.' (13)

As compared to the language used by the rest three, Shakuntala's language is more English-oriented in tone and structure. The set formula 'I hope I am not disturbing you' is essentially the English way of speaking where above all individuality of a person is maintained. However, Indian society in general prefers to be accepted and the individuality of a person is at risk when more social-oriented matters like that of family are brought in. That is why Kasturi says that she is getting modern in her thinking. Moreover, the words she uses, like 'convalescence', are not generally used by such characters who have not received enough education. The excess of Politeness shown by Shakuntala is aptly criticised by Kasturi's answer in the form of implicature—'how can family disturb?' It shows the ways in which the English and the Indian family relations are different, particularly the power and the solidarity enjoyed by different people. In the utterance—'Now you have studied and worked enough Shaadi', Kapur has broken the rules of English language and the foreigner may not be able to understand what is meant by 'enough Shaadi' unless s/he has some Indian background. Such type of features could be seen as peculiar to the language used mainly by the earlier generation characters, both men and women like Kasturi, Lajwanti, Suraj Prakash, Chandar Prakash, Lala Diwan Chand.

The language used by Shakuntala and that used by Virmati after she gets educated can be contrasted with the language used by the characters of the earlier generation. For example, the language used by the Professor and Virmati, when she is in Lahore pursuing her M.A. brings the point home:

> 'What if someone sees?' Virmati asked, trying for more sophistication in her nervous tone.
>
> 'Here, nobody cares who comes and goes,' replied the Professor soothingly.
>
> 'But suppose someone does?'
>
> The Professor pointed to the curtains. 'We are safe from prying eyes, my love,' he said. 'Take off your shoes. They must be hurting you. I know you hate shoes.'
>
> 'I bought these at a sale for three rupees, fifteen annas,' said Virmati in explanation. 'One rupee less.'
>
> The Professor did not reply. Instead he bent to slide off her sturdy black shoes. Hastily, not wanting his hand on her feet, Virmati bobbed down to take them off herself. 'It's all right', she mumbled.
>
> 'Would you like something to eat or drink? The bearer here is very nice.'
>
> More people to see. 'No, no,' Stammered Virmati, 'it's all right'.
>
> Harish sat next to her and held her hands. 'Why are you so nervous, darling? he asked. 'Do you feel you should not be with me?' (113)

The language used here is drastically different from the one employed by the characters of the earlier generation. Even the emotion like love is very effectively and successfully expressed by the Professor. What appears quite clear is that Kapur has acquired what Enkvist calls 'sense of style'—what to say when, where and to whom.

Besides, the novelist has also used Indian honorific like Baoji (9), Pehnji (9), Maji (7), Mati (10), Mumaji (7), Praji (60), Bua (15), Beti (7), Taiji (12), Chachi (13), Mamiji (45), Mamaji (45), etc. which give typical Indian sensibility to the novel. Again the interjections used by the characters are literal translations of Indian words. The English interjections would be out of place here. Interjections like *Arre* (16), *Bap re* (4), *He Bhagwan* (30), *Hai re* (13), *Arre wah* (8), *bas-bas* (73), *Are are* (73), etc. are used. It is interesting to note that most of the time these interjections are used by the characters of the earlier generation and not by the modern educated characters presented in the novel.

The Indian way of using English is also evident in expressions like:

Tell me, *na* (72)
Nice, *no* (179), etc.

Moreover, the novel abounds in the borrowing of Indian words like 'shaddi' (13), 'shann' (13), dai (8), kismet (13), Holi (21), Diwali (21), Swami (21), Kothi (21), gagjiar-mooli (44), bazzar (217), etc. There are, again, many examples of code-mixing and code-switching as and when Kapur thought they are necessary.

III

The analysis of the language of the novel underlines the ability of Kapur to use both Indian English and Standard English with equal ease as per the need of the situation. The researcher therefore thinks that the use of 'Indianized English' in the present novel is a stylistic device used with a very specific intention of providing Indian ethos rather than any lack of knowledge on the part of the writer in using English creatively. Verghese in conclusion to his book *Problems of the Indian Creative Writer in English* raises three questions to be asked for any piece of writing produced by Indian creative writer in English:

1. How fully is the writer, by using English instead of his own mother tongue, able to express the inwardness of his own culture?
2. How far can all aspects of his society be projected through English, when only a minority of his own people use English, and when vast areas of its culture

are primarily or totally linked to another language or group of languages, and to other traditions?

3. How far does the writer feel able to modify and augment the English language for his own particular purposes, and to what extent can he draw upon the other literary traditions of his society? (185)

In responding to these questions, though the answer in the present case is positive for all the questions, we need to ask the question: How long should we think of English language as the foreign language, in the sense that isn't it used now by Indian writers creatively enough to represent their cultural and social realities? The modern developments in Linguistics and Applied Linguistics and the works of Indian linguists particularly of Braj Kachru, Yamuna Kachru, S.N. Sridhar, and others have aptly pointed out that Indian English should be treated as a variety in its own right and should not be thought only as a deviance from the Standard English. Such a variety can be used by the Indian creative writer as a stylistic device to suit his purpose. Indian English as a special variety of English has its own features and characteristics which represent its culture and tradition. Why should then we ask the question whether the Indian creative writer succeeds in communicating his/her ethos in English, a foreign language, or not.

References

Enkvist, N.E., Spenser, John and M.J. Gregory. *Linguistics and Style.* London: OUP, 1964.

Hymes, Dell. "On Communicative Competence". In Pride J.B. & H. Holmes (eds.) *Sociolinguistics.* Hormondsworth: Penguin Books Ltd., 1972.

Kapur, Manju. *Difficult Daughters.* New Delhi: Penguin 1998. (All subsequent references are to this edition)

Lakoffm George and Mark Johnson. *Metaphors We Live By.* London: Uni. Of Chicago Press, 1983.

Leech, G. *Linguistic Guide to English Poetry.* London: Longman, 1969.

Levinson. *Pragmatics.* Cambridge: CUP, 1983.

Rao, Raja. *Kantapura.* New Delhi: OUP, 1947.

Selinker, Larry. "Interlanguage" *International Review of Applied Linguistics* X. 1972, pp. 209-30.

Verghese, C. Paul. *Problems of the Indian Creative Writer in English*. Bombay: Somaiya Publications, 1971.

Yule, George. *Pragmatics*. Oxford: OUP, 1996.

20

Renu Gavaskar's *Amcha Kai Gunha*? as *What's Our Crime?*: An Experiment in the Use of Translation Procedures

Manoj Gujar

The methodology of translation is dependent on the nature of the work to be translated. It is true that while translating a literary text, insistence on literal faithfulness is not always healthy, for it may produce an unreadable version.

The traditional debate on translation was centered on the problem of selecting the proper unit of translation—whether a word, a phrase, a sentence, a paragraph, a page or even (the 'spirit' of complex text) to be chosen for translation. Today, it has been widely accepted that what gets translated is not only a code but also the entire text with all its socio-cultural implications.

According to Newmark, there are two types of texts—one which would demand semantic translation and would remain as close as possible to the semantic and systematic structures of SL (Source Language) and the second set of texts would demand communicative translation and would aim to produce the same effect in the TL (Target Language) as was produced in the SL.[1] This classification is shown by Krishnaswamy et. al. as follows[2]:

Source Language Bias	Target Language Bias
Literal	Free
Faithful	Idiomatic
Semantic	Communicative

Newmark further states, "All translation must be in some degree, communicative and semantic, social and individual. It is a matter of difference of emphasis"[3]

Steiner observes that the art of translation lies in assessing:

(a) the type of translation required by the piece

(b) the right kind of strategies to be selected and integrated in the right proportion[4]

In his essay "Procedures and Strategies for the Translation of Culture", Ivir views translation as a communicative process. He further states: "Translating means translating cultures, not languages"[5]. The translator, he writes, makes use of such procedures as borrowing, definition, literal translation, substitution, lexical creation, omission, addition as well as their various combinations. What he means by these concepts is as follows:

(i) Borrowing

Borrowing means importing the source language expression in the target language. Once the expression enters the target language, it can be used freely in all the contexts and collections in which it is used in the source language.

(ii) Definition

This procedure relies on what members of the target culture know. It reduces the unknown to the known and the unshared to the shared.

(iii) Literal Translation

This procedure renders the source language expression faithfully in the target language.

(iv) Substitution

This procedure exploits the similarity between a source cultural element and its target cultural counterpart. It uses the corresponding target language expression as a full equivalent.

(v) Lexical Creation

This procedure involves coining a new word instead of borrowing a foreign word. This procedure is less frequently used than the above mentioned procedures.

(vi) Omission

This procedure involves the process of leaving out the source language cultural element.

(vii) Addition

This procedure makes explicit the implicit elements of source culture.

The present researcher selected Ms. Renu Gavaskar's Marathi book *Amcha Kai Gunha?* for his experiment of translation. This Marathi text is about personal experiences shared by Renu Gavaskar herself in the company of the inmates of Remand Home. The noted children's literature writer Dr. Sunilkumar Lavate has opined that during the last six decades of Independence, the Government of Maharashtra has not contributed anything special in reshaping, redeveloping any of the Remand Homes all over the state of Maharashtra. This clearly indicates the sad story and plight of such forced dwellings and its dwellers. The inmates of these homes have numbers instead of names which tell us about their lost identity. For the government and the police these inmates are cases and files whereas for social workers they form mere case studies. Very few try to approach or adopt these destitutes. The source text *Amcha Kai Gunha?* published by Manovikas Publication in December 2006 expresses the pangs and agonies of these suffering children. Different chapters narrate the sad and heart-rending tales of different protagonists like Vijay, Mahendra, Satya, Sunil, Narayan, Munna, Arjun, Noor, Dinesh, Pundalik and Bhairav. Renu Gavaskar's *Amcha Kai Gunha?* invites the kind attention of the people, and also of the Non Governmental Organizations (NGO's), to enrich the living standard of the unfortunate inmates. The inmates spend a very short span of their life here, but the stain of the Remand Home marks a permanent impression on their lives which disturb their social life. The translator chose Gavaskar's book for translation from Marathi into English because English translation of the book would make available Renu Gavaskar's moving and touching account to the English-knowing readers all over the world.

Taking a point of departure from Vladimir Ivir's essay 'Procedures and Strategies for the Translation of Culture', the present translator used different procedures such as BORROWING, DEFINITION, LITERAL TRANSLATION, SUBSTITUTION, OMISSION, ADDITION as well as their various combinations while translating Renu Gavaskar's *Amcha Kai Gunha?* as *What's Our Crime?*

The procedure of BORROWING, which means importing Source Language expression in the Target Language, has been used as follows:

> *Andaje chalis, panchechalis mulanna dambaleli ti kholi kinkalya, aarda-orda ani atyanta karkashya suraat mhantaleli bhajana yanni bharun geli hoti* (16)
>
> The room, in which nearly forty to forty-five children had been locked, was filled with screams, shouts and *bhajans* sung in extremely coarse voice. (24)
>
> *khokichya madhyabhagi 'Hare Rama, Hare Krishna' cha gajar chalu hota.* (16)
>
> There was a recital of *'Hare Ram Hare Krishna'* in the middle of the room. (24)
>
> *Aatmadhye chalnari dhumashchakri don-tin tas mandawalyamule baherche Mawsaab (shipayanna mulanni marnyachi haak) mulanche thode mitra hou pahat hote.* (20)
>
> The lessening of fighting among the boys also made 'Mawsaab' (peons) friends of the boys. (26)
>
> *ya saryacha shewat "Mera Bechara Andha Laal' ya shabdani hoi.* (26)
>
> On all such occasions she would call him *"mera bechara andha laal."* (30)

> *Talyanchya kadkadat mandavalyawar Khairnar hasun mhanale, "Gawkarbai" pudhchya sarva bhetit Khairnarani majha nao Gawkarach thewale.* (35)
>
> Once the clapping was over, Khairnar said with a laugh, "*Gavkarbai*," (instead of Gavaskar, Khairnar went on calling me 'Gavkar' throughout his next visits) (38)
>
> *pan aamhich sarva mulansathi batatewade anayche tharawale.* (35)
>
> we made the provision of around hundred and twenty five batatawadas for all the participants. (38)
>
> *Udaharanacha dyaycha jhala tar amchya mulanche te "bole to, mar gaya re bappa" ase shabda Varshachya ganyachya class madhun yenari mule sahaj uchalat.* (118)
>
> for example, they found their children copying the slang expressions such as *'bole toh'*, *'mar gaya re bappa'* from the boys of David Sassoon. (90)

The procedure of DEFINITION, which relies on what members of the target culture know and which reduces the unknown to the known and the unshared to the shared, has been used as follows:

> *ya janivechi pahili kal umatali ti mumbaitil Matunga stationsamor aslelya David Sassoon Industrial School ya sansthetil gajaadchi mule pahatana.* (10)
>
> I felt the falsity of what Sane Guruji said while looking at the boys behind the bars of David Sassoon Industrial School located in front of Matunga railway station in Mumbai. (20)
>
> *namanala phar tel na jalta mulani tya navin mulachi goshta sangayala suruvat keli.* (13)
>
> Without taking much time children started telling the story of that child. (22)
>
> *tyatunach vadilani aaichi hatya keli ani tila chakka purun takala.* (13)
>
> Their two sons and two little daughters used to get frightened whenever their parents quarreled. Due to

these quarrels the father killed their mother and to their shock buried her. (22)

khas parvangichi bandista sansthanmadhye agdi kshullak goshitahi parvangicha bau kela jato. (15)

The process of granting special permission was over (such prisonlike institutions **make much of permissions to do trivial things**) (23)

Helen Keller ani tichi shikshak Anne yanchi ***goshta vilakshan rangali.*** (20)

The story of Helen Keller and her teacher Anne **cast its spell on them.** (26)

mihi ***khushichi gajare khat*** *ratri nau vajta ghari paratale.* (39)

I also returned home at 9 o'clock **expecting the success of the show.** (41)

David Sassoonchya mulani natak aksharshaha dokyavar ghetala. (35)

It was an excellent performance. Indeed, **the boys** of David Sassoon **gave a thunderous response to it.** (38)

Anna buildingpashi pohochalyavar matra ***maze avasan galala.*** (40)

All of them followed us. When we reached Anna Building **I lost my control.** I asked Shri. Kakade to go ahead and I stood standing near one wall. (42)

phakta tondatun pokal khunache sudache shabda umtat hote. (44)

All that agony had starkly reflected in his eyes. **There was no real substance in his threats of destruction** of revenge. (46)

Mahendrahi aplya pahilya pagarache pedhe gheun ala. Sare kase aalbel aah ase vatale. (48)

There was a report that he was behaving well. He came to meet me with sweets after getting his first salary. He used to come frequently. **It appeared that there was no need to worry about him at all.** (48)

pan shalechya velat mhanje ek te char madheye he shakya hot nase; karan amhi baher yevun zadachya savlit basalo ki vargavargatun baina karangali dakhvun mula baher padaychi ani amchya vargat dakhal vhyachi. (66)

because whenever we started our class outside under the shade of the tree, **children from other classes used to join our class by giving a false pretext of going to the urinal to their teachers.** Therefore, we had to close down our experiment of open education against our will. (60)

pan shikayla, shikvayla konte madhyam upyogat aanave, kuthala abhyaskram parinamkarak tharel, kay kele asta mulana vargat, vargabaher abhyas karnyasathi ras vatel yavishayi vichar pakka hoina. (70)

However, I had no any concrete policy about the medium, the curriculum, and the methods of teaching inside and outside the class rooms. I was not also sure about succeeding in imparting education to the boys of David Sassoon. (63)

aapan aagitun nighun phuphatyat tar padlo nahi na, ashi shanka tyana bhedsavat ase. (72)

The boy, who has been admitted to the Remand Home, wonders, whether this inside life will be more terrifying than the kind of life he lived outside. (64)

tar asa divyatun tavunsulakhun baher yenarya mulanparyant shikshanachi ganga pohochavane he tyana asra devu karnarya sansthansathi pharach avaghad kam ahe. (73)

Definitely, **the task of imparting education to the children, who undergo several trials,** is very difficult for the institutions which provide shelter to them. (65)

chotya Anandla aplya aaicha vilakshan lala hota. itkaki shalet jaychi vel aali ki ***mayalekanna brahmand athvaycha.*** (81)

When the time of joining the school came in his life, **he found it difficult to part with the company of his mother.** (70)

Sunil eka veshyecha mulga hota va sagale purush baikade 'bai' mhanunacha baghatat ashi tyachi khatri hoti. Pan pudhe to pushakal badalala. (105)

Sunil, who was a son of a prostitute and who **believed that all men are interested in enjoying merely sexual pleasures with** women, had no interest in the festival but later changed immensely. (82)

pitrupandhravadyachya kalat *anath, garib, vanchit samajala janarya mulana dan denyachi agdi ahmhmikach lagte.* (105)

I remember one more similar occasion. During the second half of the Hindu month of Bhadrapada, which is known as 'Pitrupandhrawada' (the period of serving food to the departed dears), there is a lot of competition to offer food to the orphans and the beggars. (83)

ya vadhdiwasachya camity madhye camlinchya Dandekar aaji amchya barobar agdi suruvatipasun hotya. Yani ***oukshanacha*** *mudda upastit kela.* (110)

The old Smt. Dandekar of Camlin proposed the practice of adopting the **Hindu ritual of** moving **a lamp in a circular motion.** (86)

tyancha ***keshvapan*** *kela jat hote ha itihas mulana agdi navkha hota.* (117)

They didn't know that girls used to be married very early, they used to become widows very early, and **they used to suffer the humiliating loss of all their hair.** (89)

tyachya aaine tyala kshanbhar javal ghetale va ***'yete re'*** *ase sangun ti nighun geli.* (130)

when Dinesh went rushing to her, she took him in her embrace for a while, **bade him farewell, and left never to return.** (95)

Pundalikache ekandra vyaktimatwa ***vagale hote.*** (143)

Pundalik was a boy of an altogether different metal. (102)

aata aapli vyavastit ***'puja'*** *honar yavishayi tyachya manta kontihi shanka nasaychi.* (150)

> The boy, who used to climb up the tree with full of winning spirit, felt the shock of being identified. He knew very well that **he would be punished** by the watchman. (105)
>
> *tyachya* ***safaidar uchalegiripudhe sarvanni haat tekale*** *va sunilchi swari David Sassoonmadhye pravesh karti zali.* (154)
>
> However, all the workers of Children's Home, Chembur got faded up with his systematic methods of thefts and as a result of which, he was admitted to David Sassoon. (107)
>
> *Pravinla phatke det to mhanala, 'chori karnyapeksha bahinina pathvun de ek diwas majhyakade'.* (163)
>
> The vendor not only gave him two or four slaps but also said to him, **"Send your sisters as prostitutes to me instead of stealing things."** (113)

The procedure of LITERAL TRANSLATION, which renders the source language expression faithfully in the target language, has been used as follows:

> *tyamule malaji sayankali don tas mulanbarobar kholit 'taka' ase mhantalyabarobar tyani utsahane majhya suchaneche swagat kele.* (15)
>
> They welcomed my suggestion to 'throw' me inside along with the boys for two hours in the evening. (23)
>
> *to sagala kal mi punha ekda patiwar 'ga ma bha na' girvit hote.* (21)
>
> Throughout that period, I was once again practicing the alphabets A, B, C, D on the slate. (28)
>
> *Bahot achaha! Bahot achaha! ase mhanat nighun jai.* (24)
>
> When I began to complete it after an hour or two, he would stand up and leave saying, "Very good, Very good." (29)
>
> *'koham' . . . 'mi kon ahe?' . . . asa prashna pratyekane swatahala vicharawa ashi shikwan ahe aplyala.* (43)

> It has been taught to us to raise one question, 'koham' (Who am I?) (45)
>
> *me kahise bhay, kahishi aashanka chehryavar dakhvit mhantale, "bapre, tu jagachach khun karnar, mhanje aata mazhehi phar diwas rahile nahit ase mhan na*! (45)
>
> Pretending fear and anxiety on my face, I said, "Oh my goodness, if you are going to destroy the world, say then, that I am also not going to live for long." (46)
>
> Pungiwala. (114)
>
> Chapter Title: The Piper (88)
>
> *Ghar deta ka ghar . . .* (129)
>
> Chapter Title: Home, Sweet Home (95)
>
> *dupari char vajta shala ani karyashala yanchi vel sampali ki mule pudhacha did tas aksharshaha dhudgus ghalit.* (149)
>
> Immediately after closing of the school and workshop at 4 o'clock, the boys used to spend their time in wild wrangling for the next one and half hour. (105)
>
> *ani vartul purna jhale . . .* (166)
>
> Chapter Title: And I came Full Circle (116)

The procedure of SUBSTITUTION, which exploits the similarity between a source cultural element and its target cultural counterpart and which uses the corresponding target language expression as a full equivalent, has been used as follows:

> majhe shaleya shikshan Saneguruji Vidyalayat jhale. 'Kari manoranjan jo mulanche, jadel nate prabhushi tayache' ase sangnare Saneguruji thithe bhetale. 'Mule hi devagharachi phule' he shaleche bridavakya hote. (10)
>
> I completed my education in Sane Guruji High school. Here I met Sane Guruji who used to say, 'Whoever entertains children, will develop relationship with God'. The Motto of the School was 'Children are flowers, bloomed in the garden of God'. (20)

anandi, dukhkhi, karun, prernadayi, naitik mulye shikvanarya asha goshti tar najresamor aalyach pan ya vyatirikt parikatha, lokkatha, dantkatha, ashahi anek kathaprakarani dokyat gardi keli. (14)

My **mind was filled** with not only tales full of joys, sorrows, values but also fairy tales, folk tales, and legends. (23)

mulanna 'khairnarsab' ani tyanci ***'vadali karkird'*** *thauk aslyane talyanchya kadkadat tyanche swagat jhale.* (35)

The boys welcomed him with loud clapping as they knew 'Khairnar Saab' and his **'eventful career'.** (38)

ya shibirat don-tin goshti asha ghadlya ki tya ***dipstambhacha*** *tharavyat.* (35)

During the camp, there took place two to three activities which could be called as **milestone** activities. (38)

pan prayog karun natkatil mule damli tar hotich shivay tyanna bhukahi lagli hoti. Yamule mulanni vadyancha ***phadsha*** *padayale suruvat keli.* (35)

They began to **devour** wadas. (38)

to mulga aksharshaha oksabokshi radat hota. (36)

It was found that he had lost his shirt. The boy was crying **violently.** (39)

tya purchundikade pahtana amcha kantha datum ala. ***Lakhmolache te bakshish*** *hatat ghatta dharun amhi baher padlo.* (36)

It was difficult to control our tears while looking at that package of wada. We left holding **that most valuable gift** in our hands tightly. (39)

(sansthetil mulanni gairvartan kelyas Bhivandiche remand home kimwa david Sassooncha bagulbuwa tyana dakhvilyas ti vathniwar yetat, asa sarvasadharan anubhav ahe) (38)

(It was generally observed that the condition of the boys improved whenever they were threatened to be sent to Remand Home at Bhiwandi or David Sassoon in Mumbai.) (40)

dusre divshi sakali aath vajta david sassoonla pohochale. Praveshdarapashi mule vat baghatana disli aani ***chatit dhassa jhale.*** (39)

Next day, I reached David Sassoon at 8 o'clock in the morning. When I saw some boys waiting for me at the gate, **I was shocked.** (41)

me haslyavar hasla. Pan aajcha hasu nehmicha hasu navhata. Kahisa ***malul hasala to.*** (41)

He laughed when I laughed. But it was not his usual laugh. **It was a bit disheartening laugh.** (43)

shevati Dr. Kailash Satyarthina madhye padave lagala ***temvha kuthe sagli chakra bharabhar phirayala lagli.*** (56)

It was only when Dr. Kailash Satyarthi intervened that **the entire** machinery **geared up.** (54)

dahavichya vargachya sandharbhat asa ek baherchya jagat rahanarya manasancha ***zakas sangha staphan jhala hota.*** **(74)**

It was a very homogeneous group in which nobody would take objection to the allotment of the work. (66)

hamkhas yashachi gurukilli *konti va ti kashi milvayachi ya vishayi amhi sarecha andharat hoto.* (74)

We were absolutely in dark about **the pattern of success** at the secondary examination. (66)

pakshacha dola (88)

Chapter Title: **The** Target (74)

sari sandhyakal itha-titha bhataknyat ghalvun Arjun ***divelagnichya sumaras ghari parat yaycha.*** (90)

Arjun could not bear the idea of going home after the school. He would spend time wandering here and there and **return home late in the evening.** (75)

yache karan ase ki J.J.School of Arts la ***pravesh milnyachi swapna pahane mhanje agdi gaganala gavasani ghalnyasarkhe*** *asle tari nidan Bandra School* *of Arts che swapna aavakyat yenyasarkhe ahe, ase jamavalelya mahitivarun vatat hote.* (92)

I was planning to send him to Bandra School of Art as admission to the J. J. School of Art seemed to be an impossible affair... (76)

parantu shri Lance Dane ni ***magephude na baghata*** *Arjunla aplya ghari thevun ghenyache Kabul kele.* (93)

Shri. Lance Dane **took a very bold decision** of providing shelter to Arjun in his own house. (76)

khup varshapurvi sodun aalelya aplya ***aaila ani bhavandana*** *bhetayche hote tyala.* (96)

He wanted to meet his **mother and his family** whom he had left long long back in Bangladesh. (78)

he janun ghenyacha prayatna karit astana ek asa anubhav ala ki ***jyache nav te***! (103)

When I myself tried to know about these, **I had a very unusual experience.** (81)

Santosh Katkade ya mulakade ***Kotwalachi*** *bhumika ali.* (117)

Santosh Katakade was going to play the role of **the Police Chief.** (90)

matra Mohan agdi shant hota. Yat phar kahi viprit ghadalaya, ase tyala mulich vatle nahi. ***'Roj mare tyala kon rade!'*** (119)

For Mohan, there was nothing shocking about the tight slap because **violence was so common inside David Sassoon.** (91)

Pundalik mati kalavatana disla ki tyanchya dokyat agdi tidik jai. (143)

He used to lose his temper whenever he found him mixing clay. (102)

ha barik tap agdi mahinabhar tikla. ***Tya ajarat Pundalikachi par raya geli.*** (145)

He grew thin and later started suffering from fever for many days. He grew **very weak.** (103)

ti majhya bahinila mhanali ki dadane sadi anli ki nahi vichar. ***He aiklya barobar majhe talkacha satakala.*** *Tashich bag uchalali ani gharachya baher padlo.* (146)

When my mother saw me, she failed to notice my illness. She said to my sister to ask me whether I had bought a saree for her. After **hearing this, I lost my control.** I collected my bag and left immediately. (103)

asha ritine amcha toy libraricha ***Shriganesha*** *jhala.* (151)

Our activity of toy library **commenced** in order to provide toys to the sick children so that they could start playing with these toys when the other boys played on the playground. (106)

daruvarche avalambitwa tya kalat bhanayak vadhale. Daruchya nashet baherchi kame ti retaychi pan ghari aali ki padun rahaychi. (162)

She started depending too much upon alcoholic drinks. **She used to work hard, but lie in a drunken stupor.** (112)

atta, yavelela kuthe asava yacha andaj bandhun mi Dadar stationchya pulapashi gele. Pulachya khali mulanchi ekach gardi usalali hoti. ***Kesanchi shiptare jhaleli, aksharshaha chindhya lyayleli ti mule kaslatari jallosh karit hoti.*** (199)

Instead making a guess about his whereabouts, I went to the bridge at the Dadar Railway Station. **A lot of boys, whose hair were unkempt, and indeed, who had wore rags, were busy enjoying something.** (129)

Jyachi bhiti vatate tyachya pasun dur janyapeksha, ***'drushtiaad shrushti'*** *ase swatahachya manane samadhan karun ghenyapeksha samor jane hacha upay shreyaskar.* (203)

We feel that instead of watching it, instead of confronting it, **it would be better to ignore it.** (132)

The procedure of OMISSION, which involves the process of leaving out the source language cultural element, has been used as follows:

ya mulanni majhe bot dharun majhya ya thikancha pahila dhada girvun ghetala ase vatale. (19)

In fact, these boys themselves made me teach one lesson in their own way. (26)

manala ek navi umed labhat hot. Varvar dhatingan disnari, samajane valit takleli mule. 'yach samajat vavarne samajhitala poshak nahi' asa ingrjanni kadhalela phatava shirodharya manun tyanchich ri odhit ya mulanna bar ate athra ya atyanta samvedenshil vayat dambun taknari va tyavishayi atishaya udasin asnari yantrana. (22)

These were the boys who appeared blustering and who were ostracized by the society. They were the victims of the indifferent system, which, following the order (their free life in the society is not healthy in the interest of the society) issued by the British, locked these boys up during their prime years from twelve to eighteen. (28)

pan vargat baslay mhanun roj abhyas karil yacha matra nem nase. Ekhade diwshi sutasarkhi saral asnari hi swari dusrecha diwshi vargat mala mule tras detat he nimitta karun mulanna kharpus chop det ase. (38)

Although he attended the class, there was no guarantee of his doing studies regularly. This boy, who used to be quite obedient on one day, started beating the boys on another day. (40)

mag halkech mhanala, "aaj tumhi mala sajuk tup vadhalet mhanje mi tumchya gharchach jhalo". (133)

He then said, "It does mean that you regard me as one of the members of your family. (96)

Pundalik tyancha motha mulga. Ha porga shekel, savarel, motha sahib hoil ani aplyala char sukhanche diwas dakhvil ya ashevar prapta paristhit jhunj denari hi mandali, tyana pundalikache kalasakta man samjat nase ki tyachya botatil jaduche aaklan hot nase. (143)

The father had high expectations from Pundalik, the eldest son of the family. They fought against the adversity with the hope that one day, the eldest son after his education, would become the government officer and bring happiness in their life. They failed to appreciate their son's artistic sensibility and the magic in his fingers. (102)

Aaichya sadichya chindhya baghvit nahit ase to mhanala hota. chindhya levun vathalelya tanamanala mulane anleli navi sadi baghun duumare phutale ani punha ekda mulga distach, vijesarcha apekshecha utkantha prashna tondatun nistala. (146)

During his previous visit Pundalik had carried a saree to his mother. Once he said that it was impossible for him to see his mother wearing a torn saree. The new saree brought by her son might have given an utmost sense of pleasure to her and when she had seen her son once again, she might have expected a similar gesture from him once again. (104)

Chapter 'The Prince and the Pauper' has been omitted because it contains the translated portion of different English books. It is relevant in the Marathi version, but, is largely irrelevant in the English translation of the book.

The procedure of ADDITION, which makes explicit the implicit elements of source culture, has been used as follows:

gelya khepi jya jhanjhavatacha ullekh kela tya jhanjhavatache naav Anand. (81)

His entry there at the age of fifteen lasted only for seven to eight months only, but during that period, he became the source of a lot of excitement and uproar. He emerged like a storm and disappeared like a storm, too. (70)

The combinations of such procedures as OMISSION and SUBSTITUTION have been used as follows:

Ulti ganga (70)

Chapter Title: Remand Home (63)

Shalevyatiriktacha sara vel doghehi ekmekansobat ghalvat tarihi shalet jatana pahili ek-don varaha

Anandachya ghashat avandha datum aala nahi ase jhale nahi. (81)

Little Anand was very fond of his mother. When the time of joining the school came in his life, he found it difficult to part with the company of his mother. (70)

majhya ya vakyanantar tya kholit kharokhar smashan shantata pasarali. Kharokharach tachani padli tari aawaz yeyil yewdhi shantata. Arjun kamalicha ghabarlela hota. pan kshanbharane to ubha rahila. Tyane swatahala sawarle. Atishay kaprya awajat, jamel titkya shantpane to mhanala, 'mi ithe rahun shiknar ahe, mi punyala yenar nahi. Ani alo tari parat palun jain." (95)

In the midst of utter silence, Arjun somehow managed to regain his confidence and declared his decision 'to continue his education in Mumbai.' (77)

Nur bangaladeshcha rahivashi. Tyachya lahanpani vadil zadavarun paddle aani allala pyare jhale. (98)

Noor lost his father very early in his life. (78)

Dinesh swabhawana atyanta soumya hota. Bhandan, shivya, maryamarya yanchya vatyalahi to ubha rahat nase. Aapan bare ki apla abhyas bara asa tyacha khakya hota. (130)

Dinesh was otherwise an extremely polite child. So the officials at Children's Home would find it difficult to punish him. He was finally sent to the closed shelter of David Sassoon. (96)

tarihi tyane barach vel Pradhananshi hujjat ghatali pan ithe aapli dal shijnar nahi he janavlyavar nirupayane to parat phirla. (200)

When Pradhan refused to hand over the key to him, Balu tried to persuade him very much. When he realized that it would not be possible to get the key from Pradhan, he went away helplessly. (130)

To conclude, the present translator made use of one or the other of Ivir's procedures in his experiment taking into consideration the nature of the cultural term to be translated from Marathi into English. A non-literary text was selected for translation from Marathi into English and the methodology of 'literal' translation was preferred to that of 'free' translation. The translator first decomposed the text into single elements (or small groups of elements) and then replaced each into a corresponding element (or group) in the target language. It was observed that the procedures of SUBSTITUTION and DEFINITION needed to be used more widely than the other procedures of translation.

Notes

The following text has been used for the experiment:

Renu, Gavaskar. 2006. *Amcha Kai Gunha*? Pune: Manovikas Prakashan.

1. Peter, Newmark. 1981. *Approaches to Translation*. Oxford: Pergamon.
2. Krishnaswamy, 1992. *Modern Applied Linguistics*. Macmillan India Ltd.
3. Peter, Newmark. Opt. cit. p. 62.
4. T.R. Stainer. 1975. *English Translation Theory: 1650–1800*. Amsterdam and Assen: Van Gorcum.
5. Vladimir, Ivir. 1975. *Procedures and Strategies for the Translation of Culture*. Indian Journal of Applied Linguistics.

21

A Translator Reflects

Shirish Chindhade

(I)

I had my first foray into the translation territory at a rather unadvisable young age when the desire to be known dominates discretion. This is how it happened. When I was a callow college boy, 'Albert Camus' *The Outsider* walked into our house and despite just a nodding acquaintance with the English language I finished reading the slender book fast as its size was the main inviting feature, hardly a hundred odd pages of crown size. Initially the book angered and even repelled me because the author killed the protagonist's mother in the very first—opening—sentence of the story. Even so I waded haltingly through the whole account of a first class murder-and-suspense story spiced up with the protagonist's emotionally insensitive, almost criminally uninvolved escapades into unbecoming events and inappropriate involvement in the insignificant doings of the world. I had a sense of relief to see the protagonist eventually getting behind the bars where he unexpectedly began to suffer the slings and arrows of his outrageous conscience. What is more, he understands for the first time in his maddening isolation in the prison cell how his mother must have felt and lived all alone and distanced by the only son to an old age home. He understands for the first time in his excruciating loneliness in his cell why his mother took a companion at such an advanced age in the old age home. I was relieved, almost satisfied, he suffers mentally, physically and spiritually as he waits for the heavy blade of the guillotine to fall on his neck. I clapped that after all, poetic justice prevailed! That was the plane of understanding then.

I kept the book away but it remained in my mind long after it was returned to its owner. In due course I graduated and post-graduated with English literature and began to teach English in a rural college. It was there once again that *The Outsider* surfaced in the college library stacks. I picked it up and read it again, this time at a single go. I had by now learned the language better and had also heard words like "absurd," "alienation," "existential angst," "rootlessness" as current literary jargon. This was the time when I took up *The Outsider* for translation into Marathi....

Ever since then I have been translating all kinds of writings from and into English and Marathi, but not necessarily because they have appealed to me. I have become a semi-professional translator and most of my translations are commissioned assignments ranging over wide areas such as criticism, poems, stories, essays, biographies, autobiographies, articles, monographs, film journalism, organizational histories, political accounts, memories, literary history, children's stories and what not! I simply cannot recall all the particulars. My only recollection every time is that the labour has earned me neither lucre nor limelight!

(II)

After having declared my efforts at translating as a non-profit engagement I would like to briefly turn to one translation of mine which I did for pure labour of love and as homage. About twenty years ago I worked in Nasik for a year or so, where I got acquainted with the popular local Marathi daily *Gavkari.* The sub-editor offered me a Sunday slot to write about some Indian English poets. I jumped at the chance as it was my familiar and favourite field, thanks to my MPhil and PhD research in the area. The original plan was to introduce a poet every week and translate a couple of his poems as samples. In order to shun the spectacle of the printer's devil waiting in the courtyard for a "copy," I wrote down the entire series at a go. I selected two poems each except for three poems each of A.K. Ramanujan and Arun Kolarkar, the former being my favourite and the latter irresistible. The entire wad was duly handed over to the sub-editor who had, meanwhile, changed his mind about poetry. Only the fourteen articles, one introduction and one epilogue were published. The poems were stayed hopefully not because they were unprintable as translations but because the Sunday pull-out could not spare inches for poetry! Eventually everything was gathered into a book.

(III)

I shall, now, turn to the translations and relate a few experiences while engaged in the activity. I had never visualized that the chain of challenges would start with the titles themselves! Let me sample a few of them.

I had selected the following two poems of Gauri Deshpande, namely, "Family Portraits" and "The Female of the Species." The first title I translated as "Kautumbik-chitre" and the second, "Stree-janma". When Gauri herself saw this she cried foul, pointing out that "Kutumbia" or "Kutumb-chitre" and "baaiche jine" would have been correct. On reflection I thought that my "Kautumbik-chitre" was too wide since *kutumb* is certainly a wide concept and Gauri wrote about her first relations. But I also thought *baaiche jine* was too colloquial for the original elevated phrase, "female of the species." This I thought echoed better in my *stree-janma* as it is allusive of the well-known Marathi verse, *Stree janmaa hee tujhi kahani/Hridayi amrit, nayani paani* (O life of woman, this is your story/With nectar in the heart and tears in the eyes)

As for Gieve Patel's "On Killing a Tree" I translated it as "Jhadachi hattya." However, when I look back upon it I tend to think of two more alternatives like, *jhad todtana* and *jhad todlyawar*. In the original poem the titular preposition "on" is enigmatic. It has multiple suggestions, of which two seem to suit here. They are, (i) immediately after and (ii) about. Patel describes the act of cutting down the tree step by step and in the same systematic order in which a tree is felled by a group of cutters. So, *jhad todlyawar* is ruled out. How about *jhad todtana*? Does it not suggest a continuity of an action? My choice of the word *hattya* had a Sanskrit aura and it was prompted by the verb "killing". Consequently, I am at peace with what I have done.

Here is one more example after which I will turn to other translational casualties! When Dilip Chitre read my translation of his "Father Returning Home" he pulled me up for my Sanskritized rendering of "returning home" as *gruhaagaman.* Perhaps, he thought that *Wadeel Ghari Yetana* would have been closer to the original. As for my rendering I had at the back of my mind the word "home-coming" which I thought had an impressive ring and parallel in *grihaagaman.*

I will conclude this segment here. However, I am glad that I had no occasion to meet most of the other poets; and even if I did, I would have been spared of close encounter and close shave, for they did not know Marathi! Let me turn to a short poem of Parthasarathy which occurs as section nine in Part II called "Trial" in the long poem *Rough Passage.* It is a very erotic metaphor of reunion with one's own culture, one's own language.

Here's the original poem:

From **Rough Passage**

Trial: IX

A knock on the door:
You entered.
Undressed quietly before the mirror

Of my hands. Eyes
Drowned in the skull
As flesh hardened to stone.

I have put aside the past
In a corner, an umbrella
Now poor in the ribs. The touch

Of your breasts is ripe
In my arms. They obliterate my eyes
With their tight parabolas of gold.

It's you I commemorate tonight.
The sweet water
Of your flesh I draw

With my arms, as from a well,
Its taste as ever
As on the night of Capricorn.

It's two in the morning:
My thoughts turn to you. With lamp
And pen I blow the dust off my past.

Come in, and see for yourself.
It's taken thirty odd years.
Now, a small hand will do.

My Marathi translation is as follows:

कसोटी-9

दारावर टक्टक्, अन् आलिस तू आत
निर्वसना झालिस हातांच्या आरशात

खोबणीत माझे डोले सखोल मिटले
पथ्थरले स्नायू देहातिल या सगले

कोपन्यात ठेवुन गतकालची छत्री
टोचली स्तनांची अग्रे माझ्या गात्री।

त्या तटतटलेल्या कांचनगोलाधौनी
घेतली हिरावून दृष्टी माझ्या नयनी

डत्सवात तुझिया रात्र साजरी होत
आकंठ प्राशितो तुझ्या झऱ्यांचे स्रोत

रात्रीची घटका गडद, मनी तव खूल
शब्दांत उधलतो गतकालाची धूल

पाहण्या आपुल्या डोल्यांनी ये आत
वर्षांच्या विरहानंतर दे तव हात।

आर् पार्थसारथी

The original English poem is entirely in a triad stanza form of three short lines, unrhymed. I took some liberty as well as accepted certain restrictions while doing it into Marathi. I compressed the original twenty-four lines into fourteen lines. The restriction was a rhymed couplet with a marked metrical rhythm. I cannot tell why I did this. Possibly I felt that the original one was highly lyrical and liquid in mood which could be suitably recaptured in a conventional metrical beat only. To quote Alexander Pope, "I lisped in numbers for the numbers came." You have to tell me how my Marathi rendering sounds.

When I actually translated the poems I was not conscious of the process going on in my mind. I believe, no translator is. However, I can, at this stage of having distanced myself from the exercise for composing the present essay, think of five guiding principles that seem to have helped me for my translations.

They are:

1. Even the title of a literary unit is not a stand-alone addition; it is an extract of the total content of the unit. Therefore, its translation will have to be done mainly with reference to the content of the unit.
2. Different translators will approach one and the same unit differently for different reasons. This will depend on their individual personality and linguistic competence. In other words, there can be different translations of the same unit by different translators. (Kalidas's *Meghdoot* is an excellent case in point; there are at least one dozen translations of it in Marathi done by very well-known poets.)
3. The translation of a poem cannot cross over to any other form than a poem only without losing all the original appeal of the form. However, a translation in another sub-form within the genre is acceptable. In other words, an original sonnet can be translated as a lyric or a poem, and *vice versa*.
4. While translating a poem its "meta-phrase" (verbatim translation) can be misleading and graceless. In stead,

its "paraphrase" translation (the overall content with all other rules of rhythm, metre, rhyme scheme, musical effects, if any, taken care of) can work well. In other words, it is convenient—and advisable—to treat a whole (short) poem as a single unit and not as separate lines. A line-by-line translation of a poem is usually clumsy.

5. Neither add nor subtract: a failed translation is one in which some—important—content of the original is missed out; an "artful" translation is one in which some new content is added by the translator. An uncritical reader has no way to ferret out either the omission or the commission.

(IV)

Having reflected on my own experiences and observations about translating I would now like to turn to some more serious thinking. In fact, there are a few questions knocking about my head and I wish to put them down here for consideration. Until I sat down to compose this paper I had never given an analytical thought to my translations. I have been a practitioner and not a theorist of translation. I think that ten smart theories of translation cannot produce one faultless work. That responsibility is shouldered by persons like me who are willing to receive drubbing or are immune to neglect and indifference.

Here are the questions.

- One sees a spate of Marathi translations of pulp fiction, self-improvement and management books. Most of the modern classics in various languages of the world go unnoticed. What purpose do such (popular) translations serve beyond entertainment?
- English is emerging fast almost as a *lingua franca* in India. If at all people choose to read, will they rather go to the original or resort to a translation? Will there be any need for translations?
- Languages are being neglected the world over so much so that many of them are classified as

endangered species; many of them have already reached extinction. As teachers of literature it is our common and ubiquitous experience that even our post-graduate students of literature are scandalously bad at linguistic competence. In such a situation who will be the translators of tomorrow?

- Since as a rule translators are never elevated to the class of writers, will new translators be available?
- Reading habits are declining fast and visual media addiction is fast on the rise. Will there be any need for translations at all?
- Of all the literary forms poetry is the least preferred one for translations and eventual publication. Twenty-five years hence will poetry be read at all, far less translated (and published)?
- Computer generated translations are becoming available. When computers take over all our intellectual and–even—emotional functions in the near future, where will be the need for human translators?

22

On Translating Amritlal Vegad's *Amritasya Narmada*

Apara Tiwari

The idea to translate the Hindi version of the second book, *Amritasya Narmada,* (winner of Sahitya Academy Award 2004 for the Gujarati version) was owing to the world-wide audience of English it would reach. The translation I believed would help in transmitting the rich culture and emotions of India, helping in humanitarian causes; certainly a boost for the humble efforts. Narmada is a river of beauty for Sri Amritlal Vegad. The picturesque charm of her meandering course along the mountains, plains, through forests and rocky terrain is awe-inspiring. To capture her beauty and splendour completely, Sri Vegad embarked on a *parikrama* (circumambulation) in piecemeal and walked more than 2600 kms on foot. The journey inspired him to write *Saundarya Ki Nadi Narmada* and *Amritasya Narmada*, initially in Gujarati and then in Hindi. These two books by him are travelogues enriched by a medley of cultures, social customs and traditions and have won many regional awards in Hindi and Gujarati.

Narmada is an object of religious faith and devotion. Over the years, this ancient concept has intensified and pulsates with life, more than ever, for many. Curiosity to read the books is aroused due to Narmada's significant status of being the only Indian river around which the ritualistic tradition of holy *parikrama* (circumambulation) is performed barefoot by devotees. Sri Vegad has mentioned that the river holds a superior status to the Ganga because one gains virtue by its mere sight, while one has to take a dip in the Ganga to gain virtue. This is the reason why devotees performing the religious ritual of Narmada *parikrama* do not lose sight of it for a single moment.

The primary aim of the artist turned writer, as the titles of the books also suggest, however, is to bathe his readers in its unmatched flowing beauty. Sri Vegad has effectively portrayed its splendour through the surrounding culture and glimpses of the environmental vibrancy strewn in its entire course on both the banks. Etched by myths, anecdotes and above all by the richly coloured rustic verve, a loveliness felt and found in the tender hearts of men living in its surroundings, Sri Vegad has proved his ingenuity which has reached deep down the hearts of many. Once a student of fine arts at Shantiniketan, under the tutelage of the great painter, Nandlal Bose, he has sketched his penchant for the arts most befittingly in words.

Furthermore, this Narmada *padyatra* (journey on foot) endows the writer with a singular pleasure which he shares with his readers. The book embodies feelings of thousands of regional inhabitants around the river. Quite naturally the book offers a glimpse into the culture of rural India through poetic imagery which enhances the thrill and romance of the adventure. Personifications, exercise of wit, word-play, pun and metaphorical idioms arouse emotions of love, fear, humour, pathos and awe. The artist's creativity in the two books makes one realise that one's path to experience such a spiritual bliss is finally paved. It is amazing how he sees the river for instance, as an affectionate and caring mother at one time and a bubbly girl in her early teens at another. The author amazes all the more when he shares his bonds with the river as intimately as he would with his beloved. The river has become integral to Vegad's life for the sake of its unmatched natural beauty.

Above all, the author has included his readers in his team, and takes them with him on the journey. This way the reader is also able to perform Narmada *parikrama* with him. Sri Vegad's simple and unpresumptuous writing has inspired more men and women of all sections of society to take up one of the most arduous journeys along the Narmada banks and has generated a feeling of oneness, a means for improved humanity.

The idea to translate the Hindi version of the second book, *Amritasya Narmada*, occurred to my husband while I discussed both the books with him soon after my first reading. The idea lingered but was fated to embers. Very soon I had an opportunity to present a research paper titled "Twain's Mississippi and Vegad's Narmada: A Comparative Study", in Madurai, dated 22-23 January 2004 at a workshop organised jointly by American Consulate, Chennai and SIASN. As luck would have it, a retired Professor and Head of the Department of English (St. Joseph's Convent Autonomous College, Trichy) Prof. V. Richard present there, expressed interest in them and suggested that I should translate Sri Vegad's work in English. He had kindled those dwindling embers again. I had hardly emerged from the thrilling effect of his work when I jumped to grab the opportunity, the sooner it came. Sri Vegad's joyful consent to plunge into the venture for the second volume, *Amritasya Narmada* strengthened my already bursting enthusiasm and with pen in hand I sat with poise hardly realizing what hardships lay in store.

My prime desire to take up the challenge was owing to the world-wide audience of English it would reach. The translation I believed would help in transmitting the rich culture and emotions of India, helping in humanitarian causes; certainly a boost for the humble efforts.

The difficulties began at the outset, with the very word *parikrama*. But I could not come to terms with the English word 'circumambulation' and disagreed that it could say it all. Obviously it doesn't! The reason being, it is a word to word translation and the arousal of ethnic enrichment is instantly lost, leaving the word flat. Therefore I decided to use the word as it is, that is, I considered a transliteration of it as the best alternative to keep the ethos intact, and to show the meaning in the footnotes. In effect, a translation is creditable if it is transcreated I felt.

Other words had a similar fate. (along with the key helpers—(*parikramavasi* and the distorted local utterings; *parkamma*). Scattered throughout the book, there are words and expressions like *sadavrat, dhooni ramana, purnimasi, khichdi, dal–bati, sadhu, sadhvi, amavasya, bhai, mai, sanyasi, kutiya, chaturmas, dharamshala, shivling, pair pakharna, mahant, bindiya, rangoli, purna-kumbh, sitaram,* etc. Some words do have synonyms in English but are not complete in meaning as far as the feeling and its effect in the original is concerned. This suggests that a language of any region takes its shape depending upon its cultural set up. They can be expressed by 'full moon' for *purnamasi* or by 'rest house for pilgrims' for *dharamshala* but the cultural or religious fragrance the original term emits cannot become a pleasurable experience for the reader if articulated this way. Struggling to penetrate with the help of English into expressions like *are bhai, sadavrat, dhooni ramana, bindiya, pair pakharna* became pathetic for me. They were like losing out in an encounter. This is because these words are steeped in the genesis of one of the most ancient cultures associated with faith and devotion.

To be more precise, if Gujarati, Bangla, Malayalam or Punjabi is translated into Hindi, Marathi, Telugu or Assasmese the difference between that produced by the original and the translated version will be less because both the languages belong to a common Indo-Aryan family. But if it is translated into English there would inevitably the gaps,which a discerning reader will take note of when the two are read one after the other. This is so because English is a foreign, rather a Western language with an entirely different culture. I felt limitations of English at this stage although it is considered to be one of the most popular and most spoken languages of the world.

Then there are expressions and phrases which are nuances of human attitude in a cultural set up with a telling affect. For e.g. *are bhai*! *tapana parta hai ! kitna bojha lekar chala hai dokra!* or even *narmada maiya ki jai* and narmade *har!*

To find an equivalent of certain words proved to be a lot more of mental exercise, where I tried to coin, frame and even reframe expressions which could at least be nearest not only in meaning but also in that typical attitude and tone of speech. For e.g. — *totka ajmana, bidaai, surya-namaskar, samudra manthan, shani ki sarhe saati,* etc. Similar difficulty was encountered with the author's own coinages like, '*perchalisa*' coined from '*hanuman chalisa*' , '*sarit manduk*' coined from '*kup manduk*', '*jeerna to ho gaya hoon par sheern nahi hua. Chust bhale hi na raha par durust to hoon*'. Then there are emotions expressed which can be identified only in a particular tongue. For e.g. when he says that he felt like coming to his daughter's house; she asks "what should I prepare for your food? What would you like?" The subtle emotion is conveyed only when expressed thus; "*kaka shun banavun? Shun jamvani ichcha che?* " I kept on refining, sharpening and chiseling my work whenever I re-read extracts I was not happy with, but complete satisfaction became a remote possibility. Once Sri Vegad also advised me to be more natural as he felt I was more literary. I re-tried. I also began dropping high sounding words at his suggestion.

With metaphors, similes and application of appropriate proverbs and idioms, folk songs was another hard nut to crack. For example: choon *choon ka murabba, bhagte bhoot ki langoti, til-til kar nikalna, chulha phunkna, maara-maara phirna, gussa satven asmaan par chadna,* etc. These are offspring of culture as well, and although the meaning is conveyed through English, yet the appeal is not the same.

Dr. V. Richard once shared with me an interesting fact. He said, English was a language of warriors, hence it is male. Indian languages have their genesis in *sanskriti* and *dharma* (for convenience' sake translated as culture and religion), hence feminine.

The beauty of Sri Vegad's style I feel lies in his wit and humour, in arousing pathos, laughter, to make one smile and shock the reader by some unlikely comparison or even to make someone shed a tear, or arouse compassion, to pass a mild satirical or ironical remark. Translating all this beauty and nectar, especially in English, is not at all a child's play.

I am not even an amateur in this genre, but I plunged to try my hand in it for the sole purpose of spreading the beauty and nectar of Narmada's singularity to worldwide audience, with the ardor of Sri Vegad's simplicity. With how much success have I been able to swim across this river's simplicity I am not sure, but I am happy to have at least experienced this grueling yet enjoyable task. I also feel this was also an excuse destined for me, by which I was fortunate to learn a great deal from him.

Extracts from the English translation of *Amritasya Narmada* by me, comprising the fifth chapter has been published in Vol. xxii, No. 4, 2005 and the first three chapters in Vol. xxiii, No. 4, 2006 of a Quarterly Journal of Literature and Culture, *Pratibha India*, edited by Sitesh Aloke, published by Sneh Bharti, New Delhi. One more extract is accepted and will be published soon. An account of my experience to translate the book has also been published by a Quarterly, *Anuvad* Vol. 137, 2008 of Bharatiya Anuvad Parishad, New Delhi.

Sri Vegad continues to perform his *padyatras* regardless of his age. At present he is above 80. He has taken up *padyatras* of the tributaries of Narmada and has completed the *parikrama* of Budhner, Banjar, Hiran and is planning for Shakkar in his next trip. Hindi articles of these lesser yet not so insignificant journeys have been published in a journal Pahal. The first part of the account of Budhner venture has also been translated in English by me and published by the same journal, *Pratibha India* Vol. xxv, No. 3, 2008 and the second part is in process.

The nature of Sri Vegad's aesthetic sense combined with his simple conversational style has not only made the two books consummate but has also immortalised Narmada's beauty, loved by so many. The Gujarati and Hindi versions of the books have limited readers in the three states of India in which the river originates flows and terminates. The Marathi and the Bangla translations have expanded the horizons to a certain extent. Offers to translate are filtering from the southern states too. The need of further expansion to the readers of the larger world had led me to use English as the most read, practiced and spoken language.

It is painful to accept that human needs and greed has led to infrastructural infringement and pollution in the Narmada valley too. The day is not far when the natural beauty of this beautiful river will gradually perish. I heartily wish that my English translation of the book *Amritasya Narmada* may reach the global book enthusiasts before human advancement tolls the knell of this parting beauty. By voicing my concern through this translation I wish to appeal to the world to save its beauty. I also trust the readers to agree with my belief that although this is only a fractional contribution but as essential a contribution to save the world from the terror of climate change as any other effort.

Contributors

Sunil Sawant. Associate Professor, Department of English, Kisan Veer Mahavidyalaya, Wai (Maharashtra).

David Bellos. Professor of French and Italian and Comparative Literature, Director, Programme in Translation and Intercutral Communications, Princeton University (USA).

Sachin Ketkar. Associate Professor, Department of English, The MS University of Baroda, Vadodara.

Amar Singh. Associate Professor, Department of English, Govt. Auto. P.G. College, Chhindwara (M.P.).

Deepak Borgave. Associate Professor, PG Department of English, Awate College, Manchar (Dist. Pune).

Rajiv Ranjan Dwivedi. Guru Gobind Singh Indraprastha University, Delhi.

Meena Edith Keller. Assistant Professor Govt. Mahakoshal Arts and Commerce Autonomous College, Jabalpur (M.P.).

Laxmi Shanker. Former Editor, SYNTHESIS;

Anubha Sharma. Ph.D. Research Scholar.

Satyendra Singh. Assistant Professor of English, Govt. Mahakoshal Arts & Commerce (Autonomous) College, Jabalpur.

B.O. Satyanarayana Reddy. Department of English, Veerashaiva College, Bellary, Karnataka.

B.N. Gaikwad. Associate Professor, Department of English, N.G. Acharya & D.K. Marathe College, Chembur, Mumbai.

Mallikarjun Patil. Associate Professor, Department of English, Karnatak University, Dharwad.

Vandana Pathak. Associate Professor, Department of English, L.A.D. & Smt. R.P. College for Women, Nagpur.

Neeta Modi. Associate Professor, Department of English, Navjivan Arts and Commerce College, Dahod, Gujarat.

Sarita Mane. Associate Professor, Department of English, Mudhoji College, Phaltan, (Maharashtra).

A.K. Farakate. Associate Professor, Department of English, Kankavli College, Kankavli, Dist. Sindhudurg (Maharashtra).

J. Samuel Kirubahar. Associate Professor, Research Centre in English, VHNSN College, Virudhunagar (TN).

M. Muktha Manoj. Assistant Professor, Narsee Monjee College of Commerce and Economics, Mumbai.

Sangeetha Jayakumar. Department of English, SRM University, Kattankulathur, Chennai.

A.M. Sarwade. Assistant Professor, Department of English, Shivaji University, Kolhapur.

Manoj Gujar. Assistant Professor and Head, Department of English, Prof. Sambhajirao Kadam College, Deur, Dist. Satara (Maharashtra).

Shirish Chindhade. Principal (Retd.) Pune.

Apara Tiwari. Associate Professor and Head, Department of English, Govt. MACC, Jabalpur.